THE HORSE

A COMPLETE ENCYCLOPEDIA

THE HORSE

A COMPLETE ENCYCLOPEDIA

Pam Cary

Christopher La Fontaine

Joyce Robins

Angela Wyatt

CHARTWELL
BOOKS, INC.

A Welsh Mountain pony.

CONTENTS

Published by
CHARTWELL BOOKS, INC.
A Division of BOOK SALES, INC.
110 Enterprise Avenue
Secaucus, New Jersey 07094

© Octopus Books Limited 1987

ISBN 1-55521-129-1

Country of origin: Great Britain

FOREWORD
Angela Rippon

A few years ago I wrote my first ever book, and it was a personal account of my own very amateur experiences as a rider. During an interview for a regional television station, I was asked 'Why have you written another book about horses? Aren't there enough of them available in the bookshops?' Considering the number of books that are written about every conceivable aspect of every other conceivable sport and how the bookshelves of any store groan under the weight of cookery books, I thought it was a particularly fatuous comment. But the fact is that no one needs to justify 'yet another book about horses' on the grounds that every other sport is so well endowed in a literary sense. Quite simply there can never be too many books on the subject. No two horses are the same, and so no matter how much may have been written about their training, their minds, their role or whatever, every author will bring some new and unique dimension to his or her interpretation of the horse. And still there will be questions unanswered. After all, an interest in horses isn't a modern phenomenon like golf or football. The great Greek military commander, Xenophon, was writing about them 356 years before Christ. And the fact that people have gone on writing about horses ever since, and will presumably continue to do so in the future, is a monument not only to their grace and beauty, skill and courage, but also to the remarkable partnership forged between man and horse and the role that combination has fulfilled in every aspect of our lives, every major event in our history.

This book is concerned mainly with the power of the horse. In terms of its physical strength there is no doubt that 'horse power' has been a dominant factor in man's progress from savage to sophisticate. It's been said that the worst thing that ever happened to the horse was to be designed with a slight dip in its back, just big enough to take a man and a saddle. That 'design fault', if you will, may have been bad news for the horse, but it was certainly a happy accident as far as mankind was concerned, for that one factor, horse power, has enabled us to fight battles, open up continents, develop trade, create lines of communication, carry travellers for business and pleasure, and farm the land.

Let's just consider this: how would history's great generals have fared without the formidable striking power of their cavalry and the ability of horse drawn artillery to take the devastating fire power of cannon right up to the front line? What future would our own nation have faced without victory on the battlefields of Blenheim and Waterloo where the British cavalry turned the tide of fortune? In America, how could early pioneers have hoped to penetrate the vast interior without the horse to carry them and their waggon trains thousands of miles into the unknown, and then tame the land at the head of a plough? While here in Britain it has been said that every industrial city should erect a memorial to the horse in recognition of their role in building the commercial wealth of the country by taking the fruits of the industrial revolution to every corner of the land.

Without the horse, progress would certainly have been a very tardy affair, as I can't for the life of me see the elephant or the camel, in spite of their other excellent qualities, somehow fulfilling the same role with such a degree of success!! And yet that very success guaranteed that eventually someone would come up with a more efficient model. So, if imitation is the highest form of compliment, then surely the internal combustion engine is the greatest tribute ever to the horse. In place of four legs, there are four wheels. In place of the heart, an engine. The resultant contraption in all its modern forms is capable of carrying and moving far greater loads, faster and further than the horse ever could. Even so, this mechanical clone has not totally usurped the horse, and never could. For arguably the greatest power of all in a horse is its power to generate affection and emotion in its human partners. It demands and

deserves our respect and through the centuries has evoked that unique human condition – love. Maybe that's why we still revere the horse in music, literature and art. Why millions would rather watch The Derby than a formula one motor race, own a pony than a pair of roller skates, and spend hours riding through the British countryside in all weathers instead of being cooped up inside a family saloon.

Certainly my own association with horses has brought me nothing but pleasure. I have experienced the exhilaration and tangible surge of adrenalin from riding a racehorse bursting out of its skin with fitness and vitality. In contrast there was a moment of mild panic, overtaken by the sheer wonder of finding myself in total control of two massive shire horses, straining into their harness, and then pulling with graceful ease a fully laden dray as their hooves hit the ground with a steady and deliberate rhythm.

When I was allowed to ride the great Red Rum through the surf at Southport, he left me in no doubt that here was a character with a great heart, and great presence, while I shall be eternally grateful to Mary Gordon-Watson for allowing me to learn some of my riding skills on the back of that amazing European, World and Olympic 3 Day Event champion, Cornishman V. Through my own horse, I have experienced the rare privilege of partnership that every rider hopes to achieve. Working with another living creature and feeling a bond of trust and affection develop and grow into a relationship that fills a special niche in my life.

I'm not unique. That bond has existed between man and horse for centuries. The roots of the relationship run deep, and the emotional ties are strong. That's why it will take more than the invention of a powered machine to remove the horse from our world, and why there can never be enough books to satisfy our insatiable appetite for even more information about this brave, beautiful, and still enigmatic creature.

INTRODUCTION

There is more to owning a horse than feeding, watering and riding him. He is your leisure and enjoyment, but he is also a living creature whose welfare should be taken seriously. Just as it is sensible to know at least the rudiments of car mechanics so, to gain the greatest fulfilment from your horse, and to care and ride him to the best of your ability, you should learn about the 'mechanics', how he lives and works and later, why he behaves in the way he does and the influence your own mind and body have upon him. Be sure to read the first section of this encyclopedia, which explains the fascinating background to man's partnership with the horse through the ages.

Learning to ride is but the beginning of years of fun. Not only will you learn a lot about horses and the sport they provide, you will also learn more about yourself, physically and mentally.

On an international scale people are taking to the horse, learning to ride and, in increasing numbers, buying their own horses. Advice on buying your horse, and the pitfalls to be avoided, may be read in conjunction with the extensive section on horse breeds which indicates the purposes to which each breed or type is particularly suited.

The section on horse care tells you not just what may go wrong but, through an introduction to the biology of the horse, gives a clearer idea of why things go wrong. The care and management chapters will not teach you to be an expert – again, only experience will teach you that – but they will guide you in a basic approach to what is best for the horse, the horsemaster's primary aim. Time and experience, sometimes bitter, will make you wiser and much may be learnt from observing and questioning the experts.

The section on competitive sports covers this whole vast subject from gymkhanas to professional flat racing. Western riding is a law unto itself but the rapport western riders have with their horses, and the innate intelligence of the horses themselves is a lesson for all riders. The art of the coachman, almost lost, has made an exciting return to competitive performance trials, while side-saddle riding, showing and hunting, far from anachronisms, gain in popularity and, like driving, retain the elegance of a former age.

The ancient and classical art of dressage attracts more devotees annually while for the brave and young at heart the speed, thrills and accuracy demanded by show jumping and, to an even greater extent, eventing, have no peers.

Riding has never enjoyed so much popularity and the success and growth of international competitions is but the tip of the iceberg. For every top international 'name', there are hundreds of riders on the slippery slope (for there are always setbacks) and even more who still haven't surfaced: two-thirds of an iceberg is underwater. Most people have a competitive streak, even if competing only against themselves in a desire for exhilaration through self-discipline, and your horse will enable you to take part in one or more of the wide range of equestrian activities. The international aspect to horse breeding and riding means that similar competitions are held the world over, under much the same rules - the horse unites all nationalities in a mutual understanding.

THE HISTORICAL BACKGROUND

This first section provides a wealth of fascinating information on the historical background of the horse, from the prehistoric cave paintings onwards. Man's long association with the horse is covered in detail, from the early breeding of war horses to the Victorian heyday when horses were used for a wide variety of occupations, from ploughing to drawing trams and cabs. This section concludes with a short history of racing and the development of the modern racehorse.

Norman knights on their way to battle (detail from the Bayeux Tapestry).

GLORVM

THE ANCESTORS OF THE HORSE

The horse, more than any other animal, has shaped our history, and we in turn have shaped the history of the horse. It has been an important partnership on both sides. Richard III at Bosworth lost his horse, the battle and his kingdom, and indeed, when mounted, the horse was vital in warfare. Harnessed to carts and carriages, it ensured the expansion of trade.

The importance of the horse would never have been established if it had not been possible to form an exceptionally close bond between man and horse. As a herd animal the horse looks for guidance from a leader; removed from the herd it will not only take guidance from man but, what is more remarkable, will exert itself to the point of exhaustion without severe treatment and for no immediate reward. A Thoroughbred can be raced to its limit by a jockey it has never seen before. In the showjumping arena the rider rewards his mount with no more than a few pats. Horses are intelligent enough to carry out a complicated task, but properly treated do not use their intelligence and superior strength to defy man.

One reason for this must lie in the generations of breeding during which the animals which resented man and were unruly were given less chance to reproduce. On the other hand the degree of cooperation must also depend on the way each individual horse is treated from the moment it is foaled. There is no doubt that the build and temperament of the modern horse owe a great deal to human efforts to perfect the animal.

Selective breeding and training by man has allowed the domestic horse, *Equus caballus*, to become more varied in physique and to display a much wider range of abilities than could have developed in the wild over the same period. A species which includes individuals as disparate as a Derby winner, a champion Shire and a Shetland pony is quite remarkable. Even so, the modifications brought about by man are minute compared with those made by nature; the horse was domesticated only about 4,000 years ago, but

the horse family has been slowly altering by natural evolution for over 10,000 times as long.

The earliest known fossils of horses show the family to be at least 60,000,000 years old. Remains found show that the modern horse of that time was much smaller than the animal we know today, with a skull the size of a fox or rodent. This first horse ancestor was called *Eohippus*, meaning 'dawn horse', because it first appeared at the beginning of the Eocene or dawn period in the geological time-scale. There were several different species of Eohippus varying greatly in size. The smallest was probably little over 25 cm (10 in) at the shoulder, while the largest at about five hands (50 cm or 20 in at the shoulder) would have been about half the size of a Shetland pony. Yet it was most unlike a pony. Its backbone was slightly arched and flexible, compared with the rigid backbone of the modern horse. Its tail was long, compared with the short tail of our horse which only looks long because of the hair whisk on the end. Quite unlike a modern horse it had four toes on the front and three on the hind feet. Each toe ended in a small hoof, but the animal's main weight was carried on pads like those of a dog, which would have made it fast and nimble in the swampy forests that were the predominant vegetation of the time. Eohippus was a browsing animal living off the leaves and soft fruits of the forests.

About 25 million years after its first appearance, Eohippus was replaced by *Mesohippus*, which was starting to look something like a small horse, although in detail it was still very different. Now the toes were reduced from four to three on the front feet and it was larger, standing about six hands—60 cm (24 in) at the shoulder. The eyes were set further back, the brain was larger and the legs long and slender and a little more suitable for sustained running.

As the climate became drier, swampy forests gave way to open plains and horses had to adapt themselves to the changed conditions. Without the forest to hide in they needed to

'Buffalo Hunt Chase'. Lithograph from Catlin's North American Collection at the British Museum.

be fast enough to run away from predators, and without the leaves and fruit to feed on they had to live on grass—a food source which necessitates a special digestive system. The group of horses which managed to cope with these conditions, and which leads directly to the horses of today, is named *Merychippus*.

Merychippus appeared in North America before the browsing horses became extinct. It was well suited for life on the open plain where it was abundant. There was an increase in size, with some species reaching ten hands, the size of a small pony. There were still three toes, but the weight rested on the central large toe, leaving the other two as vestigial remains. Merychippus gave rise to a number of other groups and, in turn, about a million

years ago, one of these gave rise to our own horse family, the *Equidae*, which includes not only the horse but zebras and asses. In the members of this family known as *Equus*, the qualities that ensured the survival of Merychippus have been refined.

Today, the horse has the largest eye of any land mammal, and perhaps this is the reason for its legendary acuteness of vision. With its eyes perched high on its head, it can keep its mouth on the ground, continue grazing and still have a good all-round view. In the wild this is particularly important, for if the grazing is interrupted too often the horse will not be able to take in enough food to sustain its bulk. The pupil of a horse's eye does not contract into a smaller circle like ours but into a horizontal rectangle, and the whole eye is so

Lion hunting scene from the North Palace at Nineveh, 668–627 BC.

constructed that any movement at the edge of the field of vision is exaggerated. Horses are particularly startled by a sudden motion to the rear, and since their instinctive reaction is flight it is with good reason that when made to work in heavy traffic they are usually provided with blinkers.

The horse also has an early-warning system in its highly developed sense of smell. It is not used only to detect predators. A stallion will lay down his own scent to indicate to other stallions the territory occupied by himself and his mares.

From the point of view of survival, the most important refinement that took place in the horses living on the open plains was in their ability to run. Inevitably, breeding in the wild favoured those with speed and stamina, for any horse unable to keep up with the herd would soon fall victim to a predator. Gradually over the 20 million or so years that separate Merychippus from *Equus*, the horse became the athletic animal we know today.

The most noticeable change in the appearance of the horse was the elimination of its vestigial toes. Now it was left standing on a single toe, or hoof. When running, a human rises on to the ball of the foot to give less contact with the ground and greater thrust, but a horse is permanently poised in this position.

Then, as the horse had no need for any clasping action, all lateral movement in the legs was lost, leaving sufficient only to prevent them rubbing against each other when running. The horse's limbs, confined to a forwards and backwards movement, are a much more stable structure for carrying its weight at speed.

Finally, and most important, the bones of the legs were elongated still further to provide length of stride. Unlike humans, the horse has no muscles in its lower leg, having instead long tendons connected to the muscles above with the joints acting rather like pulleys. The expansion and contraction of the muscle is efficient by being kept to a minimum, and the small movement of the muscle is translated into the larger movement of the legs to provide the big stride. The power of the horse comes from the huge muscles of its hindquarters, and the front legs are used as supports.

At speed the horse thrusts itself along with its hind legs rather like the pumping action of two poles, and as the poles became longer so the leverage was improved and the speed increased.

Horses have been known to run at just over 65 km/h (40 mph) for short distances and at not much less for considerably longer, and although some members of the cat family can run faster, they can only do so in short bursts. If a horse saw a predator approaching, and had a sufficient start, it would almost certainly escape.

Modern horses of the *Equus* type arose in North America. There is evidence that these speedy animals prospered and roamed in vast herds in both halves of the American continent. Also, the Bering Straits were dry for a period long enough to allow migration to Asia and Europe (as earlier members of the Equidae had done), where they gave rise to the horse species that exist today. When the Bering Straits were flooded and the continents separated, the horse species of the Old World (Eurasia) thrived, whereas those on the American continent, the original home of the horse, disappeared. Today, all the horses in the Americas are the descendants of those brought over by explorers from Europe or of others introduced at a later date. The so-called wild horses were merely European horses which had escaped captivity and bred on their own.

About 10,000 years ago the earliest Indians arrived on the American continent, and at that time the original horses existed there. The reason for the subsequent disappearance of these horses could not have been a lack of food, for bison continued to thrive on the plains, as did the domestic horse much later when it escaped. Nor was there a predator capable of mass destruction apart from man, and if the Indians did kill all the horses, it is curious that the bison, which they were also fond of eating, survived. Disease cannot be ruled out, but what disease would strike down the horse and spare the antelope and bison? One possibility is a combination of causes such as disease attacking herds which had already been weakened and depleted by hunting.

In Asia and Europe Equus survived and separated into a number of different groups. When they spread down through Asia into Africa, various groups became isolated by geographical barriers and evolved differently according to the environment in which they

Przewalski's horse, the Mongolian wild horse, last survivor of the primitive horse.

found themselves. This accounts for the different groups within the horse family today. Apart from *Equus caballus*, the domestic horse, the other main groups of the Equidae are the hemiones, ('half-asses')—the donkeys and the various zebras. All these groups are closely related for it has been found that they are able to interbreed, although the offspring of a mating between two different types is usually sterile. A well-known example is the mule, a cross between a horse and a donkey.

The vocal calls of these different types are quite distinct and would seem to be one of the mechanisms for keeping them apart and preventing sterile crosses in the wild. In tests, the recorded call of a stallion played to a herd of different members of the Equidae family produced no response, but when a herd of the same family was played the call it immediately stopped grazing and started to call back.

Today, there is only one living species of truly wild horse and, whether or not it is solely or partly responsible for our domestic horse, there is no doubt that it is a more primitive type. This is Przewalski's horse, discovered in Mongolia by a Russian explorer after whom it is named. The horse bears a remarkable resemblance in both shape and colour to pictures of horses painted on the walls of caves by prehistoric people about 15,000 years ago. It is the size of a small pony, yellowish-brown, and has a faint stripe down its back. It has a short, erect mane and no forelock. In a group its behaviour is fairly aggressive and it would be unwise to go into a paddock where the group is being fed. The senior members of the herd move from one pile of food to the next, vigorously biting and kicking to assert their dominance.

The first member of the horse family to be domesticated was the onager, one of the hemiones or half-asses. The name hemione is misleading, for although they do look like a cross between a horse and a donkey, they are in fact a true-breeding group within the horse family and have no connection with the donkey, which evolved separately in North Africa. The onager was used for drawing chariots in Sumaria about 2000 BC but since the onager is a particularly unruly animal it seems unlikely that the chariots could have been properly steered.

Before long the onager was replaced by the

Detail of Sumerian standard, depicting war scene (c.2500 BC., British Museum).

horse, but looking at the rough Przewalski's horse, whose temperament does not seem a great improvement on the onager, one cannot help being surprised at how much refinement has been achieved by man in such a comparatively short space of time.

At first, the relationship between man and horse was no different from the relationship between man and any other animal that could be eaten. There is, of course, no written record describing how prehistoric man hunted the horse, but it is assumed that this was done by lying in wait for migrating herds. Huntsmen would have preferred not to have chased herds which would have had no difficulty in outrunning them, and there is evidence of large prehistoric encampments set up in areas where herds were bound to pass.

One of the most famous is at Les Eyzies-de-Tayac in central France. It is set on the slopes of a narrow valley through which the herds would have been funnelled. Up to the end of the last Ice Age, bison, reindeer and horses passed through as they migrated north in the summer and back south in the winter. On the walls of the nearby Lascaux caves there are exquisite prehistoric paintings of these animals. Unfortunately, the cave is no longer open to the public as too much exposure to light and outside air was causing the paintings to deteriorate; however, at another site in the same area, one can still see a beautiful life-sized relief of a horse carved in the limestone about 15,000 years ago. Further south at

Peche-Merle there is a cave painting of a strange spotted horse surrounded by the imprints of human hands. The meaning of this remains a mystery, but is probably connected with hunting magic or fertility rites.

The first horses were kept in captivity as a convenient source of food a few thousand years later in Neolithic times in Southern Asia. They are unlikely to have been stallions, which would have been far too dangerous to handle. Nor is it likely they were foals, as even a day-old foal can run faster than a man. In herds of wild horses it has been observed that when the herd is in flight, and a foal starts to lag, the stallion takes its dock between its teeth and forces it along. This then leaves the heavily pregnant mare as the slowest member of the herd and the one most likely to be captured alive.

This first stage in the domestication of the horse has been called 'meat and milk husbandry'. It was a simple system which was also applied to reindeer and oxen. The mares were kept for their milk and as reproducers and the foals fattened up and eaten, but since there were no stallions in the herd the problem was how to get the mares pregnant so that the process could be repeated the following year. The difficulty was solved by tying up the mares in an area where wild herds were known to run and waiting for them to be covered by a passing stallion. It was a crude, unselective, method of breeding but it was the start of domestication.

Below right: Cave painting of galloping horse from the caves of Lascaux.

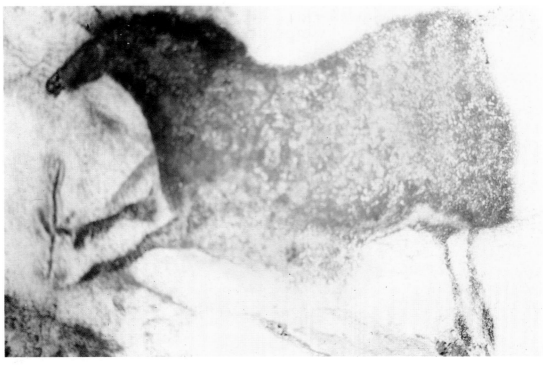

SELECTIVE BREEDING

The full domestication of the horse was achieved once colts born into the herd were kept on as stallions, and from that moment the slow process of improving the horse by selective breeding could begin. Horses which proved to be physically and temperamentally suited to their work were given the best chance to breed and pass on their characteristics. The awkward ones ended up in the cooking pot.

As nomadic tribes treated their tame horses as cattle which they drove along as a source of fresh food, it would not have been long before someone realized that they could also be used to carry cumbersome burdens such as tents, water containers and cooking pots. From that point it was a relatively short step to carrying a man. Before long, horses were selected and bred for one of two main purposes. There were those horses best suited to being led and carrying goods, and those best suited to being fitted with a saddle and carrying people. Within these two different categories they were soon selected for their aptitude for particular tasks, which varied enormously at different times and in different parts of the world.

The demands of warfare represent one of the most important influences on the breeding of horses. The horse quickly became established as the basis of military power, and the development of a horse with courageous qualities was the political policy of various rulers from earliest times. Part of Solomon's splendour was the 1,200 saddle horses and 4,000 chariot horses in the royal stables. Mohammed, a soldier and politician as well as a religious leader, made it an act of faith for his people to improve their horses.

Techniques of warfare and horses had reciprocal influences on each other. On the one hand the types of horses available affected modes of combat. The Gauls of northern Europe had small, tough, shaggy-haired horses that could not be ridden but which excelled as chariot horses, having speed and endurance, but as horses were improved by an influx of warm-blooded animals from further south, cavalry replaced the chariot. This

pattern was repeated in other parts of the world. On the other hand, changing techniques of warfare constantly influenced the types of horses needed. When armour was at its heaviest and most cumbersome the medieval knight would have needed an exceptionally strong mount to carry him, whereas the light cavalry that supplanted him needed lighter and faster horses.

There is plenty of evidence to suggest that man has used horses for sport almost as long as he has used them for any other purpose except food, and this has been a principal factor in shaping and refining the horse. Chariot races are eulogized in the Rig-Veda, part of the ancient scriptures of India that date from about 1000 BC, and racing in its various forms has been hugely popular throughout history. The culmination of man's love of equestrian sport is the supreme refinement of the modern Thoroughbred.

The development of roads and the invention of vehicles that could be drawn by a horse in harness are examples of particularly important influences on the type of horses that were bred. For transport over rough terrain on simple tracks a robust packhorse with a docile and tractable temperament was

Above: Greek vase depicting chariot racing (c. 520 BC).

Right: Mughal 16th century battle scene (Victoria and Albert Museum).

14th century combat scene from James Doyle's Chronicle of England.

All modern horses are representatives of a single species, *Equus caballus*, and the enormously varied and numerous different types that have evolved are known as breeds. All horse breeds can be traced back to groups which evolved according to the needs of the different geographical environments in which they lived. There was the forest horse, which gave rise to the slower, heavier 'cold-blooded' breeds, and the plateau horse from which came the lighter and more dashing 'warm-blooded' breeds.

As well as its breed, any horse can be classified more generally according to its use (racehorse, draught horse, hunter, and so on) and also according to its size and build into one of three categories—heavy horses, light horses and ponies. A heavy horse is a draught animal measuring well over 17 hands and sometimes as much as 20 hands (200 cm or 80 in at the shoulder); a pony is a small horse

required but, as the number and quality of roads improved, demand grew for a wide range of different horses suitable for working in harness. These might be highly specialized and vary between heavy horses, bred to draw wagons with immense loads, to light breeds like the Dutch Harddraver, well suited to pull a sleigh swiftly along a frozen canal. In England, when parish roads were little better than muddy tracks, there was a need for an easy-going, ambling horse that a farmer with his wife behind could ride to church or market. With the arrival of better road surfaces, the gig became a practical proposition and the demand switched to a faster horse with a hard, trotting action, and the carriage horse known as the Hackney became popular.

The emergence in different parts of the world of new breeds that have been developed for specific purposes has continued right up to modern times. In America, the Standardbred arose to fill the demand in the 19th century for a horse that could trot at high speeds for harness racing, while the Quarter Horse is a muscular sprinter bred for racing over short distances but also ideal for herding cattle. Another American example of a breed that developed to meet a special demand is the Tennessee Walking Horse, bred by the rich owners of southern plantations who spent many hours in the saddle inspecting their vast estates. Tall, sleek and elegant, this breed has three distinctive gaits and moves without any bump or jar.

less than 14.2 hands at maturity (144 cm or 57 in at the shoulder), and a light horse is anything that falls in between these two classes.

There are some inconsistencies in this classification: an Arab horse can be as small as a pony but is always referred to as a horse, and a full-sized horse used for polo is generally referred to as a polo pony. But ponies have distinguishing features other than size. All ponies have a characteristic 'poniness', a quality that results from learning to survive in the harsh environment in which many pony breeds evolved; this manifests as alertness, intelligence, curiosity, a sensible temperament and extreme sure-footedness—attributes which have endeared ponies to thousands of owners and riders.

Heavy horses are the gentle giants bred for their enormous strength. They are descendants of the placid northern 'cold-blooded' horses, and modern breeds were probably evolved from the warhorses of the middle ages. In Britain they are represented by the Shire, the Clydesdale, the Suffolk Punch and the Percheron (a relatively recent import from France).

The category of light horses, smaller, faster and more spirited than heavy horses, includes riding mounts and carriage horses. They are the warm-blooded breeds, and among them the Arab is supreme. The Arab's outstanding value lies not only in the excellent qualities bred into it by the desert Bedouins—exceptional courage, speed, hereditary soundness, stamina and strength for its relatively small size; it is also remarkable for the way it manages to pass on its most desirable characteristics to its offspring, and this ability (known as prepotency) has ensured that of all breeds the Arab has had the greatest influence on the breeding of horses.

Below: *Men and horses dying in battle (Bayeux Tapestry).*

Next page: *Battle of Culloden, April 1746.*

Animal breeders, whether they are dealing with horses or poultry, are always searching for hybrid vigour, commonly known as a 'nick', which occurs when the offspring of a cross embodies the best characteristics of each parent and itself shows a marked improvement. The Arab is popular because, when crossed with another breed, there is always a good chance that this 'nick' will result. The Thoroughbred racehorse is the best example of the success of an Arab cross, but the influence of the Arab is much wider. There is hardly a country in the world where an established breed does not have Arab blood, however indigenous the breed many now seem. In Britain the Welsh Mountain pony and in France the big Percheron both owe something to the Arab.

The reason for the strong hereditary traits of the Arab may have something to do with the sheer length of time over which its characteristics have been selectively bred. Horses depicted on the monuments of ancient Egypt have a distinct Arab-like appearance, as does one of the first representations of a ridden horse, a statuette found in Egypt and dated about 2000 BC.

A breed is established only when it is 'fixed', which is when the individuals belonging to it are so inbred that they will always breed true. Since the life of a human is only about three times as long as that of a horse, it is obvious that one person cannot breed a sufficient number of horse generations to stabilize a breed, and to do this properly it usually takes a sustained effort over several human generations. It has been achieved by racehorse owners—a group of like-minded people with common interests which has persisted for about 200 years. It has also been achieved by royal families, the church and, in some cases, the state. In France, Napoleon set up a system of studs for state-owned stallions which persists to this day, and in Austria the Haflinger is an example of a breed preserved by rigid state control.

The problem of pursuing a single objective over a long period of time has led to a comparatively small number of true horse breeds, and it is important to preserve as many of these as possible because this is the raw material from which crosses to suit future circumstances can be made. When the motor car appeared, the outlook for some breeds looked bleak, but today, contrary to what might have been expected, the prospects for survival of the different breeds are good.

WORKING HORSES: FULL EMPLOYMENT

The years leading up to World War I were a golden age for the horse. It was a time of high prosperity for all those in a social position to enjoy it, and a time of full employment for the horse. The horse was both an important military asset and a cornerstone of the civilian economy. Breeding societies were awarding valuable prizes to improve quality and commercial breeders were raising horses by the thousand to meet the demand for quantity.

Technological and industrial changes in this century have been so overwhelming that this golden age of the working horse now seems remote. Yet it was real enough. The motor car had been invented, but lorries were still unreliable and the railways depended on the horse to bring goods and passengers to their lines. Stations were sited within horse-transport distance of the communities they were intended to serve. The economy was based on horse transport in the cities and horse power on the land, so that thousands of people had jobs connected with horses, and everyone's life was to some extent governed by the speed at which horses moved in their various tasks.

At the turn of the century there were about four million horses in Great Britain and 300,000 of these were in London. In every town one would have been aware of the number of horse-drawn vehicles in the streets and the occupations associated with horses. Every large town had its hay market, which was usually a wide street or square where the mountainous hay carts could be turned. Heavy wagons and canal barges brought in tons of oats and took back large quantities of manure to spread on the fields. There were drivers, farriers, crossing sweepers (the polite Victorian name for the men employed to sweep up droppings) and, at the end of the line, the knackers or slaughterers. One London firm dealt with 26,000 horses a year, the average age of the horses being 11.

In London at this time there were a number of saddle horses kept by the rich. These were used for riding in the parks or by a few people who had retained the old-fashioned habit of riding a horse on business visits, or of commuting on one from a suburb and leaving it at a stable during the day; by 1900 almost all traffic consisted of some sort of horse-drawn vehicle. These harness horses varied in size and quality according to the type of work they were expected to do.

In 1893, W. J. Gordon published a detailed account of the horse world of London for the Religious Tract Society. His report stated that 22,000 horses worked drawing buses, 10,000 drawing trams and 15,000 drawing cabs. The toughest job was that of the tram horse, whose average working life was only four years, while the omnibus horse fared only marginally better with an average working life of just five years. The bus and tram horses were well cared for, as it was in the interests of the companies to do so, but their strenuous life is detailed in Henry Mayhew's account of his interview with a bus driver in 1851:

"I've been a driver for fourteen years. . . . I never have any rest but a few minutes except every other Sunday, and then only two hours; that's the time of a journey there and back. . . . It's very hard work for the horses, but I don't know they are overworked in buses. The starting after stopping is the hardest work for them, it's such a terrible strain. I've felt for the poor things on a wet night with a bus full of big people. . . . I must keep exact time at every place where a timekeeper's stationed. Not a minute is excused—there's a fine for the least delay. I can't say that it's often levied, but still we are liable for it."

The goods carriers were the next largest employers of horses. At that time the various firms, which included Carter Paterson and Pickfords, kept 19,000 and the railways 6,000. It is not strange that the heyday of the horse coincided with the high prosperity of the railways, for the railways were competing with each other in efficiency and in the towns

Hailing a hansom in South Kensington.

Mail coach by moonlight, by J Pollard.

the motor lorry was still considered un-economic and difficult to manoeuvre. The railways vied with each other in producing smart well-turned-out teams of horses:

"The Great Western prides itself on having as good a stud as any company in London, and the stables in which it is housed are admittedly excellent. In the new block in South Wharf Road there are four floors of horses one over the other, the top floor being almost as high as the hotel, with a look-out down on to the station roof.

The Great Western horses are under the superintendence of Capt. Milne, and there is a certain army precision and smartness about the management, which is not appa-rent in all railway stables. As much as

possible the colours are kept separate, one stable being of greys, another of chestnuts, another of bays, and so on; and right well do the carefully groomed animals look, standing in their neat straw litter, with a glint of sunlight on them, clean as a picture against the white background leading up to the varnished pine roof overhead, while most of the smooth arched blue-brick gangways are as clean as a man-o'-war deck.

At two o'clock on Monday morning the week's work begins. The Covent Garden vans then go out. At eight o'clock the stables are in full bustle, and the runs that slope from floor to floor are alive with the descending crowd, as, to the jingle of harness, they come cautiously down. Some

Above right: Coal mining in south Staffordshire, 1869.

of them before the day is out will have been as far as Woolwich Dockyard and back; some of them will be out for eighteen hours, to rest on the morrow, some of them for six, to take a longer turn next day.

The heaviest railway van weighs two tons, and will carry seven or more. Such a van, with its load drawn by its four-horse team, will be a moving mass of thirteen tons, one of the heaviest things going through the streets of London, as the railway parcels cart is one of the fastest. The team walks; the single horse trots, and is not supposed to go more than eight miles an hour, but he does, although it is not everyone who would give him credit for the rate at which he slips along."

About 8,000 horses were employed by coal merchants. At that time there were about five million people living in London and it has been estimated they would have burnt about five million tonnes of coal in their homes in a year. The coal merchants' horses were fed at 4 a.m. and left with their first load at about 6 a.m. The larger wagons carried two tons of coal and were drawn by a heavy horse. They would usually make a detour to avoid hills, but when this was impossible each would arrange to meet with another wagon at the bottom and hitch up the two horses in tandem on a single wagon. When they arrived at the top, both horses would return for the second wagon.

Heavy horses were also used for moving rubbish. At the turn of the century in London there were about 1,500; they were known as vestry horses because refuse collection was the responsibility of each parish. Vestry horses worked eleven hours a day, six days a week. They had to pull a load of about 2.5 tonnes and be good at backing and turning in narrow spaces, but they were properly cared for. According to Gordon, they were well fed, carried a nosebag for a midday meal and were groomed after work before entering the stable. One driver often stayed with the horse throughout his service and got a regular bonus for keeping him in good condition.

Then, as now, the best heavy horses in town belonged to the brewers. In London they owned about 3,000. A brewer's dray carried 25 barrels each weighing 200 kg (4 cwt), and to pull this load there were usually three horses. They had good feed and good stabling. They started work when they were fully mature at about the age of six and were retired long before they seriously deteriorated. The cart horse of a brewer was considered a good buy and usually fetched a reasonable price for a further period of lighter work, either on a farm or pulling the cart of some small contractor. In 1893, the brewery horses that Courage had finished with were sold for an average price of £32.

The high standard of the brewery horse was largely due to the quality of the men employed to look after them. William Miles, a contemporary writer, commented on the skill of the draymen. He noted how the horses and men understood each other so well that they could unload the beer and drive the dray to the next stop with hardly a word.

"I followed some distance to see how it was that a man who seemed as if he could be crushed at any moment by these monsters, had such control over them. I observed he never touched them; between carriages where there hardly seemed room enough to squeeze through, he went without touching, and this too by merely waving a bit of whipcord at the end of a long black rod . . . . I was quite astounded."

The welfare of this huge horse population, living and working in the unnatural con-

ditions of the city, was largely a matter of economics. At that time, working conditions for people were certainly bad, but it is unlikely that the horses would have been treated worse than humans, for most employers were sufficiently self-interested to realize that their horses were assets worth looking after. Undoubtedly there were abuses such as poor stabling, ill-fitting harness and infrequent shoeing, but there were also various benevolent societies ready to point out deficiencies in horse management. The publication of Anna Sewell's *Black Beauty* in 1877 had an enormous influence on public opinion and made people aware of the vulnerability of the horse in the city street.

In 1887, the welfare of city horses was well served when the first proper cart-horse parade was held in London. It was open to all horses

Left: *Cart-horse parade, Regent's Park, London, 1903.*

Top right: *Horse drawn barge, Llangollen, Wales.*

Below right: *Shire horse show.*

stabled within seven miles of Charing Cross. Three hundred and eighty-three attended, and there was a red rosette and £1 for every horse which reached a high standard—which that year was about a third of the entries. There were also prizes for the men with the longest service with the same firm, provided the firm could vouch for their 'attachment to, and kind treatment of the animals under their charge'. For many years the Cart Horse Parade was a popular attraction and an important event in the London calendar.

World War I marked the end of an era, but by no means the end of the working horse. Horses continued to serve commerce for many years, but when the lorries took over their role the heavy horses, on which so much attention had been lavished, seemed to have a bleak future.

SUPPLY AND DEMAND

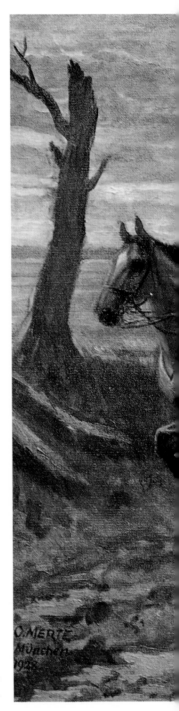

The fate of horses, both in terms of their overall numbers and the survival of different types, depends on economic factors in human society; working horses, and the heavy horse in particular, provide a vivid example of this rule.

Throughout most of the Middle Ages, the heavy horse was a warhorse and as such was highly prized. Whether these warhorses were quite as large as the heavy horses which were bred much later is a matter of controversy. There are no written records of size, and the relative proportions of horses and men depicted in tapestries and book illustrations are not reliable. In medieval times, size indicated importance rather than scale. The problem is difficult to solve, because if a horse were to carry a knight in armour, and sometimes its own armour as well, it must have been a massive animal. On the other hand, if it was the size of a Shire, it is difficult to visualize how a knight in armour could have mounted without the aid of a special mounting-block or crane, which would not always have been available on a battlefield. It is a reasonable guess that the 'Great Horse of Europe' was a somewhat shorter, stockier version of the heavy horse seen today.

The heavily armoured knight disappeared with the invention of the longbow and the introduction of fast, light cavalry protected by chain mail and leather; although there was now no need for a large lumbering horse, the cavalry still required a supply of good animals which were larger than ponies. Since the Wars of the Roses (1455–85) this supply had been low; people were reluctant to breed horses of this type because they would stand a good chance of being seized by one of the warring armies as warhorses. Owners sent many good horses to the Continent or Scotland to be sold, and in an effort to stop this and to increase the horse population, various laws were passed governing the breeding and sale of horses.

At the end of the 15th century Henry VII forbade the export of horses to foreign countries without a licence. His son, Henry VIII, enacted a whole set of horse-breeding regulations designed to improve the size of the stock on account of 'the great decay of the generation and breeding of good and swift, and strong horses, which heretofore have been bred in this realm'. Any owner of a deer park with a circumference of one mile was required to keep two brood mares, and four brood mares if the park had a circumference of over four miles. Another regulation required wealthy people to keep a number of trotting stallions according to their position. The scale ranged from archbishops and dukes who had to keep seven, down to categories such as a clergyman with a certain income, or a man whose wife wore a silk gown, who had to keep one.

The idea of improving the stock of horses by exercising some control over breeding was sound, but nothing really effective could be achieved until the land was enclosed, which put an end to the practice of indiscriminate breeding by turning all horses loose on the common land. In the reign of Elizabeth I, further proclamations were made and penalties for exporting horses were increased, but to little avail. At the time of the Armada in 1588, a mere 3,000 cavalry could be raised.

The enclosure of land in the 18th century led to a proper system of breeding. This was helped by the gradual introduction of the practice of gelding (castration), which ensured the removal of undesirable stallions from the breeding population. Gelding had been practised since ancient times (the Scythians are given the credit of inventing it) but it was not used in Britain until comparatively recently. Until then it had been considered necessary to use stallions in the cavalry, even after it had been observed that geldings were more manageable. Gelding did not become widespread until the late 19th century when there was a demand for vast numbers of tractable animals for haulage work, both in the town and country. Victorian prudery would also have played a part in encouraging the removal of entire (uncastrated) horses from the common gaze in city streets.

German cavalry patrol, from painting of World War I.

Heavy-horse breeding

The early days of heavy-horse breeding are somewhat misty; no records were kept and information was passed on by word of mouth. Many Shire horses are said to descend from the Blind Horse of Packington, which was probably foaled in 1755. Crisp's Horse of Ufford was foaled in 1768, and from him are descended 761 Suffolk horses in the direct male line.

The Friesian horse, imported from the Netherlands, played an important part in the development of the British heavy horse. These coal-black animals, which in Victorian times were known as the 'Black Brigade' because they were used by undertakers, were certainly in the country by the middle of the 17th century, and before that they were probably among the horses brought over by Vermuyden to work on the drainage of the Fens. The connection between the Friesian and the Shire is easy to trace, because the Shire was originally known as the 'Old English Black Horse', or simply the 'Black'. The name 'Shire' came about when the society promoting the breed, conscious of competition with other heavy breeds, wanted to change its name from 'The English Cart Horse Society' to something as distinctive as Clydesdale or Suffolk Punch. As their breed was being raised in the Midlands as well as the Fens, and the term 'Shire-bred' had become common usage, the name was adopted.

Robert Bakewell (1725–95) was famous for his improvement of British cattle and sheep, and was also an important figure in the development of the Shire. He farmed at Dishley, near Loughborough, and was determined to see if he could improve the local breed of horses known as Leicestershire Blacks. He travelled to Holland to buy top quality Friesian mares and crossed them with his own Leicestershire Black stallion in a system he called 'in and in'. This meant crossing the female progeny of the original cross with the purebred stallion, and then repeating the process as many times as he considered necessary. In this way the foreign blood was gradually reduced and the breed soon became stable.

The stallions which ultimately arose as the product of these crosses were greatly admired, and as they were taken to different parts of the country their influence spread widely. One was brought to the courtyard of St James's Palace so that George III could examine it and question Bakewell about his breeding methods. It is unlikely that the king learned a great deal. That particular horse was called G, and this anonymity was typical of Bakewell's secretive approach. He welcomed visitors to his stables every day except Sunday, being a strict chapel-goer, but gave few details about the breeding of his horses.

Bakewell almost never sold his Dishley stallions but instead hired them out to a group of farmers or to a landlord with a number of tenants. It was a method which suited Bakewell because he could keep an eye on the progeny, which would be concentrated in one area. In time, the hiring of stallions became a common business because hirers had the advantage of keeping their stallions in their area for a period of time, and this meant there was a greater chance of getting mares in foal.

At the end of the 18th century horses were widely used by farmers for ploughing, but there were still many who considered the use of oxen for ploughing to be more economical, and they were supported by writers who deplored what they regarded as the extravagant use of horses on the farm. One writer calculated that if all farm work were to be done by oxen, the extra meat that would be generally available would supply 100,000 people with an extra pound of beef per day. Another, Thomas Davis, in an agricultural survey of Wiltshire, wrote:

"The large farmers are, unfortunately, not only in Wiltshire but in most other counties, too fond of their stout fine horses, and their men too proud of showing them, to give them up for oxen. . . . The pride of a farmer in buying such horses is followed by the pride of his carter in keeping them as fat as possible. There are many instances where the expense of keeping up a team of fine horses amounts to nearly the rent of the farm on which they are kept."

The horse versus ox argument was widely debated. William Pitt, another country reporter, took a more objective point of view. He realized that the foundations were being laid for the horse economy of the future:

"If this subject be properly considered, it will appear that agricultural horses are here principally a nursery for raising a supply for commercial purposes. Horses are necessary in great numbers in a rich, commercial and luxurious country, for other purposes than those of agriculture. They can only be produced from the land, and therefore must be bred by farmers."

Above: Farmer Robert Bakewell, 1725–1795.

Right: Belgian horses working on Danish farm.

Below: British ploughing championships.

With the steady rise in demand for draught horses in the towns, the economic benefits of breeding heavy-horses soon outweighed both the cost of keeping them and the fact that they were inedible, and from that moment the supremacy of the horse over the ox for agricultural work was never in any doubt. Farmers realized that the resale value of a horse for town work provided them with a source of cheap labour on the farm. They raised foals or bought yearlings, broke them to harness and then worked them on the farm for four or five years before selling them at a profit as mature horses for work in the cities.

Provided the profit equalled the cost of the food the horses had eaten, the farmer had several years of farm labour for nothing. If his horses did not turn out to be large enough for heavy city work, he could always sell them to the army or retain them for agricultural work.

On the farm the horse became the main motive power. Better breeding was having the effect of reducing the number of horses needed to make a team for ploughing, and the plodding pace of oxen could not be compared with the speed of a pair of good horses pulling the light Rotherham plough. Once the farm horse had been established, all agricultural machinery was designed with the horse in mind. The benefits of the horse in the agricultural economy reached down as far as the smallholder. Horses which were considered too old for the gruelling work of the city were sold off cheaply and many found their way back to the land at a fraction of their original price. Around the city of Bristol, for instance, there was a large number of smallholdings which relied on the cheap labour of old horses.

The improvement of the draught horse by breeding took longer than it did with other agricultural livestock. The horse population was large enough to provide a good breeding pool but difficult to manage because it was so scattered. The situation improved when the railways were fully established in the middle of the 19th century, when stallion-hiring societies could inspect stallions at the various horse shows and have them sent to any part of the country in a rail box. The traditional method was to rely on the local travelling stallion: stallion owners would advertise the

route to be taken by the stallion and groom (known as the stallion-leader) and there would be stopping points, such as the yard behind an inn, to which owners could bring their mares. This had various disadvantages. A mare which is weaning a foal will come into season for only a comparatively short time, and the chance of this occurring when the stallion arrived in the village would be small. This made it unlikely that a mare would produce more than one foal every two years by this method.

There were other weaknesses in the system. Many travelling stallions were sound, especially those sent around by reputable firms, but until compulsory licensing of stallions was introduced there were also many which were simply spared from farm work to make a little extra money, and which had such defects that they should not have been allowed to reproduce. The system was also erratic on account of the stallion-leaders. Some were hard-working men who walked 60 or 70 miles a week, and put the welfare of their horse before their own. Against this, stallion-leaders had a reputation for heavy drinking at the inns and pocketing reduced fees for covering mares on the side.

The Strand, 1907.

Jutland horses in Copenhagen, Denmark.

and promote the three British heavy breeds. Each breeding society held shows, and the prizes they gave brought good business to the winners. The breeding of heavy horses was taken up by wealthy landowners such as Lord Rothschild, and the high-class Shire stallions from his stud at Tring changed hands for large sums of money. There was also royal patronage: Edward VII was President of the Shire Horse Society and owned and bred Shire horses at Sandringham, and George V twice won the championship of the London show with his Shire stallion, Field Marshal 5th.

The beginning of the end

By 1921, the year King George won the championship for the second time, the end of the golden age of the heavy horse was at hand. From then on, constant comparisons were to be drawn between the economics of transport by horse and by motor, and although the horse was not finally made redundant until after World War II, the situation had changed radically.

During World War I, in which the astonishing number of about 500,000 British Army horses were killed, every available horse was pressed into service. There was a tremendous boom in horse dealing in anticipation of prosperous peacetime conditions. In all cities, the repositories (the depots where 'used' horses were auctioned) did a roaring trade, and by 1921 the army had sold off 141,000 working horses. At shows, breeding stallions changed hands at record prices, and hiring societies were prepared to pay £1,000 for the use of a good stallion for a season.

Then came the postwar slump. In June 1921 there were over 2 million people unemployed in Britain and the bottom dropped out of every market, including that for horses. The flood of poor-quality ex-army horses now coincided with the maturity and availability of the horses foaled towards the end of the war as part of the war effort. Yet there was no employment for all these animals. Between 1920 and 1924, the horse population fell from 2.08 million to 1.89 million—a drop of almost 10 per cent.

Money was short and the economics of the working horse began to be examined. Before the war the motor car had already challenged the horse-drawn carriage, but lorries had been considered expensive and unreliable and the tractor had not been a serious competitor on the farm.

In the last quarter of the 19th century there was a great farming depression, but strangely enough this had the effect of improving the quality and numbers of the heavy breeds. A succession of very wet summers and very cold winters culminated in 1879 in one of the wettest years every recorded. The crops rotted away. This was at a time when shipping rates were low, and the market was being flooded first by cheap grain and then by cheap meat and dairy products from abroad. For British farmers the one profitable commodity was the horse. More and more were wanted in the cities and there was a good export market for British breeding stallions. Ordinary farmers could not breed hunters and carriage horses, but they could raise carthorses, and thousands kept themselves out of bankruptcy by doing just that. In 1889, the number of horses engaged in agriculture had risen 19 per cent over the past 20 years, and permanent pasture had risen by 24 per cent.

Inspired by this trend, and goaded on by a rapid rise in the import of heavy horses from Belgium, which was considered an insult to British farmers (from 12,000 in 1874 to almost 41,000 in 1876), farmers and landowners formed breeding societies to improve

*Delivery vans outside
Selfridges.*

The fight over the use of horses in towns was carried on in the newspapers, which were in favour of lorries. It was argued that the economy was losing millions as a result of traffic jams caused by horses, and it was suggested that coal and rubbish carts should be allowed to move only at night. In a debate in the House of Lords it was proposed that all London horses should be licensed, and that when each horse died the licence should not be renewed. None of these measures was introduced. The number of horses used in towns dropped considerably, but many firms and public bodies kept on their horses after calculating that horse transport was still cheaper. Selfridges, the London store, found that horse-drawn deliveries cost 3d per mile less than motorized ones, and Glasgow Corporation found that it cost half as much again to deliver a ton of goods by lorry. Nevertheless, during that period, the decline in the use of the horse continued steadily: between 1924 and 1934 the British horse population dropped by a third and in towns it dropped by over a half. But that still left 1,129,000 horses in Britain.

One of the reasons why the decline was less severe in the country was the comparative inefficiency of the early tractors. Most of them had ribbed metal wheels and were not allowed on public roads unless the wheels were changed, so, unlike the horse, they could not easily be switched between ploughing and haulage. The early tractors were difficult to manoeuvre through narrow gates and could be dangerous, as they were liable to

tip over backwards if the implement that they were towing jammed.

In the 1930s tractors were improved. Pneumatic tyres with heavy treads became available, and so did a safety linkage which disengaged before the tractor tipped backwards, but there remained the problem of the initial cost of the machine. Farmers were reluctant to pay a high price to scrap a system which continued to work, so that when World War II broke out there were still many small farms with no tractors and many large farms which worked tractors and horses together.

During the war the commercial breeding of draught horses collapsed. The supply of fodder was strictly controlled, and no breeder was allowed more than he could grow himself. Whereas a farmer might feed a single stallion along with the rest of his stock, a large firm like Foreshaws, which had been breeding Shire horses since 1863, had 75 pedigree stallions fed mainly on purchased fodder. The firm found itself in an impossible position, and there was no alternative to reducing its stock. One train carried off 23 to the knackers, and some of the best breeding stock in the country was sold for £3 a head.

Although this development signalled the beginning of the end for the heavy horse, its disappearance from farms was still delayed. During the war the severe shortage of labour and pressure to meet production targets left little time for logical reorganization. Everyone and everything that could help had been pressed into service, and often horses and tractors worked long hours side by side. With

Young's Shire horses with loaded drays making a delivery.

support the breed. John Young, a President of the Shire Horse Society, was determined to show that horse-drawn deliveries could make economic sense, and proved his point. There are 42 Young's pubs within a three-mile radius of the brewery, and accountants have worked out that it is cheaper to supply them using a dray with two horses than a lorry. Each day, five pairs of horses leave the brewery, and between them they deliver about 10,000 tonnes of beer a year.

Young's head horsekeeper is Harry Ranson. It is a position with a slow turnover, for he is only the third head horsekeeper at Young's in the last 101 years. His day starts at 4 a.m. when the horses are fed so that there is plenty of time between eating their first meal and starting work. The draymen and their assistants, called trouncers, arrive later, and the loaded drays leave the brewery at 7.30.

Harry Ranson also buys the horses, which are acquired as two- or three-year-old geldings, and looks after their training. A slow process, it takes place at the brewery stables, where there is an exercise ring and a blacksmith's shop. If the horse turns out to have the right conformation and ability he is used in the show team, and if not he becomes one of the working horses. The speed at which learning progresses depends on the horse's temperament. The horse is gradually introduced to his harness, and also to the conditions in which he is to work. He is walked and trotted around the exercise yard on long reins, while men thump crates and bang beer cans together to simulate the sort of sudden noises that he will be subjected to in the street. His hearing is acute and he learns to stop and move forwards and backwards on a single verbal command.

Eventually the young horse is put to work alongside a more experienced animal, and at first a third man goes out with the dray to hold the new horse's head. Working in the streets puts the horse's temperament to the test. He should prove himself by taking his share of the load when working, and not fret and strain when waiting around.

The breweries and farmers who prefer working with horses remain the best hope of a revival in the fortunes of the heavy horse, together with those who keep a pair of horses for the increasing number of ploughing matches. There is also a growing demand from America. Although they will never regain the importance they had before World War I, their future seems secure.

peace came the time to change the system. The government had bought tractors to help plough up 2 million acres of grassland as part of the war effort, and there were now more than three times the number of tractors on farms than there had been before the war. New methods were planned and farm buildings altered to suit the mechanization that had already taken place.

With these changes the working horse, which had held on for so long, abruptly disappeared. A slaughter started which only tailed off when there were comparatively few horses left to kill. It was reported that in one town, Rochdale, 2,600 horses were slaughtered in 12 months. The close-knit fabric of the horse economy was completely unravelled: as the horses went, harness makers disappeared, forage merchants closed down and repositories switched from the auction of horses to that of motor cars.

The low point in the fortunes of the heavy horse was reached in the 1950s when in one year the Shire Horse Society registered the birth of only three fillies and one colt. The situation then began to improve as up and down the country a number of dedicated farmers and brewers organized shows and parades, and through their efforts interest in the heavy horse was kept alive.

Among them are men such as Geoff Morton, who relies entirely on horses to run his farm of 138 acres in Yorkshire. In 1973 he held two open days on his farm to which 6,000 people came. The Young's stable of black Shires at their London brewery also

BRED FOR SPEED

No breed of horse has received so much attention as the Thoroughbred. Although Thoroughbreds are used for virtually all equine sports, it is in producing racehorses that the process of selective breeding has reached almost scientific exactitude, bringing Thoroughbreds to a stage of excellence far removed from their ancestors.

The word 'thoroughbred' is a literal translation of the Arabic *kehilan*, which means 'purebred all through'. The description is true in so far as the breed is now closed to all outside blood, but not accurate from a historical point of view. As we have seen, the Thoroughbred was created in the 18th century by crossing imported Arab stallions with native English mares.

Horseracing had been practised in England long before the appearance of the Thoroughbred, and it is believed that organized races were held in York at the time of the Roman occupation. The 'running horses' then used might well have been small Galloways, which were bred in the north and described as being under thirteen hands. It is not certain how much the Thoroughbred owes to native horses and how much to the imported Arabs, but when the two were crossed it was soon quite apparent that the progeny were faster than either of their parents.

In the 18th century over a hundred Arab, Barb (from North Africa) and Turkish stallions were imported, and although they must all have had some effect on the evolution of the breed, three stand out particularly clearly. Every modern Thoroughbred can be traced back through the male line to one of these three horses, which are known in racing as the Foundation Sires.

The Foundation Sires

The first of these, the Byerley Turk, was obtained by Captain Robert Byerley, who took him from a Turkish officer whom he killed or captured in a military campaign in Hungary in 1686. Captain Byerley took the horse to Ireland and fought with him at the Battle of the Boyne. There the Byerley Turk was greatly admired and, fortunately for British bloodstock, was not killed. The horse returned to England, was sent to stud and became the ancestor of such important breeding stallions as Herod (from whom the Derby winner Blakeney is directly descended), The Tetrarch, a brilliant but odd-looking grey horse with white spots, and Highflyer, owned by Richard Tattersall who founded the famous firm of bloodstock auctioneers. Highflyer turned out to be a brilliant breeding stallion whose progeny won 1,108 races worth a total of £170,000, an immense sum in those days. On the strength of this Richard Tattersall built a magnificent mansion called Highflyer Hall where he entertained the Prince Regent. When his horse died in 1793, Tattersall wrote on his gravestone: 'Here lieth the perfect and beautiful symmetry of the much lamented Highflyer, by whom and his wonderful offspring the celebrated Tattersall acquired a noble fortune, but was not ashamed to acknowledge it.'

The second foundation sire, the Darley Arabian, was bred by a tribe living on the edge of the Syrian desert. It was bought by Thomas Darley, the British consul in Aleppo, from the local sheikh. It is said that as soon as the money was paid, the sheikh gave instructions to his men that on no account was the horse to be removed from the palace stables. But British bloodstock was not to be denied one of its most valuable assets. Undaunted, Mr Darley arranged for sailors from a British man-o'-war to row ashore in the middle of the night, overpower the stable guards and seize the animal. The sheikh wrote to Queen Anne that his horse had been 'foully stolen from me by your subjects', but by then the horse was at stud on the Darley family estate in East Yorkshire.

The Darley Arabian sired the first truly great racehorse, Flying Childers, and his male line branches out to become the most numerous in the breed. He died in 1730, having lived to the great age of 30.

The third foundation sire, the Godolphin Arabian, was foaled in 1724, and was also remarkable for his longevity. He lived for 29

The Byerley Turk.

years and was buried at Lord Godolphin's house, Gogmagog, just outside Cambridge. When he died people came to the funeral from all over East Anglia and were entertained with cakes and ale.

A host of stories surrounds the horse. It is said that he was one of a batch of horses sent by the Bey of Tunis as a present to the King of France, but that, when the boat landed at Marseilles, the horses were so emaciated after a protracted voyage that others had to be substituted. The horse was later bought by Edward Coke of Derbyshire, who spotted it drawing a water cart in Paris. Its pedigree was known from a document found on an Arab

groom whom the Bey had ordered to stay with the horse. When Edward Coke died, the horse was bought by Lord Godolphin and put to stud where, through his brilliant grandson, Matchem, he had an important influence on the Thoroughbred breed.

The foundation sires are held in high esteem because they were outstandingly successful as breeding animals, and in the racing world there can be no higher praise. In flat racing, breeding is paramount, and the racetrack performance of a horse's progeny is just as important as his own. Fame—and the most money—goes to the owner of a horse that wins the important races and goes on to sire other horses that do the same. If the progeny of such a horse wins valuable races, his earnings at stud will be considerably greater than his prize money from the racecourse. The rapid improvement of the Thoroughbred is due to this strong emphasis on breeding, and throughout racing history the horses that are brilliant breeders are the most admired.

The Godolphin Arabian.

The history of racing

In its early days, when Charles I patronized the sport at Newmarket, racing was a test of stamina for mature horses. Races consisted of several heats, and horses were expected to carry big weights over long distances. Then came the trend towards starting a horse's racing and breeding career at an earlier age. In 1785, the first July Stakes, which is now an important race for two-year-olds, was run at Newmarket. There were one or two misguided attempts to race yearlings, but this was soon suppressed, leaving the two-year-olds as the racing novice. The modern flat-racing picture was completed when the five classic races for three-year-olds, which range over distances from 1–1¾ miles, were established.

The oldest classic is the St Leger. This dates from 1776. Racing had taken place at Doncaster since just after the beginning of the century and the St Leger, named after a Colonel St Leger who lived locally, came into being when the town decided to improve the course. This race for three-year-olds, originally over two miles, proved popular, and in the early days was an occasion for ostentation by the nobility. The Dukes of Devonshire and Portland drove over from their mansions accompanied by liveried servants. Earl Fitz-

william arrived in a coach drawn by six bays decorated with orange rosettes, and accompanied by twenty outriders. In 1813, the race was reduced to its present distance of 1¾ miles and 127 yards and, although it is still important, it has lost some of its past prestige. Run late in the season, and over a distance that stretches the limit of specialist middle-distance horses, it has suffered because of the modern tendency to send Derby winners to stud before their record is tarnished, and also from its proximity in the racing calendar to the Prix de l'Arc de Triomphe (1½ miles), France's (and Europe's) richest race and a natural target for a top-class three-year-old.

The Oaks, for three-year-old fillies, was inaugurated three years after the first St Leger as a result of that race's success. It is said to have been the outcome of a dinner-table discussion at the high-living Lord Derby's home near Epsom which was called 'The Oaks'. The race was popular, and the evening after the race it was proposed to inaugurate another race the following year, for both colts and fillies. It was to be decided by the toss of a coin whether it would be called the Bunbury, after Sir Charles Bunbury who was a leading member of the Jockey Club, or the Derby, after Lord Derby. Lord Derby won the toss and had the satisfaction of having the most famous race in the world named after him. Sir Charles Bunbury had the consolation of winning the inaugural Derby with his horse, Diomed. Diomed was not successful at stud in England, but eventually Bunbury sold him to the United States where his potency suddenly improved and he founded a line from which many of the best American racehorses are descended.

Like the St Leger, the Derby was not originally run over its present distance. The first three races were run over a mile, after which the distance was lengthened to 1½ miles and the course altered to include the sharp descent to Tattenham Corner. Much later, the start was moved to Langley Bottom to give a better view to spectators, and this also gave the horses a stiff climb for the first half-mile. This twisting and undulating race, held in front of a vast noisy crowd, is the turf's supreme test of the breeding of a horse.

The other two classic races are the One Thousand Guineas and the Two Thousand Guineas. They were first run in 1814 and 1809, respectively. They are both run over one mile and are both held early in the year at Newmarket. The One Thousand Guineas is for fillies only, and the Two Thousand Guineas for fillies and colts. In practice, fillies do not usually run in races for both sexes,

Print showing King George I at Newmarket, 1722.

although six fillies have won the Derby. On the first occasion, in 1801, it was won by Eleanor, owned by Sir Charles Bunbury.

The five races provide a test for the top class three-year-old, which should be able to win over a mile in the spring, a mile-and-a- half in the summer and one-and-three-quarter-miles in the autumn as he matures. It is a rare achievement for a horse to win the Triple Crown (Guineas, Derby and St Leger). When Diamond Jubilee won it for the Prince of Wales in 1901, there were scenes of patriotic fervour. In 1886, when Ormond performed the feat, the horse was given a special reception in London. Traffic was stopped for him as he was led from Waterloo to Grosvenor House, and there he was fed on orchids and sugar by debutantes—but that was in the golden age of horse racing. The last horse to win the Triple Crown was the Canadian-bred Nijinsky in 1970.

St Simon, undoubtedly the greatest sire of the 19th century and considered by many the greatest racehorse of all time, never ran in a classic on account of a technicality.

His owner, a Hungarian prince, died of a heart attack on the steps of the Jockey Club luncheon room at Newmarket at the start of St Simon's racing season as a three-year-old. The rules of the time dictated that under these circumstances the horse's engagements should be cancelled. St Simon was auctioned, and although he was the son of the 1873 Derby winner, Galopin, he was acquired by the Duke of Portland for only 1,600 guineas.

In 1884 St Simon won the Ascot Gold Cup by 20 lengths. The runner-up, an excellent horse called Tristram, went on to beat with ease one of the dead-heat winners of that year's Derby. St Simon then won the Goodwood Gold Cup, beating the previous year's St Leger winner by 20 lengths. His trainer, Mat Dawson, who had also trained six Derby winners, is said to have remarked: 'I have trained only one smashing good horse in my life—St Simon.'

At stud, St Simon set a record that has not been equalled in this century. For nine years he was champion sire, which meant that nine times his progeny won more prize money during a racing season than the progeny of any other sire. The breeding influence of St Simon continues to be felt today, for three racehorses which are probably among the most influential stallions of the 20th century—Hyperion, Nearco and Ribot—all owe a breeding debt to St Simon.

King Edward's horse wins the Derby, 1896.

Villains of the turf

In the 19th century racing acquired the popularity it has held ever since. The sport of kings became the sport of the general public, and it was also a good hunting ground for unscrupulous gamblers and crooks. One of the most notorious was William Crockford, the son of a fish merchant, who died in 1844 worth half a million pounds. He ran gambling dens and was at the centre of the most unsavoury side of racing.

One of Crockford's exploits was to rig the St Leger in order to settle a score with his arch enemy, John Gulley, who owned a horse called Mameluke which he had backed to win £40,000. Jockeys were bribed, unruly kicking horses were included in the runners sent to the start, and the starter, who was also involved, was responsible for seven false starts before the horses were finally sent on their way with Mameluke left too far behind to catch up.

Racing at Epsom, 1836.

Crockford was also involved in one of the greatest frauds in racing history. Running Rein, who won the Derby in 1844 with the help of bribed jockeys and 'pulled' horses, turned out to be a four-year-old. Through the efforts of the Jockey Club, and in particular Lord George Bentinck (later described as 'dictator of the turf'), most of these excesses were removed. Then, at the turn of the century, the bad days returned with an outbreak of wide-scale doping.

Doping was not unknown previously, but had been dealt with severely. Daniel Dawson, a petty crook paid by others, had been publicly hanged in Cambridge in 1812 for putting arsenic into drinking troughs in Newmarket. It was hard to believe that doping would again provide a serious threat, and when George Lambton, the most eminent trainer of his time, warned a Jockey Club steward that doping was being so widely used to pull off gambling coups that the system of bloodstock breeding was in danger, the stew-

ard took no notice. Lambton then demonstrated the effect of doping by giving drugs to five indifferent horses. Four won and one came second. The result was the passing of a rule that anyone administering drugs or stimulants would be 'warned off the turf'!

Today, there is a sophisticated dope-testing laboratory at Newmarket, and this receives routine samples from racecourses from all over the country. It is an expensive operation which costs the Horserace Betting Levy Board, responsible for the distribution of funds raised through the betting tax, about £500,000 a year to run, but it is effective as a deterrent. In 1986, there were 2 positive results out of 6,590 samples and some were cases of horses ingesting minute amounts of caffeine or theobromine in horse nuts accidentally. So accurate are dope tests in Britain today that in a recent case a horse was found to have traces of caffeine in its blood after eating a stable lad's chocolate bar on the way to the races. Although no blame was attached to the trainer or his staff (the horse had snatched the chocolate from the lad's hand) the horse, No Bombs, was still disqualified from first place.

Today the Jockey Club, in common with other European racing authorities, has listed those drugs it considers to be non-normal nutrients, and stringent security checks make malpractices less of a threat. The future of the Thoroughbred is more likely to be influenced by changing economic circumstances. Rising costs and the emergence of the Thoroughbred as a commodity in an international market are putting pressure on the traditional pattern of breeding and racing.

The economics of racing

The current value of bloodstock can be gauged by the prices paid at the yearling sales. In Britain the most important is the Houghton sale held at Newmarket in November, attended by buyers from all over the world. The auction is held by Tattersalls, the firm founded by Richard Tattersall in 1766.

The Houghton sale lasts a week. Unlike the hurly-burly of a racecourse, the atmosphere is discreet and serious. The catalogue, a large hardback volume listing the pedigree of the horses, indicates the order in which they will be brought into the elegant sales ring. There they are disposed of at the rate of about one every five minutes. Tattersalls takes no heed of decimalization. The bidding is in guineas, usually rising in steps of 1,000, and the odd shilling on top of the pound, the five per cent, is Tattersalls' commission.

There are obvious clues to observe when buying a yearling. A good horse should have well-developed quarters, which are its driving power, and walk straight with an athletic movement of the shoulders. Its back legs should reach well forward so that they pass the mark made by the front legs, indicating a good stride. Its head should be of a good size, well set on the neck, with a bold, clear eye, indicating an alert presence. Even if all the signs are right, however, there is no guarantee that the horse will win back its costs. Very few yearlings ever pay their way in prize money, while the yearling Canadian Bound, by the American triple-crown winner, Secretariat, was sold for $1.5 million, and when racing in France ran only twice without winning.

In 1979, the 427 yearlings in the Houghton sales realized about 13 million guineas, an average price per horse of 30,403 guineas. In the previous year, about two out of seven horses sold won a race, and the earnings of the average horse were less than £2,000, so a horse from the Houghton sales would have had to have been well above average to recover its purchase and training costs. Keeping a horse in a reputable training stable, and paying for transport to racecourses, race entry fees and jockey fees would, in 1987, cost the owner about £10–12,000 over the year.

Against a background of rising expenses, however, there is the prospect of rising rewards at the top end of the scale. In 1978, Shirley Heights, bought by Lord Halifax for £60,000, won the Derby and was syndicated to shareholders for breeding purposes for £1.6 million. This figure seemed less astonishing when Troy, who was bred by his owner and won the English and Irish Derbies in 1979, was syndicated for £7.2 million. Troy had earned the equivalent of 60 per cent of all prize money available to horses in Britain in 1979.

The tendency of rising rewards for the successful was confirmed in the Houghton sales of 1979, when 525,000 guineas was paid for a yearling sired by the successful stallion Lyphard. There were three other yearlings by

Right: Newmarket—Sale at Tattersall's, 1887.

Below: Portrait of gentleman on horse, with hunting scene in background.

Lyphard in the sale, and the four together achieved a total of 1,083,300 guineas, which shows how much faith is placed in a popular stallion.

Even if an owner does succeed in buying a good yearling, problems can develop during training. The horse may turn out to be a 'bleeder' or 'roarer'—that is, to have weak blood vessels or a respiratory defect which shows itself by a roaring noise. Prolonged snowfall, a virus infection, or a simple injury might hold up training. The horse might have all the physical abilities, but not the temperament to win. The best horses, like the best athletes, need to be mentally in tune, for when the general standard is high, mental attitude often tips the scales. Young horses sometimes lack the mental strength to stand up to the noise and tension of racing.

For the breeder, a major problem is the low fertility of the Thoroughbred. This is not surprising in a breed of horse which has been developed for maximum athletic performance rather than reproductive capacities.

On a national basis, the conception rate is only about 70 per cent, and twins, which are useless for racing, and spontaneous abortions reduce the rate of successful foalings to about 60 per cent. A mare only produces one foal a year, so a breeder will be lucky if he has seven foals in the approximate ten years of a mare's reproductive life.

The situation is not improved by the demands of the sport. For administrative reasons, all Thoroughbred foals are deemed to have been foaled on 1 January of the year of their birth, and it is important that the foal's real birthday should fall as near as possible to that date. The later in the year it is born, the less mature it will be when it comes to competing against its contemporaries. The mare's eleven-month pregnancy means that she should be covered as soon as possible after 15 February, the start of the covering season, but since in nature mating would occur later in the year, this early covering brings a drop in the conception rate.

Conception is also hindered by infections transmitted by the stallion, although these could be eliminated if artificial insemination, as used in cattle breeding, was allowed. The subject has been widely debated, but the Jockey Club has so far ruled against artificial insemination on the grounds that it would be difficult to police a system which could put pedigrees in doubt. It might also lead to popular stallions dominating the breeding population, which could result in excessive inbreeding and also, if the popular stallions turned out to be less good than anticipated, an unnecessarily large crop of poor foals. Artificial insemination would improve the fertility rate, but its drawbacks have so far remained unresolved.

The breeder's aim is to produce the best horse he can with the available material, and to do so he selects the sire and dam on the basis of past performance, of previous matings between the two families, and of conformation. The owner of a mare will look for a stallion whose conformation will correct any faults his mare may have.

He will hope that the genetic mix will produce the desired 'nick' and that the off-spring will have a brilliant racing and breeding career. Commercial breeders, who are to the fore in an economic climate which curtails the activities of all but the richest or most devoted of owner-breeders, will aim to sell their produce at the yearling sales and will therefore need to anticipate the trends in fashionable sires, choosing stallions for their mares more than two years before the off-spring are sold.

There are two main breeding theories: in-breeding and out-crossing. In-breeding is the process of mating stallions and mares which have the same ancestors. In practice, this duplication rarely appears before the second or third generation; the stallion and mare might have the same great-grandmother or great-great-grandfather, for example. Federico Tesio, the great Italian breeder who bred Ribot and numerous other good horses, was a masterful exponent of the theory.

Out-crossing is the process of mating stallions and mares who have no duplication of each other's ancestors in their pedigrees, although each parent may have a horse appearing more than once in its own pedigree. The theory is that an infusion of a fresh family's blood into a mare's pedigree will produce a nick, and there are recognized out-cross stallions for certain dam's families which have produced nicks in the past.

However, these theories have proved to be inexact, and although breeders adopt as scientific and logical an approach as possible, there is no guarantee of success on the racecourse—as the sorry list of high priced yearlings' subsequent racing careers shows.

Steeplechasing

Steeplechasing, as its name implies, arose out of the sport of matching hunters in cross-country races in which church steeples were the landmarks. In the early days of hunting, the sport consisted of a lengthy struggle in which slow hounds and large men on big, slow horses wore down the fox by sheer persistence. At the end of the 18th century, the time when the Thoroughbred was being established as a breed, an obsession with speed changed the character of the hunt. Horses and hounds were improved, the fashion for fast hunting became popular and riders liked to match their horses. The early contests were rough. An account of a match between two horses, Clinker and Clasher, for a prize of 1,500 guineas, makes exciting reading. After crashing through fences, falling into bogs and sinking into dung heaps, Clasher snatched the race at the last moment: 'They held Clasher up, and they flung water into his face, and he won in the last hundred yards from superior training.'

Eventually steeplechases were run over enclosed courses with artificial fences. This meant that admission could be charged and prize money increased. At first there was considerable opposition to these artificial courses on the grounds that, because they were less strenuous, they were not a proper test for hunters and would merely provide

Above: Racing at St Moritz.

Left: 'Little Owl' at the final fence, Cheltenham Gold Cup, 1981.

nerable to injury while jumping. The result is, of course, that champion male steeplechasers cannot sire offspring and pass on their genes.

Top-class stallions tend to be either flat-race sires or National Hunt sires. But another difficulty facing breeders is that, because a steeplechaser takes six to eight years to reach his best (unlike flat racers, which are racing after two or three years), a stallion can take almost a decade to prove himself as a sire of steeplechasers.

A good steeplechaser need not, however, be jumping-bred on both sides of his pedigree. The celebrated Red Rum, who won the Grand National three times and was second twice, was not bred to be a jumper at all but a sprinter on the flat, being by the miler Quorum out of the sprint-bred Mared. He did in fact dead-heat for first place in a poor race at Liverpool over five furlongs on the flat as a two-year old, the first time he ran. But he can fairly be described as having been a hopeless flat horse, not realizing his great potential until much later in life when put to fences and extreme distances, thus belying his breeding. It is also true to say that Quorum did not sire another National Hunt horse remotely as good as Red Rum, who was something of a fluke. Similarly, Night Nurse, who won the Champion Hurdle in 1976 and 1971, run over two miles, was by the sprinter Falcon, although his dam, Florence Nightingale, was by the stayer Above Suspicion.

Arkle, one of the most famous steeplechasers of all time, was a grandson of Nearco, one of the great sires of flat racing. Arkle won 22 races, including the Cheltenham Gold Cup (a 3¼ mile steeplechase), three times. Unfortunately his owner, the Duchess of Westminster, never ran him in the Grand National because she considered the risk of injury too great, so it was never known how this famous steeplechaser would have done in the longer and more gruelling race.

The Grand National, with its 4½ miles of very tough fences, used to be the one race which every owner of a steeplechaser hoped to win. But since World War II increased prize money has raised the status of races such as the Cheltenham Gold Cup (perhaps the greatest 'chase for the connoisseur), and owners have been less inclined to risk their horses on the hazardous Aintree course. Now that the fences have been lowered to improve safety, one must hope that this great sporting spectacle will return to its central position in the steeplechasing calendar.

employment for cast-off horses from flat racing. This has not proved to be the case. For racing over hurdles (a series of low obstacles which the horse must jump without losing the rhythm of its stride) a horse which has graduated from flat racing is usually the most suitable, but in steeplechasing, where each fence must be considered and deliberately jumped, the best horse is generally the steeplechasing type of Thoroughbred.

Naturally, in steeplechasing breeding is important, but it does not dominate in the way that it does in flat racing; steeplechasing is regarded more as a trial of the skill and stamina of a particular horse than as a test of its breeding. One complicating factor in the breeding of steeplechasers is that almost all male steeplechasers are geldings. It takes many years of training for a horse to carry heavy weights over a course of difficult fences, and stallions are not suitable because, as they get older, they become less and less amenable to the discipline needed. They are also vul-

THE PARTNERSHIP OF MAN AND HORSE

Selective breeding has been the fundamental influence in the more recent history of the horse's development; but this gradual improvement and refinement of the species might never have begun had man not learned to ride on the horse's back. The feasibility of equitation caused the horse to prosper and proliferate in the past, and the pleasure of equitation is the main reason for its survival today. It has been estimated that in Britain there are now about two million people who ride regularly.

Riding is fundamentally a partnership between man and horse, and the satisfaction lies in the subtle communication and interaction between the two. One has only to witness a dressage competition to see how the combination of a well-trained horse and rider raises equitation to the level of an art. The instructions, known as 'aids', which pass from rider to horse, are invisible and the horse and rider move fluently and precisely as one unit. Not many riders achieve this perfection, but many aim for it.

A trained horse is constantly looking to the rider for guidance and reassurance. The rider 'talks' to the horse through physical contact with the horse's body and the horse interprets every change of pressure. At a basic level, the banging of heels on the horse's flanks drives it forward, and the pressure of the bit on its mouth holds it back but, on a more subtle level, every small change of pressure of the rider's legs and every slight shifting of his centre of gravity will mean something to the horse. The horse is sensitive to movements which are so small that the rider is unaware of them. Involuntary body movements rapidly communicate the unease of the rider to his horse and undermine its confidence, and, by the same path of communication, the horse is able to understand when the rider is confident and in tune with its needs.

A good rider develops not only physical skills but also a temperament that responds to the temperament of the horse, and this applies to every type of riding. In a racing

stable the apprentices who are the most technically skilled riders do not necessarily turn out to be the best jockeys. Many races are lost when a potentially good horse frets and wears himself out in the early stages through lack of communication between horse and rider. A great jockey like Steve Cauthen or Pat Eddery is able to mount a horse which he has never ridden before and, in spite of his style of riding which gives him very little physical contact with the animal, he manages to keep the horse calm, well balanced and ready to give its supreme effort at the moment it is asked.

The development of saddlery

The art of equitation depends on the rider understanding the physical capabilities and behavioural tendencies of the animal that he is sitting on. It also depends on various

Above: Assyrian hunting scene from the North Palace at Nineveh, c. 640 BC.

Right: Mughal miniature depicting Shah Jahan out riding with his son, 1630 AD.

Greek vase showing horse race, 500–480 BC

mechanical devices which make the control of the horse simple and effective.

In ancient Greece the riding horses were a luxury reserved for the rich. The young men who rode them had no stirrups, no saddle (except possibly a cloth) and usually wore no clothes. The only bit they had for riding under these difficult conditions was the snaffle, and when this proved inadequate to control their horses, which were usually stallions, they made the bits more severe by adding spiked rollers to the mouthpiece or even spikes to the cheekpieces, which could be squeezed into the side of the mouth. It was not until the 3rd century BC that the invention of the curb chain was introduced by horsemen from Gaul who settled in Asia Minor, and this later became an important element in the Roman cavalry.

The curb chain (often a bar or leather strap) fits under the horse's chin and, acting in conjunction with the bit, enables the reins to press the bit downwards on to the bars of the horse's mouth rather than pull it upwards into the corner of its lips. This means that the horse is forced to tuck in its chin and bend its neck at the poll. Without its neck extended, a horse is unable to bolt, so spikes and other forms of cruel restraint became unnecessary. At the same time, the curb bit made possible the collected style of riding. When the head, which weighs about 35 kg (80 lb) and which the horse uses as a balancing weight, is drawn into the body, the horse is in the collected position and alert; in this position, as the British Army's *Manual of Horsemanship* puts it, 'he has the maximum control over his limbs and is in a position to respond instantly to the least indication of his rider.'

Both the saddle and stirrups were introduced by nomadic groups who lived and hunted on horseback. Roman and Persian saddles were no more than a pad laid over the horse's back, so unless the horse was what early writers described as 'hollow-backed'— that is, with the spine sunk between the dorsal muscles—the friction between the spine and pad would have soon produced sores. The Scythians, a warrior tribe who scalped their enemies, improved the situation by introducing a saddle of two cushions resting either side of the horse's spine and connected by straps, and soon after that the Scythians or another tribe introduced the saddle tree, the framework which effectively takes all weight off the horse's spine.

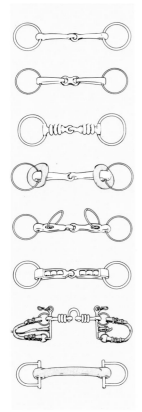

Above: Types of bits
described from top to
bottom. The vulcanized
jointed snaffle suits a young
horse, as rubber creates
more sensitivity than metal.
The French Bridoon is a
soft, lightweight bit for a
good mouth. The roller
snaffle is fairly heavy, and
suits a bad, hard mouth.
The German snaffle is a
hollow, lightweight bit that
only works on a good
mouth. The Cornish, or
Scorrier, is very tough, but
not severe, and is useful for
strong horses. The
Magennis works on the
cheeks and lips to create
more feeling in an insensitive
mouth. The Hannoverian
Pelham, which can be fixed
or jointed, prevents the horse
jolting the bit and the tongue
port helps stop the tongue
going over it. The rubber
snaffle is excellent for
sensitive but strong mouths.

Stirrups were introduced by the Huns, the horsemen from Mongolia who in the 4th and 5th centuries pillaged their way through the civilized world under their leader Attila, 'the scourge of God'. Stirrups not only made mounting easier and long journeys more comfortable; they were also an enormous advantage for the warrior fighting from the saddle. With his feet in the stirrups he could freely twist and turn to strike blows, and he could give himself leverage against the horse when drawing a bow or throwing a weapon.

It is not known who invented the horseshoe, but some of the earliest examples were found in Britain. Also found in Britain was the Roman *hipposandal*, an iron-soled boot which was fastened to the horse's hoof with straps. The concern of the Romans for their horses' feet was probably due to the combination of the damp British climate and the hard Roman roads. In ancient Greece shoes had not been essential because in a hot, dry climate hooves remain hard. In the damp climate of Britain they are still not essential provided the horse keeps to grass and soft ground, but when the horse has to move along metalled roads, shoes are needed to protect the soft horn of its hooves.

An early writer on horsemanship was Xenophon, an ancient Greek historian and military hero, born in the 5th century BC. Despite having lived before the invention of the stirrup and the curb bit, Xenophon made great contributions to the science of riding with his belief that kindness and understanding produced better results than force. He was convinced that 'what is done by compulsion is done without understanding, and there is no more beauty than in whipping or spurring a dancer.'

Among his many written works Xenophon, a disciple of Socrates, produced two books, *Hippike* and *Hipparchikos*, for the guidance of his two sons who entered the cavalry, and much of the advice he gave would be considered sound today. If a horse suspects some object and will not approach, it should be persuaded with the voice, but if that fails,

"you should yourself touch the object that he considers dangerous, and lead him up to it gently. But those who compel the horse with blows make him more frightened than ever. For whenever horses receive any harsh treatment in such circumstances, they think that the suspected objects are responsible for that too."

Haute École riding

A great leap forward came with the Renaissance, when the partnership between rider and horse was elevated to the level of an art. Books were written laying down methods of training and describing exercises, called 'airs', which the horse should perform to demonstrate its agility and obedience. Many of the exercises, especially the kicks and leaps known as 'airs above the ground', were extravagant and, in the opinion of the English, seemed more appropriate to the circus; according to the exponents of the art, however, the movements were no more than a heightened expression of the normal actions of a stallion and were useful from a military point of view. The *capriole*, which is the most advanced and spectacular of all the airs, consists of the horse leaping into the air and then, when all its four legs are off the ground and its body is horizontal, launching a kick backwards so that its 'hind legs shoot out like arrows'. If this was meant to clear a space in battle and knock down nearby soldiers, the English were not impressed. Thomas Blunderville, who was commissioned to translate Grisone's influential book, *The School of Horsemanship*, wondered who would want to be in a battle on a horse which when spurred forward, 'fell a-hopping and dancing up and down in one place'.

In spite of this scorn, the influence of Grisone, and the School of Naples where he taught, spread out to all the Courts of Europe. Even Henry VIII employed a riding master at Hampton Court who called himself 'sometime Grisone's scholar', although this was before the English found out more from the publication of Grisone's book. The Italian School initiated a style of riding which was essentially a grand spectacle, and it was seen at its best when performed by aristocratic people in a formal setting.

The displays were carried out in a *manège*, or indoor riding school, which was often an elegant building complete with chandeliers and a royal box. The same manège was also used to train the horses and was fitted with the special pieces of equipment considered necessary. The most important was the pillar, which was devised by Pignatelli, Grisone's pupil, and perfected by later teachers. The horse was tied to the pillar by a long rein and exercised round it in circles or with its head tied to it so that, when it could not move forward, it was stimulated to produce impulsion. In the latter situation the horse's energy released itself in the desired kick or leap.

Unfortunately, the School of Naples seems to have paid little attention to Xenophon's recommendations about teaching by kindness. Grisone's advice on how an untrained horse should be brought to the mounting block for the first time seems guaranteed to put it off learning for good. It is the exact opposite of the gentle approach used today:

"But if he be so forward and so stubborn as he will not come to the block, then all to rate him with a terrible voice, and beat him yourself with a good stick upon the head, between the ears, not leaving him until you have made him come to the block, whether he will or not."

Grisone attached great importance to the use of footmen armed with cudgels or, in an extreme case, a cat with sharp claws tied to the end of a pole. It was their job to beat and shove an obstinate animal until it followed the trainer's instructions. The answer to any difficulty was usually to increase the severity:

"If their corrections do not work, truly the fault is in the footmen, lacking perhaps rough terrible voices, cruel looks and gestures as should serve the purpose." Later exponents of this advanced training, known as *haute école* (high school) riding, rejected the cruel methods but the system still called for a much sterner discipline than would be used in the course of normal training of a horse today.

In England, where for a long time horsemanship was regarded as the outcome of inborn ability rather than of serious study, it was inevitable that *haute école* would be looked on as a fashion in which the horse was called on to perform antics. The critics failed to appreciate that, although the movements themselves had little practical application, horsemanship would be greatly improved by being the object of serious attention by intelligent people. François Robichon de la Guérinière, the court riding master of Louis XIV and one of the greatest exponents of *haute école*, firmly believed that horsemanship was a proper subject for scientific study: 'Every science and every art has its own principles and rules that lead to new discoveries and

Pellier's riding school, Paris 1836.

perfection. Why should horsemanship be the only art for which practice alone is needed?'

In England, the one man who actively promoted *haute école* was the Duke of Newcastle, Governor to Charles II and a strong supporter of the Royalist cause. He was an incompetent military commander, largely responsible for the loss of the battle of Marston Moor, but was a brilliant horseman. During his subsequent exile on the Continent he studied scientific equitation, ran a riding academy, and had a great following. When his master was restored to the throne the Duke returned to England, built a circular manège at Bolsover Castle and published an impressive book entitled *A General System of Horsemanship in all its Branches*. Here he both set out his views and anticipated the criticism they would provoke:

"Some wag will ask, what is a horse good for that will do nothing but dance and play tricks? If these gentlemen will retrench everything that serves them either for curiosity or pleasure, and admit nothing but what is useful, they must make a

hollow tree their house, and clothe themselves with fig leaves, feed upon acorns and drink nothing but water..."

His teaching fell on deaf ears. The English were only interested in hunting and racing, and the Duke of Newcastle was honoured abroad but not in his own country.

Today, the situation has changed and formal exercises are accepted as a normal part of many a horse's training. Some of the high school 'airs on the ground' can be found in modern dressage—the name given to the formal exercises now used to test the obedience and suppleness of the horse. The names of the 'airs' have not changed. Included in the modern routine is the *passage*, the balanced high-stepping trot defined by de la Guérinière as 'more sustained and precise than the ordinary trot, so that there is not more than one foot distance between every step he takes.' The *piaffe* is a way of marking time 'when a horse passages in one spot without advancing or retiring or moving to one side, raising high and flexing his legs with a graceful action.'

A Lipizzaner of the Spanish Riding School performing the 'capriole'.

Some of the 'airs on the ground' such as the *terre à terre*, which is a kind of slow gallop in two-time, have not passed through to modern dressage, but those which have are included in international competitions. Today, the use of dressage as basic training for cross-country events is widely accepted, and it has been suggested that it should be used by racehorses which could improve their performance by learning how to lengthen their stride. This seems impractical so long as horses start to race before they are sufficiently mature to be trained in this way.

Haute école in its complete form, including the 'airs above the ground', is only performed by two schools. These are the Spanish School in Vienna and the Cadre Noir at Saumur, in France. The older, and the more famous, is the Spanish School, whose present building was completed in 1735. After the French Revolution many important riding schools disappeared, but the Spanish School continued and Vienna became a focal point of the art of equitation. At one time there were 20 riding schools in the city. Today, the Spanish School remains faithful to the teaching of de la Guérinière, and its performances of the advanced art of equitation on its grey Lipizzaners are famous throughout the world.

The Cadre Noir has had a more chequered history. The name comes from the traditional black uniform of the French Cavalry Riding School which is worn by the *ecuyers*—the instructors who perform the displays. Originally the school was both civilian and military and was subject to continual dispute between the civilians, who were interested in pure academic equitation, and the military, who were more concerned with producing a horse and rider which could cope with the rough conditions of a military campaign. In spite of a dominant cavalry influence, the practice of *haute école* continued together with the other forms of training, and today one can still see the Cadre Noir perform high school riding in Saumur on the square in front of the elegant 18th century Cavalry School. The 'airs above the ground' are carried out both unmounted and mounted by a special group called *sauteurs*. When mounted, they use an old-fashioned white-buckskin saddle with no stirrups so that there is no possibility of levering the horse upwards. The impulsion must come entirely from the horse.

The Cadre Noir is now a part of the state-funded French National Riding School which has magnificent buildings opened in 1976 just

outside Saumur. From all over France, instructors from local riding schools and competitors in equestrian sports come to be taught by the Cadre Noir. The school belongs to the Ministry of Sport and includes two indoor schools with facilities for videotape analysis, extensive cross-country courses and stabling for over 400 state-owned horses.

Eventually the general style of English and Continental riding converged, but right through the 19th century the English largely ignored the more collected style practised by Continental riding schools. They relied on their own quite effective style of riding with fairly long stirrups and the horse extended, which was more suitable for fast hunting over open country. But in 1907 came a shock. That year the exponents of the riding style of Captain Caprilli, an officer at the Italian Cavalry School, had an overwhelming success at the International Horse Show at

The Spanish Riding School in Vienna.

The dressage horse, Sun and Air, ridden by Miss Sheila Wilcox, in an advanced dressage competition at Goodwood.

Olympia. In one class for officers in uniform the British were not among the first thirteen.

Caprilli's new system became known as the 'forward seat', or, as he put it, 'accompanying with the body the forward thrust of the centre of gravity.' He realized that when jumping (and when racing, too) the horse could not give its best performance unless the rider adjusted his position by closing the angle of his body and leaning forward to keep himself over the horse's centre of gravity, and that if the rider leaned back while jumping this would throw his mount out of balance and could prevent the horse lifting its quarters up over the fence. Hunting men who leant back in the stirrups when jumping were carrying out the instinctive movement of bracing themselves against a shock, but if the horse fell, nothing would save them and, unless they defied the law of gravity, no amount of tugging on the reins would hold the horse up.

After the show of 1907 Caprilli's system gained acceptance and there was some determination by the British to do better in equestrian trials, but progress was slow. Up to World War II the majority of British horsemen concentrated their efforts on hunting and polo.

During that time an important test for the horse and rider had emerged. Known as the *militaire*, or at one time as the military versatility test, it was the outcome of the type of training that had been going on in Saumur, where dressage was combined with a stiff cross-country course. The militaire, consisting of dressage, a steeplechase, road and track riding and showjumping, became increasingly popular. In 1912 it was included in the Olympic Games.

After the end of World War II the militaire was opened to civilians and became the modern three-day event. The Duke of

Beaufort organized the first annual three-day event competition at his home at Badminton in 1948, and this is now one of the most famous fixtures for this sport.

'Eventing' is a word that has passed into the English language. The combination of dressage, cross-country riding and showjumping on the third day is a real test of the skill and endurance of both rider and horse. It has been argued that eventing encourages the production of a horse which is a mediocre all-rounder and good at nothing in particular, and it is true that, in the dressage on the first day, the horse is often too wound up for the next day's endurance test to perform to the highest standard, and on the final day, when the horse is tired, the showjumping is little more than a test of the horse's obedience and willingness to continue. But eventing is not just a test of the horse. It is a test of the partnership of rider and horse which requires intelligence on the part of the rider and physical skill and courage on the part of the horse.

In the early days of showjumping, riders usually indicated to the horse its stride and the moment it should take off. After Caprilli, things changed. He believed that, provided

Left: Richard Walker riding Accumulator at Badminton, 1984.

Right: *Harvey Smith at the Royal Show 1984.*

the horse was properly balanced, it would do best if it was left to its own devices. Today, the situation is changing back again: with higher jumps in the showring and complicated courses, made more testing by jumping against the clock, the horse needs the intelligence and guidance of the rider. Before an event the rider must walk the course and plan his strategy to suit his horse's capabilities. One thing he must not do is to ask so much from his horse that it makes mistakes at jumps and loses confidence. The confidence of the horse is the rider's most valuable asset.

Partnership between man and horse is an exhilarating experience which is enjoyed by thousands of riders and, thanks to television, by millions of spectators. The pleasure it gives ought to assure the future of the horse, especially when it is combined with the incurable optimism of every horse owner, eloquently expressed by Xenophon more than 23 centuries ago:

"If a man buys his horses wisely, feeds and handles them, exercises and trains them well, there is nothing but the interposition of some divinity to prevent him from owning a famous horse and becoming himself a famous horseman."

WORLD BREEDS

This section gives a description of the world's most popular breeds of light horses, heavy horses and ponies. Each breed is illustrated in full colour, with a short easy-to-consult summary of the main characteristics of the breed. Each entry gives the history and derivation of the breed in some detail, as well as indicating the purposes for which each breed is particularly suited. For easy consultation the breeds are listed alphabetically, country by country.

The gentle and courageous Welsh pony has roamed the Welsh hills since pre-history. These agile ponies are natural jumpers and have always been favoured as good breeding stock for larger ponies and horses.

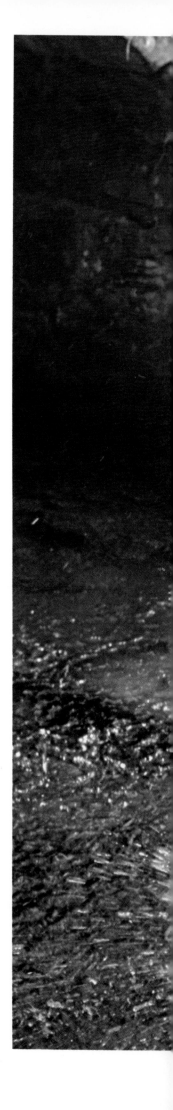

THE WALER

Australia was almost entirely without horses until about 200 years ago when European settlers imported stock from Europe and South Africa including good English Thoroughbreds, and Arabian stallions which were in much demand by the breeders. The Waler receives its name from its place of origin, New South Wales. All newly inhabited areas of Australia were given the name New South Wales and consequently all saddle horses from these settled parts became known as Walers. Eventually, when Australia was divided into separate states with their own names, the general term Waler was retained for the Australian Saddle Bred Horse.

The Waler originated from crossing English Thoroughbred, Arab and Anglo-Arab stallions with the best local mares. Today, the best examples of the Waler breed have many characteristics of the Thoroughbred. As the breed continued to flourish, it proved itself to be one of the best saddle horses in the world.

During World War I, good chargers were in great demand by the Indian army and Walers were supplied in huge numbers throughout the campaign. Australia herself provided a cavalry division made up almost entirely of Walers. The tremendous stamina and endurance of this breed undoubtedly played a major part in the defeat of the Turks. Unfortunately, because of strict Australian quarantine laws, these horses could not return to their homeland and many were destroyed. Today, in Sydney, a memorial honours these brave horses.

Many modern Australian saddle horses of uncertain breeding are given the name Waler. Their height on average is 16 hh and all solid colours can be found. They possess a very kind nature, tremendous endurance and stamina and a natural instinct for survival.

The Waler is named after its place of origin, New South Wales.

CHARACTERISTICS
Height Average 16 hh.
Colour All solid colours.
Conformation Varied, though they possess many Thoroughbred characteristics.
Temperament Very good. Equable disposition, hard working and willing.
Use Very good general all-purpose saddle horse.

THE HAFLINGER PONY

Haflingers all look remarkably alike, due to close in-breeding.

A native of Austria, the Haflinger was extensively bred in the district of Hafling which is now part of Northern Italy and from which it took its name. All Haflingers carry the brand of an Edelweiss, the national flower of Austria, with an 'H' in the middle.

A combination of Nordic and Oriental blood and extreme mountain temperatures produced an exceptionally strong, hardy and sure-footed animal, used extensively for farm and forest work. Also, the steep, rugged slopes of their natural habitat has helped to develop good lung and heart capacity as well as sound feet and legs. Because of close inbreeding, the Haflinger has developed into a fixed breed of definite type. Always chestnut in colour with white facial markings and a flaxen mane and tail, the Haflingers are all very similar in appearance. The ponies are now bred throughout Austria and are in demand all over the world, especially in Germany and Switzerland. Colt foals have to pass strict official inspections before they are chosen as future stallions and are kept at the government stud farms. Individual breeders are only allowed to keep mares.

Averaging about 13.2 hh, these ponies are not worked until they are about four years old and invariably live to a grand old age. In fact, they have been known to be still working at the age of forty. Under saddle and in harness, the Haflinger can work long and hard and survive on very little food and in difficult conditions. They make excellent trekking ponies and are a popular tourist attraction for showing visitors the beautiful Austrian countryside.

Their placid temperament, suitable for beginners, their strength of body and character, their free action and very attractive appearance have made Haflingers very popular and they are now bred in many other countries.

CHARACTERISTICS
Height 13 hh—14.2 hh.
Colour Various shades of chestnut with flaxen mane and tail and white markings on the face.
Conformation Small, slightly dished head, strong neck and good riding shoulders. Broad chest, strong back, muscular quarters. Clean, strong legs, hard feet.
Temperament Excellent. Very docile and ideal for beginners.
Use All-purpose pony under saddle and in harness. Trekking and general riding.

THE LIPIZZANER

The Lipizzaner has come to be known world wide as the most outstanding performer of high-school riding or *haute école*. Small in stature (averaging about 15 hh–15.2 hh), these beautiful grey horses of spectacular grace are famous for their association with the Spanish Riding School of Vienna.

The Lipizzaners of today can be traced directly back to the founding of a stud in Lipizza, then part of Austria but now of Yugoslavia, in 1580 by Archduke Charles II. He imported horses of Spanish Andalucian breeding believed to be descendants of the Spanish horses used on ceremonial occasions by the Roman emperors. The importing of these horses continued until the 17th century with the inclusion of some Arab blood.

The stud was all but destroyed during the Napoleonic Wars, but Franz Joseph I gave the breed a permanent home at Lipizza and there the Lipizzaners flourished in ideal breeding conditions. Today at the famous Piber Stud in Austria the Lipizzaners are bred for the Spanish Riding School.

The Lipizzaner is an exceptionally strong and compact horse with shortish legs and powerful quarters. Its unique athletic ability is demonstrated when performing brilliant movements such as the *croupade*, *courbette* and the *capriole*. With its docile temperament, the Lipizzaner also makes a fine carriage horse. Although predominantly grey, the foals are born brown or black and it takes up to 10 years for them to change colour.

CHARACTERISTICS
Height 14.3 hh–16 hh.
Colour Predominantly grey, few bays. Foals are born black or brown.
Conformation Good, well-shaped head, good, strong neck, compact, muscular body and deep girth. Very powerful quarters, short, strong legs and hard, well-shaped feet.
Temperament Excellent. Docile and placid.
Use High-school riding, good riding horse, under saddle and driving.

Above: the Lipizzaner has a well-shaped head and large expressive eyes.

Left: this breed is noted for its excellent conformation.

THE NORIKER

The Noriker's sturdy build is well suited to mountainous regions.

The Noriker takes its name from Noricum, which formed part of the Roman Empire and roughly corresponded to the present state of Austria. This was the native country of the tough mountain ponies of the Hafling district, the Haflinger ponies, of which the Noriker is a descendant. The Noriker was first bred near Salzburg, the best of the breed being found in the Gross Glockner mountain region. However, it was not until after 1565 when the breed came under the jurisdiction of the monasteries and later the Imperial Court that infusions to improve the breed were made. Blood from Neapolitan, Burgundian and Spanish stallions were introduced to produce what we see today in a good, medium-sized working horse.

The modern Noriker averages between 16 hh and 16.2 hh, is sure-footed and well adapted to work in these mountainous regions both as pack transport and in harness. It has a heavy head set on a short, thick neck, deep chest, short, strong legs and good hard feet. The Noriker has a clean, sure action and a kind, willing temperament and is found throughout Germany, Austria and Bavaria, hence it is also known as the South German Cold Blood. The colours generally found are chestnut and brown.

In order to maintain and improve the standard of the breed, stallions are carefully selected before they may stand at stud. The tests include willingness in harness, the ability to pull a heavy load and walking and trotting trials. Some breed societies also carry out tests on mares carrying their first foals.

CHARACTERISTICS
Height 16 hh–16.2 hh.
Colour Generally chestnut and brown.
Conformation Heavy head, short, thick neck and broad chest. Good, clean legs with plenty of bone and hard feet. Strong, muscular shoulders and powerful quarters.
Temperament Very good. Kind and willing.
Use As pack horses and working in harness.

THE CANADIAN CUTTING HORSE

This is the Canadian version of the American Quarter Horse, from which it was developed.

As far back as 1665, Canada began importing draught horses, trotters and pacers from Normandy and Brittany and by the mid-18th century a definite type of Canadian Draught Horse had been established. It was a horse very similar to the Percheron, an excellent general all-purpose animal that possessed a superb temperament and particularly hardy constitution. The popularity of the light Canadian Draught Horse spread widely through America and in both America and Canada it was crossed with the versatile American Quarter Horse. It is from this American breed that the modern Canadian Cutting Horse has inherited an innate talent for working cattle.

In 1885, the official stud book was opened and within 10 years a breeders' association was founded. Horses are only accepted for registration upon inspection. Today, the Canadian Cutting Horse is found throughout Canada although mainly in the province of Quebec, the main breeding centre being at the Agricultural Research Station at Deschambauld, Quebec.

The modern Canadian Cutting Horse closely resembles the American Quarter Horse in appearance and disposition. It is extremely intelligent, quick and agile and, like its American cousin, is used extensively for competition work. Standing between 15.2 hh and 16.1 hh, it is generally bigger than the Quarter Horse but is compact and muscular, with powerful quarters and short, sound legs. The Canadian Cutting Horse can be found in almost any solid colour and is a very popular all-round riding horse.

CHARACTERISTICS
Height 15.2 hh–16.1 hh.
Colour Any solid colour.
Conformation Kind head, muscular neck and strong shoulders. Short back with powerful quarters, strong, sound legs.
Temperament Excellent. Very kind, willing and intelligent.
Use Good all-round riding horse.

THE FREDERIKSBORG

The Royal Frederiksborg Stud was first set up in 1562 by King Frederik II of Denmark and was one of the most highly regarded and successful studs to be founded in that century. The foundation stock consisted of Andalucians imported from Spain and Neapolitan blood. Further Eastern and British blood was introduced and the Frederiksborg was developed.

As the demand grew for lighter, more active military horses, the Frederiksborg proved itself most suitable for this occupation as well as fully capable of working in harness on the farms. The breed showed tremendous courage and obedience in the line of duty and those that had been schooled to high standards of *haute école* proved the most suitable as military chargers. In addition, the Frederiksborg was considered one of the most elegant riding horses in Europe during the popular times of the European riding schools. With its active and obedient temperament and its superb, agile action, the popularity of this breed spread throughout Europe. Without careful control or any regard for the future, breeding stock was sold in great numbers in order to upgrade breeds throughout the world, including America where it was the forerunner of the American 'pleasure horse'. As a result, the Royal stud was forced to close in 1839 as it had seriously depleted the best of its stock and no longer housed any suitable breeding material. However, a considerable number of Frederiksborgs still exist throughout Denmark thanks to the private breeders who continued their enthusiasm for the breed. They are still extremely useful as both riding horses and harness horses.

In 1923, official registration of the Frederiksborg began and every year about 100 stallions and 1000 mares are registered. This medium-weight working horse stands about 15.3 hh and is generally chestnut in colour. It possesses particularly powerful, muscular shoulders and chest, and strong legs with plenty of bone. Its head is slightly convex in outline, showing its Spanish heritage, and its temperament is kind, willing, hard working and very courageous.

This strong active horse was first developed for use as a military charger.

CHARACTERISTICS
Height Average 15.3 hh.
Colour Predominately chestnut.
Conformation Face convex in outline, muscular shoulders and powerful chest, powerful quarters. Good legs with plenty of bone.
Temperament Excellent. Kind, willing and hard working.
Use Good under saddle and in harness.

THE ARAB

The typical refined 'dished' face of the Arab.

The Arab, originally bred in Arabia, is the oldest purebreed and has undoubtedly made the most substantial contribution to the development of the equine world. Today, the Arab is bred throughout the world and is generally considered to be the most refined and beautiful of all horses. The Arab was established as a breed many centuries before any other due to the determination of the tribesmen that their breed should remain pure and that no foreign blood should be introduced. The extraordinary pure qualities of the Arab are unsurpassable and, because of the prepotency of the breed, have been preserved since ancient days. During the 17th and 18th centuries, the Arab was of vital importance to the development of almost all European breeds, though it was first imported to Europe in the seventh century when the Moors crossed into the Iberian Peninsula from North Africa. Breeds such as the Percheron, the Lipizzaner, the Austrian Haflinger pony and the Russian Don and virtually all British native pony breeds owe many of their characteristics to the Arab which was first taken across the Atlantic with the Spaniards.

Even with all this cross-breeding, the pure-bred Arab is well established all over the world, though types of the breed vary slightly. Arab studs have been established particularly in Europe, America and Australia.

Although the demand for equestrian sports such as show jumping and eventing have perhaps overtaken the scope of the Arab, it remains, nevertheless, a superb riding horse with an amenable disposition and a will of iron. It possesses unequalled stamina and strength most suitable for endurance riding, and remarkable speed for racing. The Anglo-Arab (or Arab cross Thoroughbred) has often proved itself to be a performance horse of the highest class.

The Arab, though small, averaging 14 hh to 15 hh, combines a delightful gentle temperament with a spirit and liveliness that is not only beautiful to watch but also very manageable to handle. The lovely characteristic head with dished profile, large eyes, elegant neck and muscular body set off by a silky coat and high-carried tail gives an impression of pride and majesty.

CHARACTERISTICS
Height 14 hh–15 hh.
Colour Bay, brown, chestnut, black and grey.
Conformation Short, fine head with dished profile, large eyes and small ears. Long, elegant neck slightly curved and sloping shoulders. Short, concave back, deep girth and chest and good, strong quarters. Clean, strong legs with dense bone and good, hard feet.
Temperament Excellent. Kind, gentle and willing, though high spirited.
Use Good all-round riding horse; racing and long distance riding.

THE FINNISH

The modern Finnish is a very similar breed to the native ponies found in the north of Scandinavia and is the only recognized breed of Finland. The Finnish is a descendant of the Finnish Draught and the Finnish Universal, two closely related breeds developed by crossing imported stock with the native ponies.

The Finnish was bred primarily as a working horse, and the result of careful, selective

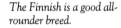

The Finnish is a good all-rounder breed.

breeding produced a very versatile, powerful yet agile type particularly noted for its tremendous endurance and excellent constitution.

The modern Finnish is a good all-purpose horse and two slightly different types have emerged. The lighter version is used as a very capable and versatile riding horse. The draught type is slightly more common and tough and is predominantly used for timber hauling and heavy harness work. The latter type is capable of tremendous, endless work which it does willingly in the most extreme of conditions. Trotting races are also very popular in Finland and the best trotters of this breed have been selectively bred.

In 1907, the official stud book for the Finnish was opened and only one stud book is maintained. Within 53 years, 70,000 stallions and 100,000 mares were registered. In order to be accepted for registration, at the age of 4 years each horse must pass the selection test. These tests are on pulling power, soundness and conformation, temperament and action.

The Finnish stands about 15 hh and is very powerful for its size. It is usually found in chestnut, bay, brown or black and is a horse with good, strong bone. What the breed may lack in looks and quality, it gains in its superb temperament, disposition and endurance.

CHARACTERISTICS
Height Average 15 hh.
Colour Chestnut, bay, brown and black.
Conformation Thick, strong neck and powerful, muscular shoulders. Deep girth, powerful quarters and legs of good, strong bone.
Temperament Excellent. Kind and hard-working.
Use Good all-rounder under saddle and in harness. Trotting races.

THE ARDENNAIS

This Ardennais well demonstrates the stockiness of the breed.

Surviving the harsh and severe winters of the French Ardennes produced this adaptable and thick-set breed that is best suited for heavy farm work. The Ardennais is an enormously tough horse, standing up to 15.3 hh. Although a smaller, finer type can be found around Chaumont, resembling the Ardennais of former times which are believed to have been the only horses to carry back the troops of the Emperor Napoleon from the failed Russian campaign, it is the heavier type that is the most preferred. The popularity of the Ardennais is growing to such an extent that the stud organization has had to limit further expansion in order to preserve the quality of the breed.

The breed suffered badly during and after World War II and there was heavy importation from other European countries including Belgium and the Netherlands in order to build up the depleted French stock.

The Ardennais is an animal of such gentle-ness and docility that even a child can handle one, and it is perfectly adapted to its surroundings and occupation. It is of extremely heavy build with enormous bone structure, and is more thick-set than other heavy horses, standing close to the ground on short, but extremely strong, legs with well-covered muscles. Found usually in bay, chestnut or roan, the Ardennais is one of the most admired of all French breeds.

CHARACTERISTICS
Height Up to 15.3 hh.
Colour Bay, chestnut or roan.
Conformation Large head set on a thick neck. Extremely muscular throughout with powerful quarters, short, strong legs and compact, stocky all-over appearance.
Temperament Excellent, extremely docile and gentle.
Use Agricultural work.

THE BRETON

This small draught or carriage horse, indigenous to Brittany in North-West France, has developed unique qualities of appearance and endurance so that it cannot be compared to any other breed in the world. The original pony-like character of the Breton still exists today, despite the numerous infusions of foreign blood which have resulted in the emergence of three distinct types. The Postier, standing about 15 hh, is one type of Breton that possesses a good, active trot as a result of Norfolk Trotters and Hackneys being infiltrated into Normandy to encourage and develop trotting abilities. The Corlay was influenced by Arabian and Thoroughbred blood and produced a lighter, and today rather rare, carriage and riding horse. The third and most common type is the Draught Breton, which stands about 16 hh and contains infusions of Percheron, Ardennais and Boulonnais blood.

The Breton is a horse noted for its excellent disposition and is similar in looks to the primitive horse of the Steppes. The breed has been used quite extensively and successfully to produce very useful half-bred work horses, especially in North Africa where it has upgraded the local horse in agriculture. Military remounts have played a particularly active part in Brittany and the Breton has been used extensively by the Horse Artillery. The capital of Brittany is Landivisiau in the centre of north Finistère and it is here that the extensive buying and selling of the breed throughout the world takes place. Countries such as Japan, Switzerland, Italy and Spain are particularly keen to acquire this extremely adaptable horse which is loved especially for its willingness and hard working attitude.

CHARACTERISTICS
Height Up to 16 hh.
Colour Blue and red roan, bay, chestnut and occasionally black.
Conformation Thick-set throughout. Extremely strong neck and shoulders, short back with powerful quarters, good strong legs with plenty of bone.
Temperament Excellent. Willing, kind and adaptable.
Use Draught or carriage horse.

The Bretons are often used for work in the French vineyards.

THE PERCHERON

A Percheron taking part in a Heavy Horse competition.

The Percheron is the best known variety of heavy horse and is also the most widely exported throughout the world, including America and Britain. The breed originated in a region of France known as Perche, hence the name, and today the Percheron stud book restricts its entries to only those bred in the departments of Perche, that is, Sarthe, Eure et Loir, Orne and Loir et Cher. Horses bred in other regions have their own stud book.

The Percheron is of Arab ancestry, dating from the time when the Lords of Nogent, Belleme and Mortagne kept Arab stallions on their land and so began the tradition of Arab infiltration. The Percheron is more highly strung than other heavy horses due to the Arab influence and has inherited a relatively fine head, as well as qualities of grace and endurance.

This is a working breed. Mares are scattered around the various farms and only stop working when foaling, whereas the stallions are kept by a few select breeding families who control the breeding and sale of the stock. Farmers of Perche are offered semen from the best quality stallions but must return an option on the animal when born. Foals sold as stallions can only be bought by the breed's stud organization or the breeders. As a coach horse, the Percheron was invaluable, combining strength and stamina with grace, freedom of movement and a love of work. As the demand for this type of work declined, the breed returned to work on the farm. Even though selective breeding produced a carthorse type better suited to farm duties, it retained much of its original quality and character, though perhaps it lost some of its activity of step and compact frame. When castrated, however, the breed tends to lose much of its power and nobility of movement.

The Percheron is an extremely well constructed horse, averaging between 15.2 hh and 17 hh. With careful, firm handling it shows extreme talent and a willingness to work. Despite its immense size, strongly built frame, wide body and powerful quarters, the Percheron, which can weigh up to 1 ton, moves with perfect balance, poise and even elegance.

CHARACTERISTICS
Height 15.2 hh–17 hh.
Colour Grey or black.
Conformation Relatively fine head, muscular neck, good sloping shoulders. Pointed chest with pronounced breastbone, wide body and good, strong quarters. Sound legs with good bone.
Temperament Good. Slightly highly strung and needs careful handling.
Use Agricultural work.

THE SELLE FRANCAISE

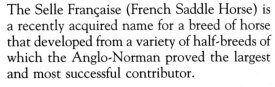

This breed has a good conformation and temperament.

The Selle Française (French Saddle Horse) is a recently acquired name for a breed of horse that developed from a variety of half-breeds of which the Anglo-Norman proved the largest and most successful contributor.

Standing between 15.2 hh and 16.3 hh, this quality horse with an excellent temperament and good, strong conformation can be found in regions of France such as Vendée, Charblais and Angevin. Its ancestor, the Anglo-Norman, was a descendant of the big Norman Draught Horse which was originally bred as a draught animal but was later used as a war horse.

During the 17th century, German, Arab and Barb blood was introduced to produce a good, strong all-purpose saddle horse and still further infiltrations occurred through the following two centuries with the introduction of Norfolk Trotter and English Thoroughbred blood. And so the Anglo-Norman came into existence, developing into two rather distinctive types: The French Trotter and the Anglo-Norman Saddle Horse—which has been used in harness, as a cavalry mount and as a good riding horse.

The quality hunter-type Selle Française we know today was bred primarily as a competition horse and is a result of more recent Thoroughbred influence. A large percentage of Selle Française have been sired by Selle Française and Thoroughbred stallions, fewer by Anglo-Arabs and a small percentage by French Trotters.

CHARACTERISTICS

Height According to its weight-carrying capabilities:

Medium weight: Small 15.3 hh and under.
Medium 15.3–16.1 hh.
Large over 16.1 hh.

Heavyweight: Small under 16 hh.
Large over 16 hh.

Colour Any solid colour, predominantly chestnut.

Conformation Fine head, long, elegant neck and good riding shoulders. Deep chest, strong, powerful quarters and legs of good bone.

Temperament Excellent. Willing, kind and sometimes spirited.

Use Good all-purpose riding horse, jumping and eventing.

THE FRIESIAN

The Friesian's willing temperament makes it an idea all-rounder.

The Friesian is one of the oldest breeds in Europe. In Friesland, from where this breed takes its name, excavations have shown that a heavy horse was domesticated there some 3000 years ago, enduring extreme weather conditions. It was during the crusades that Eastern stallions were brought back to Friesland, greatly improving the then rather rough and heavily built breed. It was, however, during the 17th century that the Friesian became much sought after as a highly reputable weight carrier.

As the breed flourished on the rich Friesian pastures, they proved themselves excellent trotters and during the 19th century when trotting races became very popular in the Netherlands, the Friesians excelled. However, as production concentrated on lighter, faster horses, the Friesian became less suited for its occupation as an agricultural worker and the breed began to decline in numbers. With the adoption of a new breeding plan and the establishment of the Friesian Society (which in 1954 was awarded the title of 'Royal'), this breed has never looked back.

The Friesian today is a smart and attractive animal of about 15 hh with a good nature and willing disposition. Very compact and muscular with a fine head, strong body and short, feathery legs, the Friesian makes an ideal all-round working and pleasure horse and is very popular at horse shows throughout Europe.

CHARACTERISTICS
Height Approximately 15 hh.
Colour Jet black with no white markings.
Conformation Bright, alert head, longish, muscular neck and strong shoulders. Short, strong back and powerful quarters. Short legs with good, clean bone, hard feet and feathered heels.
Temperament Excellent. Kind nature, willing and easy to handle.
Use Working and pleasure, under saddle and in harness.

THE HANOVERIAN

Hanoverians have been bred for equestrian sports since World War II.

As with many other breeds, the Hanoverian originally developed by combining the blood of Spanish, Neapolitan and Oriental stallions with native mares to produce what today is considered to be the most popular and successful of Germany's warm-bloods. Although the breed is believed to trace back to the Great Horse of the Middle Ages, the breed largely owes its existence to the House of Hanover who promoted and supported its development.

When George I, the Elector of Hanover, inherited the British throne in 1714, British collaboration with breeding was already taking place with the introduction of Thoroughbred blood into the German studs. In 1735, George II founded the Landgestüt at Celle and installed 14 black Holstein stallions to be crossed with Holstein, Neapolitan and Andalucian mares. It was later that more Thoroughbred blood was introduced to produce a lighter horse but still with the strength and endurance capable of working under saddle and in harness.

The Napoleonic Wars seriously threatened the breed and in order to reinstate its former population, much more Thoroughbred blood was introduced. Up until World War I, the objective of the breeders was to produce an all-purpose horse of quality and stamina, but, as the role of the horse in agriculture declined rapidly after 1940, the breeders concentrated on producing an exceptional competition horse by introducing Trakehner and Thoroughbred blood to upgrade the breed.

Today, the Hanoverian is in great demand, particularly as a show jumper and dressage horse. As with many other European breeds, the Hanoverian stallions have to pass rigid selection tests before they are accepted for stud duties.

A big, powerful horse of exceptional competitive ability, the Hanoverian may lack the speed of the Thoroughbred but possesses all the quality and presence to dominate the warm-blood breeding in Germany.

CHARACTERISTICS
Height 15.3 hh–16.2 hh.
Colour Any solid colour, usually chestnut, bay, black or brown.
Conformation Fairly plain head; long, well-placed neck. Large, sloping shoulders, deep girth and powerful quarters. Well-muscled legs with good, hard feet.
Temperament Very good. Well mannered and easy to handle.
Use Exceptional competition horse, particularly show jumping and dressage. Driving; a good riding horse.

THE HOLSTEIN

The origins of the Holstein can be traced back to the great horses which carried knights in armour into battle in the Middle Ages. As with the Hanoverian, the Holstein was developed by crossing Spanish, Oriental and Neapolitan stallions with the native mares of the Schleswig-Holstein region, the breed's birthplace and from whence its name derived. As a war horse, the Holstein was invaluable but, as the need for these declined and the demand for harness horses increased, British Yorkshire Coach Horses and Cleveland Bay stallions were imported to produce a strong, high-stepping carriage horse with an exceptionally good temperament. The introduction of English Thoroughbred blood upgraded and refined the breed to produce a dual-purpose animal suitable for riding and driving and also developed a more compact horse with shorter legs and a more refined head. Since World War II, the Holstein has seen still further changes with the introduction of more Thoroughbred blood to produce the multipurpose riding horse that we know today.

At the age of three or four, all Holstein stallions must pass performance tests before they are accepted to stand as stallions.

This strong, large (averaging between 16 hh and 17 hh) horse has proved its talent and versatility in eventing, dressage and particularly show jumping, reaching international levels in several cases, and exhibits the quality of an excellent hunter with a kind and

sensible temperament suitable for the not so experienced rider. Its popularity reaches around the world and as early as 1892 the Holstein stud book was opened in America. Holsteins such as the famous dressage horse, Granat, ridden by Christine Stuckleburger of Switzerland and the eventer, Magrigal, bronze medal winner for Germany at the 1976 Montreal Olympics, are just two examples of the competition stars of this breed.

Above: *the Holstein brand is clearly visible on this horse's flank.*
Below: *the Holstein's attractive, expressive head.*

CHARACTERISTICS
Height 16 hh—17 hh.
Colour Any solid colour, particularly bay and black.
Conformation Bright, well-shaped head, long, muscular and slightly arched neck. Good, deep chest, strong back and powerful quarters. Short, strong legs set square; clean hocks and sloping shoulders. Good bone and hard feet.
Temperament Excellent. Well mannered, willing and docile.
Use All-purpose riding horse, particularly jumping.

THE OLDENBURG

Above: the Oldenburg is Germany's largest and heaviest warm-blood.

Right: crossing with Thoroughbreds has produced an all-purpose horse.

This strong, heavy type of horse based on the Friesian originated in the region of Oldenburg during the 17th century. The Oldenburg was founded by Count Anton Gunther (1603–1667) who owned the celebrated grey stallion, Kranich.

Originally bred as a strong carriage horse, the demand for lighter, faster harness horses encouraged breeders during the 17th century and early 18th century to import stallions from Spain and Italy and the resulting crosses greatly improved the quality of the Oldenburg. In the second half of the 18th century, further infusions of Spanish, Neapolitan, Barb and English half-bred blood consolidated the breed. By the end of the century, Thoroughbred, Cleveland Bay, Hanoverian and Norman horses were also being imported, resulting in powerful, all-purpose riding and coach horses.

The Oldenburg Horse Breeding Act passed in 1819 and revised in 1923 delegates the responsibility of licensing the breed to the Society of Breeders of the Oldenburg Horse and their strict selection methods contribute to the uniformity of the breed. All three-year-old stallions are sent for testing to a centre in Westercelle before they are approved for breeding.

During the present century, as the need for carriage horses saw a rapid decline, more Thoroughbred blood (particularly that of the Thoroughbred stallion Lupus), Norman blood (from the stallion Condor), Hanoverian and Trakehner blood has been introduced to produce the very useful, strong, versatile all-purpose riding horse that we know today.

Although perhaps lacking the hardiness and endurance of other German breeds, the Oldenburg once again is becoming a very popular harness horse, now often seen competing in combined driving competitions. The Oldenburg is noted for its very tall stature (often reaching 17.2 hh), short legs, strong back and good bone, coupled with a very kind and bold nature.

CHARACTERISTICS
Height 16.2 hh–17.2 hh (sometimes exceeding).
Colour Bay, brown, black or grey.
Conformation Large head with Roman nose, thick and strong neck, sloping well-muscled shoulders, deep chest and powerful quarters. Short legs with good bone.
Temperament Excellent. Bold and willing yet kind and docile.
Use All purpose riding horse; driving.

THE TRAKEHNER

Trakehners are the most elegant and handsome of the German warm-bloods.

The foundation of the Trakehner breed, also known as the East Prussian, traces back to the order of the German Knights, but it was not until 1732, when King Friedrich Wilhelm I of Prussia established the main stud of Trakehnen in North-East Prussia, that the Trakehner began controlled and selective breeding. By importing quality Arabians from Poland and carefully selecting the stallions and foundation mares to produce offspring for various purposes, Trakehnen became the breeding centre of East Prussia. However, in 1786 the stud was taken over by the State and the breeding policy was modified to concentrate more on developing cavalry horses, for which the Trakehner proved excellent.

At the beginning of the 19th century, the type of Trakehner we see today began its development when further Arabian and English Thoroughbred blood was introduced and by 1913 at least 80 per cent of all mares had been sired by Thoroughbred stallions. By the end of World War II there were 15,000 breeders and about 25,000 Trakehners registered with the Trakehner Stud Book. In 1945, as the Germans retreated from Poland, breeders and horses desperately fled to West Germany, saving only 1,200 horses. It is here

that today the Trakehner is privately bred and takes fame as the only national horse in the Republic.

The superb conformation and disposition of this top-class riding horse has established its excellent reputation throughout the world. Breeding is controlled by the society of Breeders and Friends of the Warm Blood Horse of Trakehner Origin in Hamburg and it is evident that the admiration and demand for this quality horse is very likely to be maintained.

Standing between 16 hh and 16.2 hh with tremendous stamina, versatility and a big heart, the Trakehner has proved a successful competition horse.

CHARACTERISTICS
Height 16 hh–16.2 hh.
Colour Any solid colour.
Conformation Large, refined head, elegant neck, sloping shoulders, strong body and well rounded and powerful quarters. Strong, hard legs with good feet.
Temperament Excellent. Generous, kind and docile.
Use All-purpose riding horse; jumping.

THE WÜRTTEMBERG

This sensible breed goes very happily into harness.

During the 16th century, the royal studs of Germany were very influential in the development and breeding of the Warm-Blood horse, both in the mountainous region of Württemberg and at the main stud at Marbach, founded in 1593. The chalky, hard environment of the Rauhe Alb mountains helped develop the Württemberg into an extremely hardy, all-purpose animal that was easy to handle and suitable for working the small farms of the area. But in order to improve the breed still further for this purpose, the breeders introduced Arab blood as well as infusions of East Prussian, Norman, Oldenburg and Nonius. For a very short time Clydesdale and Suffolk stallions were also introduced to increase the strength of the breed, but this was later discontinued.

The type of Württemberg we know today was largely influenced by the Anglo-Norman stallion, Faust, a medium-sized, compact cob type. He produced useful horses of excellent temperament and hardy constitution. It was not until 1895 that the official stud book was opened, once the required type had been achieved. Experiments with infusions of Thoroughbred blood and that of Holsteins were considered unsuccessful, though influences from Brandenberg and Hanover have been advantageous.

Since World War II, the breed has been improved still more with East Prussian blood (of Thoroughbred and Arab background), most notably that of Julmond, an East Prussian Trakehner who passed on reliable and approved characteristics and conformation, resulting in today's all-purpose performance horse. The Württemberg is a very strong, sound and sensible cob-type, standing about 16 hh and has proved versatile under saddle and in harness. It is a very economical feeder that willingly works long and hard and has a very kind and generous nature.

CHARACTERISTICS
Height 16 hh maximum.
Colour Bay, chestnut, brown, black.
Conformation Good, strong cob-type. Stocky with deep girth, strong legs and powerful quarters.
Temperament Excellent. Very willing, hard working and kind.
Use Good all-purpose horse ridden under saddle and in harness.

THE CLEVELAND BAY

Above: an excellent all-round competition horse.
Below: the handsome Cleveland Bay head.

The Cleveland Bay is a large horse that comes from the area around Cleveland in Yorkshire and, as its name implies, it is a bay with black points and no white except for a small star on the forehead. It is a strong horse, and since medieval times has been used extensively both as a pack-horse and in agriculture. Today its power is valued in the hunting field where a strong leg action allows it to move swiftly over heavy ground.

The Cleveland Bay has been popular with breeders for, like the Arab, it tends to be prepotent. When crossed with another breed its qualities are stamped on the offspring and re-appear in successive generations. For this reason, the Cleveland Bay has been widely used as foundation stock for crossing with the Thoroughbred, and this has filled the demand for lighter hunters and a faster carriage horse. The pure-bred Cleveland is still found both in the hunting field and in harness—the Royal Coach is sometimes pulled by a team of Clevelands—although at one time it seemed that, in its pure form, the breed was becoming increasingly rare. Today, a lighter horse continues to be more popular, but fortunately there is still a good demand for the pure-bred Cleveland overseas.

CHARACTERISTICS
Height 16 hh–16.2 hh.
Colour Bay.
Conformation Bold head, long neck, good shoulders, deep girth, long back with powerful quarters, short legs with good strong bone.
Temperament Excellent. Intelligent and well-mannered.
Use Riding horses, show jumpers, eventers, hunters, driving, light draught work.

THE COB

The Cob gives a very comfortable ride, ideal for a day's hacking or hunting.

The Cob is not a breed but rather a type of horse that tends to be typically British, though it is also found in many other countries. There is no basic breeding pattern to produce a good Cob though many of the best results come from chance crosses. However, a good result will most likely be because of crossing a heavyweight hunter, or perhaps one with some heavyweight blood, or an Irish Draught horse, with a Thoroughbred.

A good Cob can be a wonderful ride, comfortable, obedient and placid, especially good for the beginner, elderly or nervous rider. Although their stocky build and short legs impose certain limitations to the scope of the Cob, they are by no means dull, sluggish animals. Their compact and sturdy build along with their safe and calm disposition, certain gaiety and willing attitude will give their riders an enjoyable safe day's hunting and they can take part, though perhaps at a limited level, in many different competitive events. Many of the best Cobs today can be seen in the show ring. Their powerful quarters ensure some good jumping ability while their short, strong backs and short, sound legs mean they are capable of carrying a fair amount of weight.

Up until 1948 when the Docking and Nicking Act was passed, the Cob was usually shown with a docked tail, and today it is still usual to see a Cob with a hogged (roached) mane. With its relatively small head set on an elegant, arched neck, deep body and well-rounded quarters, this well-mannered and obedient horse is a pleasure to see. With its high action and straight shoulder, the Cob is also very good in harness.

CHARACTERISTICS
Height Up to 15.2 hh.
Colour Any solid colour.
Conformation Small, quality head with a strong, arched neck and muscular shoulders. Short, strong back, deep girth and sound legs with plenty of bone.
Temperament Excellent. Perfect manners, safe and kind.
Use Showing under saddle and in harness, hunting, hacking and jumping.

THE CONNEMARA PONY

The Connemara Pony is the native pony breed of Ireland, and is one of the most beautiful of the mountain and moorland breeds. Although its exact origins are unknown, this hardy pony developed in the wild, mountainous region of Connaught, surviving the extreme climate by eating herbs, rushes and reeds as well as grasses. The minerals in this diet contributed significantly to the strength and endurance of these ponies. The environment also helped produce their hardiness, agility and sure-footedness, with good, strong feet to survive the rocky slopes and the bogs.

A descendant of the Celtic pony, the Connemara has over the years had an infusion of Andalucian, Barb and Arab blood, and Arab characteristics are still apparent in the modern breed. In 1923, the existing stud book was opened by the local pony society and the Department of Agriculture. No animal is accepted for registration until the age of two years when it must be passed by the inspection committee at various centres in Connemara. They are not accepted on breeding alone. They must be sound, true to the breed and possess a good, kind temperament and an easy, calm disposition. The pony must be short in the leg (over 14 hh is not accepted) with good shoulders, well-balanced head and neck, good strong legs and an easy and true action. All stallions in Ireland must also be licensed with the government.

Today, the Connemara makes an ideal riding pony for both children and adults. It is fast, sturdy, a natural jumper and good in harness. When crossed with the Thoroughbred, the Connemara produces a large, good all-round riding horse that has proven itself as a very high quality, successful competition animal. Little Model, out of a Connemara mare, represented Britain at dressage at the Rome Olympics and Dundrum, also out of a Connemara mare, won many international show jumping titles ridden by Tommy Wade, including the King George V Gold Cup.

Demand for the Connemara pony reaches around the world, particularly in America where the smaller type is preferred. Ponies are also exported in large numbers to Britain, Sweden, Germany, Holland, Belgium and France.

CHARACTERISTICS
Height 13 hh–14 hh.
Colour Predominantly grey but also black, brown, dun and occasionally roan and chestnut.
Conformation Small head with large eyes, well-balanced neck. Good sloping shoulders, deep girth, compact body with strong quarters. Short cannons of hard, dense bone.
Temperament Excellent. Ideal child's pony.
Use Good all-round riding pony and in harness and jumping.

The Connemara is one of the most beautiful of the mountain breeds.

THE DALES PONY

Below: the typical alert, expressive face of the Dales Pony.
Right: the pony is noted for its strong, stocky build.

For centuries, the Dales pony has been bred in the area east of the Pennines in North Yorkshire, Northumberland and Durham from where it takes its name. Only at the end of the 19th century was it recognized as a separate breed because of its similarity to its near, though smaller, relative, the Fell. The two breeds also share a likeness with the Welsh Cob and in fact all modern Dales can be traced back to the Welsh Cob, Comet, foaled in 1851. Comet competed in trotting races, putting up some remarkable performances, and was bred extensively with Dales ponies. The trotting ability is still evident today in the modern Dales pony, making it a good working animal, good in harness and capable of pulling extremely heavy weights.

The Dales also make ideal family ponies, sensible and kind enough for children to ride and handle, yet their short, strong backs and stockiness make them capable of carrying even the heaviest adult. Although not very fast, the Dale is a natural jumper and makes an excellent trekking pony, safe and sensible over any type of country, and a superb harness pony. Their hardy constitution means they can live out in the worst of weathers.

CHARACTERISTICS
Height Averaging 14.2 hh.
Colour Mostly black. Also bay, brown and occasionally grey.
Conformation Small head, bright eyes and alert expression. Deep shoulders, short, strong back, deep girth and powerful loins. Strong quarters, short, strong legs and good, hard bone.
Temperament Excellent. Docile and sensible yet active and bright.
Use Hacking, trekking, jumping and harness.

THE DARTMOOR PONY

For thousands of years this tough, hardy little pony has occupied the moorlands in the Dartmoor area of Devonshire. This area of rugged, bleak, windswept slopes, mostly over 1000 feet high, has developed a race of strong and enduring ponies.

It was not until the end of the 19th century that the Dartmoor became recognized as a native breed and until then, when registration was introduced, the breed varied considerably. In 1899, the Dartmoor section of the National Pony Society was opened and since then the standard of the Dartmoor pony has remained relatively unaltered, though infusions of Arab and Welsh blood were introduced at the beginning of this century.

Because of its kind, sensible temperament, sure-footedness and delightful personality, the Dartmoor makes an ideal first pony. The short, compact body with good front and an excellent head carriage means that children feel very secure. A natural jumper, this good looking pony, when crossed with larger ponies, is a useful foundation stock in many studs throughout Britain and produces excellent riding ponies for the older child. Interest in the breed has meant that many have been exported to the United States, Canada and throughout Europe.

The Dartmoor has a kind, equable temperament.

CHARACTERISTICS
Height 12.2 hh.
Colour Black, bay or brown—few white markings accepted.
Conformation Fine, pretty head, large intelligent eyes, small, pricked ears. High set neck, good front and sloping shoulders, short compact body, strong quarters, well set tail, good, strong legs and hard feet.
Temperament Excellent. Sensible, alert and kind.
Use Ideal for a child's first pony. Hacking and jumping.

THE EXMOOR PONY

The Exmoor pony is probably the last survivor of the original Celtic ponies, and the breed was first recorded in the Domesday Book. The Exmoor is a native of the south-west regions of Devon and Somerset where today there are only three principal herds actually running on the moor. In this wild and solitary area, the Exmoor has developed into a particularly hardy pony that can survive the harshest of winters.

This pony should not exceed 12.3 hands (51″) and should not have any white markings. Its distinguishing characteristics are its oatmeal coloured muzzle with black nostrils and its 'toad' or slightly hooded eyes. The texture of its coat is unlike that of any other horse. Thick, springy and rough, it gives protection during the harsh winter on the moor. The foals are protected by a kind of double coat. They have a thick woolly lower layer and a top layer of long waterproof hairs.

This small and exceptionally strong animal makes a good child's pony though it is quite capable of carrying a fully grown man. In fact the Exmoor can carry extraordinary weights quite beyond the capabilities of other ponies. Tough and hardy and with tremendous endurance, the Exmoor is noted for its well set head, good sloping shoulders, deep girth, short back, powerful quarters and good, strong legs.

When crossed with a Thoroughbred a superb quality horse results, inheriting the best qualities from both sides and making a useful larger horse for older children and teenagers. The Exmoor is a highly intelligent and wilful animal that can be quite a handful if not correctly managed. Quick witted and agile, it is particularly suited to the more experienced child. Exmoors provide the finest foundation stock and for this reason they have been exported to horse breeders around the world, particularly Canada and Denmark.

CHARACTERISTICS

Height Height limit 12.2 hh for mares, 12.3 hh for stallions.

Colour Bay, brown and mousy dun. No white markings permitted.

Conformation Short, thick head well set on the neck, good sloping shoulders, deep girth, short back, strong quarters. Short legs with good bone and hard feet. A distinctive tail called 'ice' tail that is thick with a fan-like growth at the top.

Temperament Good. Very intelligent, independent and highly wilful.

Use Good child's pony, though also capable of carrying a fully grown man.

An Exmoor mare at pasture with her foal.

THE FELL PONY

The Fell Pony is noted for its hardiness, well adapted to its rugged mountain habitat.

larger, stronger animals for hauling the heavy materials needed to build roads and forts. The Fell today is a direct descendant of those hard working, weight-carrying ponies. Slightly smaller than the Dale, the Fell pony was originally bred for draught and light farm work and was used extensively during the 18th century as a pack pony working the lead mines, for farm work and participating in the local trotting races. Since 1900, when the National Pony Society opened its stud book to the Fell, very little alien blood has been introduced.

As with most working breeds, the Fell was seriously threatened with the introduction of mechanization, but fortunately interest in the breed after World War II guaranteed its survival. The Fells have truly come into their own as driving ponies as they are exceptional under harness. They make excellent all-purpose ponies and a safe ride for all ages because they are sensible, hardy, strong and sure-footed with a good riding shoulder and native good sense. Agile and clever, though lacking speed and much scope to jump, they are competent across country and do very well in handy pony classes. When crossed with the thoroughbred, the Fell produces a very good hunter with a deep girth, plenty of good bone and good movement. As with other larger mountain and moorland breeds, the Fells make excellent all-round ponies for those who do not aim to compete at a very high level.

Until the end of the 19th century, the ponies bred on either side of the Pennine range in the north of England were indistinguishable. Since then, the ponies bred on the northern side in the Cumberland and Westmorland areas of the Lake District are known as the Fells and their close relations, the Dales, breed to the east. It is believed that when the Romans arrived in the north of England they imported many Friesians to cross with the native ponies they found in order to produce

CHARACTERISTICS
Height 13 hh–14 hh.
Colour Black, dark brown, dark bay and occasionally grey. No white markings.
Conformation Small, well-set head, bright, intelligent eyes. Good strong neck, sloping, strong and well-developed shoulders. Short, strong back, strong quarters. Straight legs with good bone.
Temperament Excellent. A good child's pony.
Use Hacking, trekking and driving.

THE HACKNEY

Right: the Hackney's small neat head.

Far right: the extravagant, elevated trot of the Hackney.

Although today the Hackney is chiefly seen being driven in the show ring, the breed was first developed during the 18th century as a saddle horse. The breed was developed in the East Riding of Yorkshire and in East Anglia, using two rather different trotting breeds—the Yorkshire Hackney, which showed the more quality, and the Norfolk Roadster, more cob-like than its partner. Both breeds shared a common ancestor called The Original Shales, said to be a Hackney, by the thoroughbred Blaze by Flying Childers and can be traced back to The Darley Arabian. Thus, with both Thoroughbred and Arabian blood in its veins, the Hackney came into demand during the 19th century for two main uses. First, as roads were being improved for the use of faster and lighter carriages, these fast horses with their distinctive, high-stepping action and spirited disposition switched roles from the saddle horse to elegant carriage horses. Secondly, the Hackney proved itself a good quality military horse.

Today, the Hackney horse with its extravagant, elevated trot is a popular attraction on the British show scene. Although the trotting action is partly inherited, it is also carefully taught with the use of heavy shoes. The action must be absolutely correct. With a free shoulder action the foreleg reaches well forward as well as up and down. The movement is given a look of flight and particular grace as the foot pauses lightly at each stride. The action of the hindlegs is the same but to a lesser degree. The small, neat head of the Hackney, carried elegantly high on an arched neck, and the high-set tail provide an extraordinary impression of pride, alertness and energy. The Hackney now provides this thrill around the world as the breed has been exported in great numbers to the United States, Canada, Australia and South Africa, as well as throughout Europe.

CHARACTERISTICS
Height 14.1 hh–15.2 hh (occasionally over 16 hh).
Colour Dark brown, black, bay, chestnut.
Conformation Small, neat head, arched neck, powerful shoulders. Compact body with deep chest, short legs, good feet.
Temperament Good. Lively, spirited and intelligent.
Use Driving.

THE HIGHLAND PONY

The Highland Pony is a native of the highlands of Scotland and the Western Isles. Until recently, the breed consisted of two distinctive types: the bigger and heavier mainland type and the lighter and more active Western Isle pony. Both types still exist today but are no longer recognized as such by the Highland Pony Society.

The Highland pony was originally bred to work the crofts taking farmers to the market and carrying the peat for the croft fires. Their proven hardiness and strength together with their docile, steady temperament means that they are very versatile. Even today the Highland Pony is used to carry the great weight of shot stags down the mountainside. Over the years, the Highlands have had infusions of outside blood, particularly Arabian. When crossed with the Thoroughbred, the Western Isle type produce some excellent hunters.

The founding of the Highland stud in Britain by the Dukes of Atholl marks an important step in the breed's history. A fine, grey Highland pony called Herd Laddie stood at stud from the age of six and is best known as the grand-sire of the famous Highland pony called Jock, owned by George V and used by him on shooting expeditions.

In recent years the Highland pony has become very popular as a good all-round riding pony. One of their best-known qualities is their ability to survive very well on even the sparsest of vegetation, making them very economical as a family pony living out!

Because of their calm and willing disposition, they are well suited for the beginner or nervous rider. They may not be fast but they are honest jumpers, good in harness, safe across country and, being handy for their size, they make very popular pony club and riding club ponies.

Highland Ponies appear in various shades of dun, as well as grey, brown, black and occasionally chestnut.

CHARACTERISTICS

Height Not exceeding 14.2 hh.
Colour Wide range of colours, predominantly grey and dun with a dark 'eel' stripe down the centre of the back.
Conformation Broad, alert face set well on a strong neck. Pronounced withers, compact back with a natural curve. Deep chest, powerful quarters. Flat hard bone, good strong cannons, well shaped hooves.
Temperament Excellent. Ideal child's pony or for the nervous rider. Calm, docile, sensible and very safe.
Use Good all-round pony. Excellent for pony club activities, general riding, trekking and in harness.

THE HUNTER

The English Hunter is a type rather than a breed, but has received just as much attention as a breed and is admired throughout the world for its quality.

There is no common specification for a hunter, which can be one of four sizes. The heavyweight is able to carry riders over 14½ stone, the middleweight carries between 14½ and 13 stone, the lightweight carries less than 13 stone and then at the bottom of the scale are the small horses which are larger than ponies but not over 15.2 hands.

The hunter, which is usually cross-bred, varies in type according to the area in which it is expected to work. A hunter should be able to carry a rider safely, comfortably and quickly over the countryside during the hunting season, but as the countryside varies from region to region, so does the type of horse needed to fulfil these requirements.

In the Shires—that part of the Midlands considered to be the best hunting country—there are large grass pastures which give good scenting conditions and sturdy hedges to be jumped, so here speed and endurance are necessary if the horse is to keep up with the hounds. For this sort of country the hunter should be a strong athletic horse with a big stride, and this usually means a predominance of Thoroughbred blood.

In rough, hilly country where there are small pastures and deep gullies, a horse with too much Thoroughbred blood would be inclined to be impatient, and the better hunter might be a cross involving one of the large pony breeds. Such a horse is likely to be more sure-footed and long-suffering in these difficult conditions. For big, open ploughland such as is found in East Anglia, a good horse should have short, active legs, which enable it to skim over the top of clinging soil into which a heavier horse with a measured tread might sink.

At its annual show in Newmarket, The Hunters Improvement Society maintains standards both by studying the appearance of horses and by riding them to assess how well they move and respond. It awards a number of cash premiums to approved Thoroughbred

stallions whose owners are thus able to keep to a minimum the cost of the stallion's service fee. In some countries, the United States for instance, the horses are required to prove their jumping ability in the ring. One of the best types of Hunter produced is the Thoroughbred/Irish Draught cross.

The Hunter has the strength and agility to withstand a day's hunting or eventing.

CHARACTERISTICS
Height Over 15.2 hh.
Colour Any colour.
Conformation Deep girth, well-sprung ribs, nice sloping shoulders. Shortish back, strong loins and powerful quarters. Short cannon bones, big, flat knees and hocks, well-shaped feet.
Temperament Patient, willing, calm, safe and sensible.
Use Hunting, eventing, jumping and endurance riding.

THE IRISH DRAUGHT

Irish Draughts make top-class competition horses.

The Irish Draught has experienced several setbacks over the years. The 1847 Irish famine seriously depleted the breed, and the subsequent infusion of Shire and Clydesdale blood caused a coarseness in the breeding until control was taken to approve Irish Draught and stallions. During World War I, the Irish Draught also experienced serious depletion when the army requisitioned a great many mares. In recent years the breed has suffered from the unrestricted export of mares to the Continent, until a law was passed to prevent the export of the breed for working purposes.

The Irish Draught stud book was introduced in 1917 by the Department of Agriculture and Fisheries at which time 1,180 mares and 270 stallions were inspected and 374 mares and 44 stallions were accepted. In 1976, the Irish Draught Society was formed to promote and preserve the breed, and in 1979 the British Irish Draught Horse Society was formed to work with its Irish counterpart and to introduce controlled inspection and a registration scheme of stallions and mares with and without papers.

As well as being capable of doing all agricultural work on the farm, with their good, strong and level action the Irish Draught are fast travellers on the road. They are natural jumpers and, without being extravagant, their action is free and easy, straight and true.

Originally bred for riding and for light-draught work on the farms in Ireland, the actual origin of this horse is uncertain. It is believed that the Irish Draught evolved by crossing the native Connemara pony with imported Thoroughbred stallions (they themselves carrying Spanish and Arab blood), the offspring being bred up on the good, lush grass of southern Ireland. Whatever the beginnings, the Irish Draught today, when put to Thoroughbred stallions, produces the best of top class, up-to-weight hunters and competition horses. Because of their tremendous popularity they are being exported from Ireland across the world.

CHARACTERISTICS
Height 15 hh–17 hh.
Colour Bay, brown, chestnut, grey.
Conformation Small, intelligent head, deep chest, good shoulders. Clean, good legs and well-shaped, smallish feet. Smooth coat with very little hair on the legs.
Temperament Good. Strong, willing, bright and intelligent.
Use Farm working, jumping, hunting, eventing and general riding.

THE NEW FOREST PONY

New Forest Ponies are ideal for children.

Herds of ponies have lived in the New Forest since before the Roman invasion, but unfortunately, towards the end of the last century, this long line was broken when there were misguided attempts to improve the stock. In 1852, Queen Victoria loaned an Arab stallion for covering New Forest pony mares and it remained in the Forest for eight years. Later, a Thoroughbred stallion was introduced. Eventually the New Forest pony began to fail to breed true to type, and was threatened as a breed because it was losing the hardiness it needed for survival in the wild. This led to the formation of the New Forest Pony Breeding Society in 1938, and from that moment no 'foreign' blood was permitted. The breed has become more stable and there is now a good trade for the better ponies for riding and breeding, although the poorer ones are still sold as meat.

They are true family ponies, easily handled by children because of their docile and generous temperament. Every autumn, the ponies in the New Forest are rounded up by their owners and by the New Forest verderers. They are wormed and checked over and each tail is cut in a certain pattern to show that the fee payable for grazing has been paid. The foals that are to be sold are removed and the mares are re-released until the following year.

Today, the New Forest pony is in great demand abroad and large numbers are being exported to the United States, Australia and New Zealand, as well as throughout Europe. Both Holland and Denmark have imported so many that they have their own New Forest stud book and now the New Forest pony has been accepted for registration in the Australian Stock Horse stud book as well.

CHARACTERISTICS
Height Not exceeding 14.2 hh.
Colour Any colour, especially bay and brown. Skewbalds and piebalds not found.
Conformation Well set, pony head, good, sloping shoulders, short back. Powerful quarters, straight legs with good bone and round, hard feet.
Temperament Excellent. Good child's pony, generous and docile.
Use Good all-rounder. Riding and driving, hunting, jumping, dressage, and eventing.

THE SHETLAND PONY

Shetlands are noted for their thickset, sturdy build.

The Shetland is well known as the smallest native pony of the British Isles. It is rarely more than 10.2 hands (3′6″) and can be any colour. This pony comes from the remote northern island groups of Orkney and Shetland, where the weather conditions are particularly severe. On the isles of Shetland there is hardly a tree to provide shelter. The Shetland was used to pull small carts and carry panniers of peat, and away from its native habitat was used in mines on account of its small size. Now it is best known as a harness pony in shows, or as a mount for a very small child.

Unfortunately, the Shetland is difficult to school for riding as it is too small to carry an experienced adult trainer, and it can also have a stubborn temperament which may make it difficult to handle. It may be that its small size causes it to be indulged like a pet when, like any other horse, it should be trained by being treated kindly but firmly.

Today, about 100 Shetland ponies remain on the islands though they are being extensively bred in England, north and south America, Australia, Canada and most countries throughout Europe. Holland, Sweden, Denmark, Belgium, and France have their own stud books for this breed. Their gentle temperament, courage and character enable them to adapt to a wide range of climates and occupations. They make ideal children's ponies and companions as they are easy and economical to keep and make excellent driving ponies. Shetlands can be found in any colour, although the favoured colour is black. Their huge abundance of mane and tail hair gives them a cheeky, almost comic, appearance.

CHARACTERISTICS
Height 26–46 inches.
Colour Almost any colour, though black is favoured.
Conformation Short, strong back and very deep girth. Short, strong legs, abundance of mane and tail.
Temperament Excellent. Wilful yet docile, gentle and courageous.
Use Ideal child's pony. Riding and driving.

THE SHIRE

The Shire, originating in the Midlands and Lincolnshire, is the tallest of the British breeds. The attraction of the Shire lies in its mass and prodigious strength, combined with a remarkable docility. At the Wembley Exhibition of 1924, a pair of Shires were attached to a dynamometer and exerted a pull equivalent to a starting load of 50 tons.

The Shire stallion is usually between 17 and 18 hands, weighs about a ton and has a girth of between six and eight feet. The mare is slightly smaller. It has more hair, or 'feather', on its lower legs than other heavy horses, but less than at the turn of the century when the hair of both its legs and mane was coarser and longer.

Preferences have also altered in respect of colour. The Shire horses from which the breed originated were black, but cross-breeding allowed for other colours and black became unpopular. Now black is quite acceptable again, and Young's, at their bewery in South London, have 21 fine black Shires. Feelings have also changed about white legs, which at one time were regarded with suspicion. Today, horses with four white socks are eagerly sought after and most colours are acceptable. Whitbread's team of Shires which pulls the Lord Mayor of London's coach is grey.

At the start of the century the tails of heavy horses were docked. The most extreme form, known as bung-tailing, consisted of severing the tail at the rump and at one time was regularly practised on Suffolk Punch stallions. However, since the beginning of the century even the less severe forms which left part of the tail were objected to on humanitarian grounds, although farmers and breeders argued passionately that the tail harboured dirt and disease and was liable to be caught up in farm implements.

Left: Shire horses at pasture.

Right: Shire horses are popular at shows.

CHARACTERISTICS
Height Up to 18 hh.
Colour Bay, brown, black or grey.
Conformation Relatively fine head, thick neck, strong muscular shoulder. Big barrel, powerful quarters and long legs with pronounced feathers.
Temperament Excellent. Gentle giants.
Use Working the land; draught horse; showing.

THE SUFFOLK

The Suffolk originated in East Anglia in the 16th century. All present-day Suffolks can be traced back to one horse, foaled in 1760, so the Suffolk is also one of the purest of breeds of heavy horse.

The success of this breed is largely due to the controlled and selective breeding by the breeders of East Anglia and the rigid rules set by the breed society for registration. Consequently, the Suffolk has developed into a strong, compact and hardy animal whose kind disposition and strong constitution has found fame all over the world. Countries such as the United States, Australia, Africa and Russia favour this breed for all its attributes mentioned here. Standing between 16 hh and 16.2 hh and weighing over a ton, the Suffolk has seen a decline in numbers over the years as mechanization has replaced the breed on the farms. However, these active horses with big, weighty frames (a girth of over 8 feet) set on short, sound and clean legs can still be seen working on the farms in certain areas and are also used by brewers for short haulage.

The Suffolk is also renowned for its longevity and ability to live well on very little food. There are several records of Suffolk mares breeding well into their 20s. And one Suffolk gelding was shown at the London Cart House Parade by his London coal merchant owner for seventeen years in a row. The horse retired when he was 21!

A team of Suffolks at a show.

> **CHARACTERISTICS**
> **Height** 16 hh–16.2 hh.
> **Colour** Chestnut. About seven shades can be found.
> **Conformation** Kind face set on a thick neck. Very wide girth, short back and powerful quarters. Good, strong, clean legs with much bone. Strong, well shaped feet.
> **Temperament** Excellent. Kind, intelligent, honest and well mannered.
> **Use** Showing; farm work.

THE THOROUGHBRED

The Thoroughbred is the preferred breed for almost all equestrian sports.

In England during the 17th and 18th centuries, racing enthusiasts had one ultimate objective—to produce the fastest horse in the world. They wanted a racing machine. Today we can see their dream in reality—the Thoroughbred. Not only a racehorse of tremendous ability, capable of galloping a mile at about 40 miles per hour, but also one of the most beautiful, elegant and most admired horses in the world.

The English Thoroughbred can trace its ancestry back to three founding fathers, imported Arab stallions: the Byerley Turk, imported in 1689; the Darley Arabian, imported in 1705; and the Godolphin Arabian, imported in 1728. It is from the Arabic 'Kehulan', meaning purebred, that the Thoroughbred earned its name.

Within a very short time, the Thoroughbred was being exported all over the world and has firmly established itself wherever racing is popular. In America, a son of the Darley Arabian arrived in 1730 and from there the vast American racing industry we know today flourished. However, each country has established its own slightly different racing world. In England and Europe, the Thoroughbred has concentrated more on middle and long distance racing with the emphasis being on stamina. In America, although the trend is moving towards the long distance horse, the quick starter, short-distance runner has been favoured and much emphasis has been put on speed and precocity. In Australia and New Zealand, the Thoroughbreds have become more tough and enduring than their European cousins as the smaller animal with tremendous stamina and huge jump is favoured. Although the Thoroughbred, with its fine, proud head, sleek neck and powerful quarters is instantly associated with the racetrack, the Thoroughbred cross has established itself as a top-class winner in a wide variety of equestrian activities. Although in Britain the more substantial, hunter-type Thoroughbred has proven itself very successful in sports such as show jumping and eventing (and superb as a hunter galloping all day across any country), its highly-strung and often flighty temperament can cause it to be quite a handful, requiring careful and experienced managing. Crossed with the native pony, Cleveland Bay or Irish Draught, the result will be a hardier, rather more even-tempered and economical animal to keep, while still retaining the flowing action, good paces and natural jumping ability for which the Thoroughbred is favoured.

CHARACTERISTICS
Height 14.2 hh–17 hh.
Colour Any colour, usually bay, brown, black and chestnut.
Conformation Fine, intelligent head, bright eyes, elegant, arched neck. Good, sloping shoulders, deep body, short, strong back, powerful quarters. Strong, long legs.
Temperament Usually good, though it can be highly strung and spirited.
Use Almost any equestrian activity.

THE WELSH COB AND WELSH PONY OF COB TYPE

Right: the Welsh Pony of Cob Type.

Far right: a Welsh Cob stallion.

There are four breeds of Welsh pony: The Welsh Mountain Pony (probably one of the most beautiful of all the native breeds); The Welsh Pony (developed by crossing the Welsh Mountain and the Welsh Cob Section C with an infusion of Thoroughbred blood); the Welsh Cob, and the Welsh Pony of Cob Type.

The Welsh Cob and Pony of Cob Type can both be traced back as far as medieval times although their exact ancestry is unknown. By the 15th century, both breeds were firmly established, and it is believed that the Welsh Mountain Pony influenced their development.

When the Welsh Pony and Cob Society stud book was first opened in 1902, the cobs were split into two sections: Section C for the smaller pony known as the Welsh Pony of Cob Type and Section D for the larger and stronger Welsh Cob.

For centuries the Welsh Cob has been an indispensable part of Welsh country life, especially on the farms, ploughing the fields and working under saddle and in harness as the major form of transport for the farmer and his family. Trotting races were also a familiar sight in rural Wales and after a hard day's work, the great trot of the Cob would be put to the test in races over long distances. The infusion of high-stepping breeds such as the Hackney and the Yorkshire Coach Horse is certainly evident in the Cob today. During World War I, Welsh Cobs were in great demand by both the British and German armies for use as pack horses and remounts.

Between the wars the numbers of the smaller Welsh Pony declined dramatically until only three stallions remained. Happily, their numbers are now on the increase again, due to their popularity as children's ponies.

The Welsh Cob is bright, active and intelligent. With its superb temperament and natural jumping ability, it makes an ideal family pony, strong enough to carry a full-grown man and gentle enough for a young child. With its courageous and sure-footed qualities, the Cob is ideal for hunting, trekking, and as an all-round ride and drive animal. Crossed with the Thoroughbred, they produce excellent hunters, dressage and performance horses. Enormously popular, they have been exported worldwide.

CHARACTERISTICS

Height The Welsh Cob:14.2 hh–15.1 hh. The Welsh Pony of Cob Type: up to 13.2 hh.

Colour Any solid colour.

Conformation Quality, pony head set on a lengthy, well-carried neck. Strong shoulders, muscular back though lengthy and strong. Powerful quarters. Long, strong forelegs set square; large, flat and clean hocks. Well-shaped hooves.

Temperament Excellent. Ideal family pony. Bright with good character.

Use Riding and driving, hunting, trekking, jumping and dressage.

THE DUTCH DRAUGHT HORSE

The Dutch Draught Horse is a relatively new breed that has only been in existence since World War I. Small farmers farming on both the clay and sand soils of the Netherlands needed a good, heavy working horse with a quiet temperament and sufficient power and turn of speed to cope with both types of land work. Today, the Dutch Draught horse is the most popular draught horse in the Netherlands and is exported throughout Europe.

The breed was developed by crossing Zealand-type mares, who carried a distant cross of Eastern blood, with Brabant stallions (the breed that the Dutch Draught closely resembles) and later on, to a lesser extent, with Belgian Ardennes stallions. The modern Dutch Draught is one of the most heavily muscled breeds in Europe. It is a massively built horse with heavy, sound legs, well-developed shoulders and powerful quarters and has great stamina and endurance. But despite its size and strength, the Dutch Draught also possesses a kind, willing temperament, good action at all paces and tremendous agility when required. Standing, on average, up to 16.3 hh, the breed is usually found in chestnut, bay or grey.

A stud book for the Dutch Draught was opened almost from the beginning, in 1925, and no horse can be registered until the age of two and a half years and until its pedigree has been carefully checked and its conformation has been approved. Each year there is also a National Show where judging takes place on conformation, breeding and pedigree.

CHARACTERISTICS
Height Up to 16.3 hh.
Colour Usually chestnut, bay or grey.
Conformation Large head, thick, muscular neck and powerful shoulders. Deep chest and girth, short back and short, heavily built legs. Plenty of feather around the heels.
Temperament Excellent. Kind, willing and hard working.
Use Agricultural work.

The Dutch Draught is noted for its strong, powerful build.

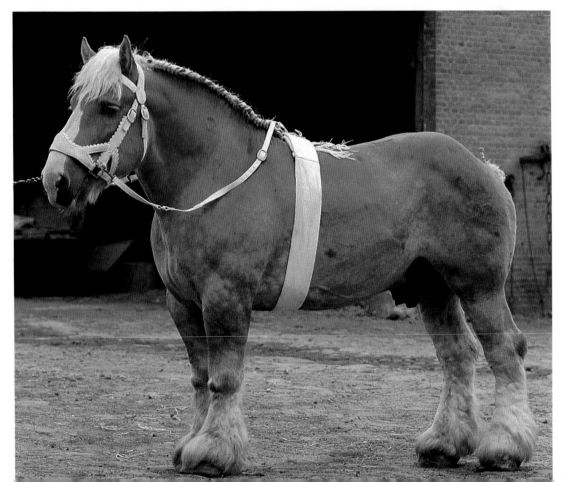

THE DUTCH WARM-BLOOD

In 1958, the stud book for the Dutch Warm-Blood was opened making it one of the most recently established breeds of this type in Europe. In less than 30 years, however, the breed has established itself, though not yet with any easily described features, as a breed capable of producing top quality and versatile competition horses for riders of all standards competing in equestrian sports of all types.

Based on the Groningen, a tremendously strong horse with powerful quarters, used under saddle and in harness, and the Gelderland, a lighter horse with an outstanding forehand, the Dutch Warm-Blood combines the best qualities of these two older and well-established Dutch breeds. When crossed with selected Thoroughbreds and later with French and German Warm-Bloods, these horses produced an animal averaging about 16.2 hh of a slightly lighter type than its German Warm-Blood cousin and one that is noted for its extremely docile and willing disposition suitable even for the less experienced rider.

As well as the careful selective breeding that has taken place to ensure the top quality of this breed, the Dutch Warm-Blood stallions must pass a series of performance tests before they are approved for breeding. These tests involve 100 days of training including riding under saddle and in harness, jumping loose and under saddle and cross country during which time the stallions are assessed and marked on temperament and manners. Only those that pass the scheme are used as stallions for breeding and their offspring will also be tested under identical conditions. Mares, however, are assessed only on conformation and action and the foals that they produce. There is no doubt that this scheme is proving a success as we can see from the number of this breed reaching international levels, competing at extremely high levels, particularly in dressage and show jumping.

The Dutch Warm-Blood's versatility makes it equally useful under saddle or in harness.

CHARACTERISTICS
Height Average 16 hh.
Colour Any solid colour.
Conformation Not yet easily recognized. Good, strong shoulders, high withers, strong body and powerful quarters. Good strong bone.
Temperament Excellent. Docile, kind, willing and versatile.
Use Good all-rounder under saddle and in harness. Dressage and show jumping.

THE GELDERLAND

Above: the stylish action of this carriage horse.

Right: Gelderlands are no longer bred officially.

The Gelderland as a breed was first created in the last century in the Gelder province of Holland from which its name derived. This outstanding carriage horse was first produced by cross breeding native mares with imported stallions from Britain, Germany, Poland, Egypt, Hungary and Russia—the most notable being the Norfolk Roadster and the Arab. Breeders in the Gelder province, noted for their experimentation with new breeding systems and for producing animals especially suitable for their own locality, took the best of the descendants and in later years introduced Oldenburg, Friesian and Hackney blood and still later, in this century, Anglo-Norman blood to produce a very strong and active horse much admired throughout the world.

The Gelderland of today is unsurpassed as a carriage horse, although as a popular riding horse the new breed of Dutch Warm-Blood, whose evolution is greatly indebted to the Gelderland, has taken its place. The Gelderland will always remain in demand for its proud carriage, energy and vitality. Its strength in body and character also lends this breed to light draught and agricultural work. Usually standing about 15.2 hh, the colour is predominantly chestnut and grey although skewbalds are also found. Those Gelderlands that have been broken for riding have proved themselves very good, natural jumpers.

CHARACTERISTICS
Height 15 hh–16 hh.
Colour Usually chestnut or grey although occasionally skewbald.
Conformation Long, strong neck, good, strong build with excellent forehand, powerful shoulders, deep girth and strong back. Powerful quarters and shortish legs of strong bone. Hard feet.
Temperament Good, very willing and active.
Use Primarily as carriage horses, also good jumpers.

THE FURIOSO

The Furioso breed inherited its name from the foundation sire, the English Thoroughbred Furioso, foaled in 1836. This stallion was imported to mate with the local mares of Nonius type—from the French Stallion Nonius, foaled in 1810, itself the result of a

This handsome horse is descended from Thoroughbred blood.

mating between an English half-bred stallion and a Norman mare. Between the years 1841 and 1851 Furioso produced 95 stallions whose subsequent distribution to studs throughout the old Austrian empire spread the popular English half-breed far and wide.

Infiltration from British stallions continued to reinforce the breed, the most famous being the Norfolk Roadster stallion, North Star. Foaled in 1844, this horse was noted for its handsome, elegant looks, compact stature and short, strong legs and he produced a number of descendants who found fame as trotting horses. The families of the Furioso and North Star are now interwoven and the result today is a versatile, quality horse particularly adaptable to all equestrian sports. They are excellent, all-purpose saddle horses and have proved successful in dressage, show jumping, and eventing as well as racing and steeplechasing. It is also an imposing carriage horse. The breed is active, intelligent and extremely tractable. It has a medium-sized attractive head on a long, strong neck, together with powerful, sloping shoulders with a deep chest and prominent withers. There is a long, strong back with well-sprung ribs, and muscular sloping hindquarters with a rather low-set tail.

Today, the breed is found throughout Austria, Czechoslovakia, Poland, Hungary and Romania. Because they are so widespread, these horses tend to vary in colour and size, averaging about 16 hh and usually black or brown. The heavier Furioso type sometimes found is used for light draught and agricultural work.

CHARACTERISTICS
Height Average 16 hh.
Colour Usually brown or black.
Conformation Reasonably good conformation with a free, though slightly exaggerated, action.
Temperament Excellent, willing and adaptable.
Use Excellent all-purpose saddle horse. All equestrian sports including racing.

THE ICELANDIC PONY

This pony is noted for its strength and endurance.

The Icelandic pony is generally considered to be the prototype of the Celtic pony which may be the common ancestor of all pony breeds of northern Europe. It was first introduced in to Iceland from Scandinavia by the Norse settlers and with injections from imported Scottish, Irish and Isle of Man pony breeds developed into what is known today as the Icelandic pony.

With careful selective breeding, two types of the breed have emerged: a lighter type for general riding and a heavier type mainly used for light draught work and as pack ponies. Until about 50 years ago, both these types were used extensively as the only form of transport on the island and were invaluable especially during the harsh winters. Because of their toughness, tremendous endurance, strength and handy size, the Icelandic pony was in great demand until the beginning of this century to work the British coal mines.

As export trade declined, so did the numbers of ponies bred on the island and today many are bred for meat instead of cattle which would not survive the extreme weather conditions. The Icelandic pony remains today much the same as the tough, rugged pony of centuries past. They move with a distinctively fast pace, a comfortable ambling gait which covers much ground.

The Icelandic pony is small, ranging between 12 hh and 13 hh but what it lacks in height is more than compensated for in intelligence, a kind temperament and independence. It is one of the hardiest breeds of pony with a rather large head, short, thick neck, deep girth, stocky appearance, and the characteristic abundance of mane and tail and thick feather on the heels. The colours most usually found are grey and dun, although most other solid colours do exist.

CHARACTERISTICS
Height 12 hh–13 hh.
Colour Usually grey and dun but also all solid colours.
Conformation Large head set on a short, thick neck, deep girth and tough, stocky appearance. Abundance of mane and tail hair and feather on the heels.
Temperament Excellent. Docile, kind and intelligent.
Use Good riding pony. Also bred for meat.

THE ITALIAN HEAVY DRAUGHT

The Italian Heavy Draught has a fine head for a heavy horse.

The Italian Heavy Draught is the most popular horse in Italy. Also known as the Italian Agricultural Horse, this medium-sized draught horse provides about 35 per cent of the stallions at stud in Italy. The breed is of French Breton ancestry and although it is now bred throughout central and northern Italy, it is chiefly bred in the region of Venice.

The horse was originally bred for agricultural work, a job for which it was ideally suited and where it found great popularity. Unfortunately, with the increase of mechanization and the growing demand for good meat, breeders began to look at this breed more as a provider of food and this trend continues today.

Noted for its speed, power and extremely docile temperament, this rather striking horse stands between 15 hh and 16 hh and is very often of a dark liver chestnut colour with a flaxen mane and tail, although roan and a light chestnut do occur. The Italian Heavy Draught has a finer head than is found on most heavy horses, a short and very thick neck, compact body and extremely strong quarters. Today, at Verona, two and a half year old Italian Heavy Draughts can be seen in a special competition held annually.

CHARACTERISTICS
Height 15 hh–16 hh.
Colour Liver chestnut with flaxen mane and tail. Also roan and light chestnut.
Conformation Relatively fine head, short, thick neck, deep chest and girth. Compact body and strong quarters. Strong, rather boxy feet.
Temperament Excellent. Very docile.
Use Agricultural work and meat.

THE BARB

The Barb has had a great influence on European breeds over the centuries.

The Barb originated in the north west corner of Africa, in what is now Morocco, Tunis and Algeria, formerly known as the Barbary Coast. It is a breed of ancient origin—the Barbary Coast has been noted for its horses for over 2000 years—and, like the Arab, has had a considerable influence on other breeds, notably the Thoroughbred, the Lipizzaner, and the Andalucian. It was certainly used extensively to improve light horse breeds and types. However, when the Moslems conquered Barbary in the 10th century, Arabian blood was introduced and the Barb and Arab of today have many similar characteristics.

The Barb was first exported to Britain during the reign of Elizabeth I, and thereafter the breed was exported to Europe in great numbers. Although small, not exceeding 15 hh and not the handsomest of horses, the Barb was regarded as good breeding stock for race horses, because of its endurance and remarkable speed over short distances. As they were being constantly cross-bred with Arabians and horses of other Eastern bloods, the pure-bred Barb is hard to find today. The best pure-breds can be seen at the Royal Stud in Morocco.

These good, all-round riding horses are extremely tough, capable of carrying great weights and are very economical feeders. Unfortunately, in North Africa today most of the breed are worked too young, fed insufficiently and prematurely weaned so their extraordinary characteristics are not developed to the full.

Usually found in bay, brown, black, chestnut or grey, the Barb is also known for its rather bad, fiery temper and ability to kick.

CHARACTERISTICS
Height 14 hh–15 hh.
Colour Bay, brown, black, chestnut and grey.
Conformation Long head, flat shoulders, sloping quarters and low-set tail.
Temperament Not very good. Tendency to be bad-tempered and to kick.
Use Good all-round riding horse.

THE DØLE GUDBRANDSAAL

This breed has a neat, pony head and straight profile.

The Døle Gudbrandsaal is now widely spread throughout Scandinavia, though it is believed to have originated in southern Norway and is far and away the most influential and widespread breed of that country. Very similar to the Dales pony in Britain and the Friesian from Holland, the Døle is of mixed origin, having evolved from heavy draught blood and from the Thoroughbred Odin and his stock, imported in 1834. This stallion has had the most influence on the breed and all Døles today can be traced directly back to him.

This very strong, fairly small horse, standing between 14.2 and 15.2 hh, developed on the rich mountain valleys into a very useful agricultural worker and general all-purpose riding horse. With a pony-like head, strong shoulders, long back and powerful quarters, the Døle proved to be a hard worker, willing, versatile and full of endurance. Active, patient and dependable in temperament, it is ideally suited to all farming tasks, and equally suited as a sure-footed saddle horse. During the 18th century, however, interest in the breed as it was dwindled, and it was not until

the 19th century that infusions of heavy draught and Thoroughbred blood improved the quality of the breed to such an extent that societies were formed to promote the breed and its role in competitive sports encouraged. The demand for Døle horses in Norway suddenly surged in World War II because of the scarcity of motor fuel. Further importations of stallions of Norwegian Trotter stock gave us the quality horse we know today.

CHARACTERISTICS
Height 14.2 hh–15.2 hh.
Colour Black, brown or bay.
Conformation Small, neat pony head, straight face, long silky mane and tail, strong, muscular shoulders, wide chest. Long back with powerful quarters and deep girth. Good, strong, short legs with much feather.
Temperament Very good, willing and kind.
Use Good all-purpose riding horse.

THE NORWEGIAN FJORD PONY

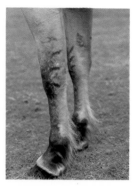

Above: zebra stripes are often seen on the legs.

Left: this primitive-looking breed has inhabited Norway since prehistoric times.

The Norwegian Fjord Pony, also known as the Westland pony, is very easily recognized because of its characteristic dun colouring, a dark 'eel' stripe down the centre of the back, black, zebra markings on the legs and rather primitive, overall look. The Fjord can be traced back to prehistoric times in Norway and, later, ponies of this type were used by the Vikings for the barbaric sport of horse fighting, a pastime that has been recorded on stone engravings.

A very strong and sure-footed pony, the hardy Fjord is now being bred extensively in Norway, as well as throughout Scandinavia and Germany. Denmark, especially Jutland, has been importing the breed from the beginning of this century to be used for light agricultural work and further afield the breed is gaining popularity as an ideal riding pony under saddle and in harness.

Even with the introduction of mechanization, the Fjord continues to be very useful working on farms in mountainous regions where the use of a tractor would be imposs-ible. With their tremendous endurance and tireless energy, the Fjords are invaluable for a variety of jobs from ploughing to carrying heavy loads up the mountains. Ranging from 13 hh to 14.2 hh, the Norwegian Fjord pony has a lovely temperament to match its un-usual and attractive looks.

CHARACTERISTICS
Height 13 hh–14.2 hh.
Colour Dun, occasionally bay and brown. Characteristic black 'eel' stripe down centre of back and black zebra-like stripes on legs. Silver mane and tail with black through the centre. Mane cut to stand upright and curve.
Conformation Pony head with flat fore-head and small ears. Short, thick neck, and short, compact body well-muscled all round. Short, very strong legs.
Temperament Excellent.
Use All-purpose riding pony and in harness.

THE POLISH ARAB

The Polish Arab has a beautiful head and neck.

For centuries, Poland has bred some of the finest Arabs in the world. Arab stallions were first brought to Poland with the returning crusaders, and it is known that pure-bred Arab stallions were held at the Royal Stud at Knyszyn in 1570. Through the Turkish wars all varieties of Eastern stock were captured by the Poles and horse breeding soon came to depend on the improvement they effected. In subsequent years the Poles continued to travel to Asia Minor in order to import horses from Aleppo, Baghdad and Damascus. In 1845, three pure-bred mares were imported to the Jarczowce stud and each of the female lines they established still survive today.

In 1926, the Polish Arab Stud Book was opened under the patronage of the Ministry of Agriculture and many modern Polish Arabs can be directly traced back a full 10 or 14 generations. Some of the most famous Arab studs in Europe existed in Poland before World War I. The invasion of Poland destroyed many of the best breeding stock but, with dedication and initiative, the Polish breeders worked hard to restore their valuable legacy. Disaster struck again during World War II, devastating the breeding centres. Fortunately, by this time Polish-bred Arabians had been exported to other countries where they continued to survive and flourish.

The Polish Arabians have had a tremendous effect on Arab breeding throughout the world, and stallions are exported to America, Britain, Canada, East Germany, Hungary, Italy, Czechoslovakia and Russia. Offspring of the famous grey stallion, Skowronek, bought by the well-known Crabbet Stud in Britain in 1920, still have prominent descendants in Britain, South and North America, Russia and Spain. Today, Arab racing, introduced in 1927, is ever growing in popularity all over the world. Racing stock is specially bred in the district of Kielce at Michalow, though the main Arab stud at Janow, where Arabs have been bred since 1817, is government-owned.

Polish Arabs are now highly valued in many countries and have won important championships in the UK, Sweden, Netherlands and Canada. Their greatest success has been in the USA with tremendous victories being won by the stallion Bask and his progeny. It was Bask who won the American National championship on three successive occasions, and he was followed by his daughters twice winning the mare championship and reserve. It is notable that the 1972 stallion and mare championships were won by Polish Arabs.

CHARACTERISTICS
Height 14 hh–15 hh.
Colour Any solid colour.
Conformation Beautiful head with dished profile, elegant neck, compact muscular body. Slender but strong legs.
Temperament Very gentle but yet high-spirited.
Use Good, all-purpose riding horse; racing and long-distance riding.

THE WIELKOPOLSKI

The Wielkopolski is a good all-rounder.

Although in recent years there has been a considerable decline in horse breeding in Poland, nevertheless the country still rates as one of the top horse-breeding nations in the world, with a horse population of nearly 3,000,000. The great historical traditions of breeding and horsemanship, together with military and sporting achievements, still pervade many aspects of Polish life today and horsebreeding has a genuine basis, rooted as it is in agriculture. The Polish Ministry of Agriculture is directly involved in improving the general standard of horses in the country and has adopted a regionalized system.

The Wielkopolski is a combination of two breeds from central and western Poland, the Poznan and the Masuren. The Poznan horse, the older of the two breeds, contained Arab, Hanoverian and English Thoroughbred blood. Though this actual breed no longer exists, it was at one time an officially recognized breed and studs for the stallions were made available. The Masuren was based on the Trakehner, from what is now East Germany, and came from the Masury District. In 1947, a new stud was founded by the Polish Ministry of Agriculture at Liski in the Masury District. It was here that this breed was developed and proved a most successful horse in international equestrian competitions.

Polish Warm-Bloods are all known now as the Wielkopolski, although those still bred in the Poznan district are regarded as being of a distinct type and are distinguished from those bred in the Masury district. So, although the two breeds now exist as one, variations do exist and Polish breeders are conscientiously eliminating the differences. The Wielkopolski is a good quality, dual-purpose horse suitable for riding and driving. The heavier types make good agricultural workers. It has a sound constitution and excellent temperament, standing about 16 hh, and is particularly noted for its good, fluid movement.

CHARACTERISTICS
Height Average 16 hh.
Colour Any solid colour.
Conformation Quality head, slender neck and muscular shoulders. Shortish back and strong quarters. Good, strong legs.
Temperament Good and very sensible.
Use Good riding and driving horse.

THE ALTER-REAL

A herd of the Alter-Real breed which has been much improved by culling.

In 1748, the House of Braganza founded the Alter-Real Stud at Ville de Portel by importing 300 Andalucian mares of the finest quality selected from around Jerez de la Frontera in Spain. (The breed continues today to retain many of the original characteristics of its Andalucian ancestors.) Eight years later the stud moved to its present home at Alter, and the breed continued to flourish and became best known for its tremendous ability as an *haute école* horse. About 150 were sent to Lisbon and drew tremendous interest by displaying the same style that we see today at the Spanish Riding School in Vienna.

The Alter-Real breed was seriously threatened in 1821 when the stud was sacked by Napoleon's army who stole much of the best stock, and in 1834 with the abdication of King Miguel a great part of the land was confiscated and the Royal stud abolished. Reorganization and redevelopment of the breed was begun by introducing Arabian blood and infusions from English, German and Norman horses. However, this rather haphazard and uncontrolled breeding caused the Alter-Real to deteriorate. The quality of the breed continued to fall due to further infusions of poor quality Arabian blood.

Fortunately, at the beginning of this century, an attempt was made to reintroduce Andalucian mares of the Zapata strain as well as some Spanish stallions in order to restore the breed to its former quality. In 1932, when the Ministry of Economy took over the stud, careful control and selection breeding was instigated and the breed is now, once again, fully established. Despite the traumas and cross breeding that the Alter-Real has suffered through the years, it is still today a beautiful saddle horse especially suited for *haute école*. Often difficult to handle, with a highly-strung temperament that needs careful management, this compact and powerful horse has a superb, elevated action that always draws enthusiastic spectators.

CHARACTERISTICS

Height 15 hh–15.2 hh.

Colour Bay, brown and occasionally chestnut and grey.

Conformation Small, convex head, short, well arched neck. Deep chest, broad, powerful quarters. Short legs, well set, very strong hocks.

Temperament Often difficult to handle and highly-strung.

Use Good riding horse especially suited to *haute école*.

THE LUSITANO

The Lusitano is an ancient breed of Portugal but of unknown origin. However, since it is not dissimilar to the Spanish Andalucian, although perhaps lacking the natural presence, it is believed that this splendid old Portuguese breed descended from the Andalucian and Arabian and was originally bred to be used for light farm work. Standing between 15 hh and 16 hh, the Lusitano is usually grey in colour and compact in stature. It has an alert expression and possesses intelligence, tremendous agility and great courage for which it is particularly noted. Because of these three qualities, the Lusitano was formerly in demand as a cavalry horse, working for the Army Remount Division for supplying cavalry regiments. Today, the highest quality Lusitano horses are required for the native bull-fighting ring. Because Portuguese bull-fighters, or *rejoneadores*, conduct the fight on horseback, it is essential that their mounts are schooled to an extremely high standard in *haute école* to respond instantly, athletic enough to swerve at the last possible moment and courageous enough to stand facing a charging bull. Because of the importance of its job, the bull-fighting Lusitano is a highly prized and valuable animal. Lusitanos also make superb riding horses and today some are being bred in Suffolk, England, to train as Grand Prix dressage horses.

Above: the Lusitano looks similar to the Spanish Andalucian.

Right: Lusitanos were used at one time as replacement horses for the Portuguese army.

CHARACTERISTICS
Height 15 hh–16 hh.
Colour Usually grey, although any solid colour permitted.
Conformation Small, straight head, short, thick neck and long, sloping shoulders. Compact, strong body with strong, clean legs.
Temperament Excellent. Intelligent, bold and willing.
Use Good all-round riding horse; used for bull-fighting and sometimes dressage.

THE CRIOLLO

The Criollo can now be found all over South America.

The Criollo is descended from Spanish stock, including Andalucian, Arab and Barb, brought over the conquistadors to South America in the 16th century. The breed gradually spread throughout South America, acquiring slightly different characteristics according to the environment. Because of their stamina, hardiness and tremendous endurance the Criollos were used by the settlers to carry their owners over vast distances and through harsh country with relative ease.

About 100 years ago, when importations of American and European blood were introduced to 'upgrade' these tough ponies, the breed suffered drastically. However, since the beginning of this century, breeders have worked collectively to re-establish the breed to its former glory, by selectively breeding from the best stock, and in 1918 a society to promote the breed was formed.

The Criollo is an extremely muscular and sturdy pony that varies in height, averaging about 14 hh, and type throughout South America. Its name also varies as follows: In Argentina it is known as Criollo; in Brazil as the Crioulo; in Chile as the Caballo Chileno; in Venezuela as the Llanero and in Peru as the Costeno, the Morochuco and the Chola (three different types).

The most popular colour of the Criollo is dun with black points and an 'eel' stripe down the back and zebra-type markings on the legs, although other solid colours can also be found including skewbalds and piebalds. The neck and quarters should be strong and well developed, the shoulders sloping and the legs short but with good bone and extremely hard feet. The pony is well adapted and capable of carrying a great weight willingly and with tremendous endurance. The Criollos are used principally by the *gauchos* as stock horses and for general riding.

CHARACTERISTICS
Height Average 14 hh.
Colour Mostly dun, also bay, brown, grey, chestnut, palomino, skewbald and piebald.
Conformation Well-developed neck, short, broad head and wide chest. Fairly sloping shoulders, short back and powerful quarters. Very compact and muscular with good legs and hard feet.
Temperament Very good. Willing, hard working and intelligent.
Use General riding; stock horses; pack ponies.

THE PASO FINO

Although small, the Paso Fino has an exceptionally strong conformation.

This small breed of horse, standing no more than 15 hh, is bred in Colombia and Peru as well as Puerto Rico. The Paso Fino resembles the Andalucian which, during the 16th century, arrived in large numbers in South America along with other Spanish breeds.

The Paso Fino today is a very intelligent horse admired for its good and sensible temperament. This breed displays three particular gaits which, although inherited, have been perpetuated over the years by careful and selective breeding. The Paso Fino is a collected and highly elevated gait of 4-time; the Paso Corto is also 4-time but it is not collected. It is very comfortable for the rider and as such was used primarily for covering long distances; the Paso Largo is an extended 4-time gait which is very fast and can reach speeds of up to 16 mph.

The Paso Fino is a very strong little horse capable of carrying a heavy man. It is particularly useful and popular on the South American ranches because of its comfortable gaits.

CHARACTERISTICS
Height Not exceeding 15 hh.
Colour Primarily bay, brown and chestnut.
Conformation Strong, thick neck, good muscular shoulders and short back. Powerful quarters and good, strong legs.
Temperament Very good. Intelligent and willing.
Use Saddle horse, especially comfortable for long distances.

THE PERUVIAN PASO

Above: the distinctive gait of the Peruvian Paso.

Right: the attractive head of this good-looking breed.

The Peruvian Paso, like the South American Paso Fino and Criollo, is a descendant of the Spanish horses, including the Andalucian, imported during the 16th century. Inevitably, some of the imported stock escaped and turned wild, but with careful select breeding and further controlled importations, the Peruvian Paso developed into a national breed.

Also known as the Peruvian Stepping Horse, this breed is of Criollo type that has been systematically developed for its distinguished action, believed to be unique to South America. It is this extravagant action in which the forelegs display an exaggerated elevation and the hindlegs are driven forward with great power with the quarters lowered, that distinguishes the Peruvian Paso from the Criollos and has for generations made it a highly prized horse. This breed is comfortable enough to ride over vast distances, hardy enough to survive all types of conditions, including mountains, and has plenty of stamina and endurance. To add to all these qualities, the Peruvian Paso can travel at steady speeds of about 11 mph over the roughest country.

The National Association of Breeders and Owners of Peruvian Stepping Horses was established soon after the last war. The modern Peruvian Paso stands between 14 hh and 15.2 hh and is strong enough to carry a heavy man all day. It is a very good looking breed of horse, powerful and very proud. It has a kind and intelligent temperament and is usually found in bay or chestnut.

CHARACTERISTICS
Height 14 hh–15.2 hh.
Colour Bay or chestnut.
Conformation Attractive head set on a strong, muscular neck. Very powerful shoulders and quarters; good, sound legs.
Temperament Very good, willing, hard working and intelligent.
Use General riding under saddle and light agricultural work in harness.

THE ANDALUCIAN

The Andalucian is a strong, active horse of enormous presence.

The Andalucian is an attractive, flamboyant and extremely agile little horse which developed in Spain, most probably by the crossing of native mares with Barb stallions, brought over by the Moors.

Carthusian monks from the 15th century onwards strove hard to ensure the purity and indeed survival of the breed by selective breeding and by such dramatic acts as disobeying a Royal Edict ordering the introduction of European blood, and hiding their horses from Napoleon's armies.

Today there are relatively few Andalucians left but the breed's popularity in the past (especially as a mount for European monarchs and for haute école riding) has had a significant influence on the development of other European breeds.

In Spain the Andalucian's brilliant, active paces make it the ideal choice of the Rejoneadores or mounted bullfighters, but is fairly uncommon in other European countries and America. In recent years, however, it has become increasingly popular in Australia, where pure and part-breds (especially crossed with Thoroughbred) have achieved considerable success in dressage, show jumping and cross country events.

CHARACTERISTICS
Height 15 hh–15.2 hh.
Colour Predominantly grey or bay.
Conformation Handsome head with straight profile, broad forehead and large eyes, set on elegant neck. Long sloping shoulders with well-defined withers, short, strong body, broad chest and well-sprung ribs. Broad hindquarters, the tail set low.
Temperament Excellent. Easy to handle.
Use As a mount for Spanish bullfighters; dressage, show jumping, haute école.

THE GOTLAND PONY

Gotland ponies have small heads, a straight profile and a low-set tail.

The Gotland pony, also known as the Skovr-gruss, is the oldest of the Scandinavian breeds, having originated in Stone Age times on Gotland Island where it is still extensively bred today. Also bred on the mainland, it is believed to be a descendant of the Tarpan and some still run wild in the Lojsta forest lands. The Gotland possesses a primitive appearance, despite the fact that oriental blood was introduced in to the breed about 100 years ago. They are in fact very similar to the Hucul and Konik ponies of Poland.

The Gotland pony ranges from 12 hh to 12.2 hh and is rather lightweight and narrow in build with strong, short neck, long back and sloping, relatively weak, hind quarters. Despite their lightness they make very fast little ponies and possess a natural ability to jump.

Today, the Gotlands are not only bred for light agricultural work, for which they are ideally suited, but are also being selectively bred for the very popular trotting races. Found in a variety of colours, ranging between bay, brown, black, dun, chestnut, grey and palomino, the Gotland can be a little contumacious but overall is a pony easy to handle with a sweet temperament.

CHARACTERISTICS
Height 12 hh–12.2 hh.
Colour Any solid colour.
Conformation Small head, short neck and rather narrow. Long back, sloping quarters and poor hind legs. Low set tail.
Temperament Overall good, though can be obstinate.
Use Light agricultural work, trotting racing and general riding. Good jumpers.

THE SWEDISH WARM-BLOOD

The Swedish Warm-Blood has good riding characteristics, easy paces and an amenable temperament.

The Swedish Warm-Blood has been carefully and selectively bred for the past 300 years as a versatile riding horse of tremendous quality and presence. Selective breeding first began at the Royal stud at Flyinge. Oriental, Friesian and Spanish stallions were imported in order to produce good cavalry horses. More recently, Thoroughbred, Arab, Hanoverian and Trakehner have been introduced, enhancing the breed's all-round ability, excellent temperament and good conformation.

The breeding of the Swedish Warm-Blood continues to be tightly selective. All mares and stallions must first pass inspection before being approved for breeding or as performance horses at Flyinge. This highly-controlled selection system maintains and enhances the quality and outstanding ability of the Swedish Warm-Blood we see today.

Also known as the Swedish Half-Bred, this breed has produced horses of the highest aptitude seen especially in dressage and three-day eventing.

CHARACTERISTICS
Height Up to 16.2 hh.
Colour Any solid colour.
Conformation Up to weight, good, deep girth and short, strong legs.
Temperament Excellent. Easy to handle and friendly.
Use Good, all-purpose riding horse, also dressage and eventing.

THE EINSIEDLER

The name of the Einsiedler, also known as the Swiss Anglo-Norman, originated from the stud principally associated with the breed—the stud at Kloster Einsiedel. With the onset of chivalry in the 10th century, certain cloisters and abbeys were founded by the Holy Roman Emperors and were occupied by monks and young men aspiring to knighthood who gave property in the form of corn and horses brought with them from their own distant estates. Such a cloister was that at Einsiedeln, which founded one of the oldest studs in Europe (the name means hermitage). The Benedictine abbey of Einsiedeln was founded about 934 on the site of the cell of St Meinrad, and is now the most famous pilgrim-resort in Switzerland.

The breed appears regularly throughout the history of Switzerland, the best years for the stud being from 1500–1800. After the French Revolution, however, almost all the breed were taken as loot to France and breeding rapidly declined.

The Anglo-Norman stallions were first imported into Switzerland 150 years ago to improve the breed and meet the Swiss demand for horses of good quality, and it is the Anglo-Norman that has been the main modern influence on the Einsiedler. The need for general-purpose horses was greater than the breeders could supply and the Anglo-Norman satisfied the requirements, including those of the cavalry. Today, the Einsiedler is still regularly bought by the Swiss army.

The breed can now be found widely spread throughout Switzerland. However, a large number of stallions, about 100, are held at the Federal stud at Avenches where they are controlled and distributed around the country during the breeding season. About the same number of stallions are home-bred and privately owned and are sustained by nine breeding societies. Mares still continue to be imported but are selected from recognized Anglo-Norman stock from France.

The Einsiedler averages about 15.2 hh to 16.2 hh and is a very versatile horse, excellent for riding and in harness. Often described as a horse *à deux mains*, it possesses good

conformation with a deep girth, powerful quarters and good, strong legs. It has an active and willing temperament and an easy and elegant action, combined with strength and endurance that has made the Einsiedler one of the most common and most popular breeds of Switzerland.

The Einsiedler is an exceedingly good all-round riding and driving horse.

CHARACTERISTICS
Height 15.3 hh–16.2 hh.
Colour Any solid colour, mostly bay or chestnut.
Conformation Generally very good. Very deep through the girth, strong, powerful quarters and strong legs with good bone.
Temperament Excellent. Very willing and active.
Use Good all-purpose riding and harness horse.

THE AMERICAN SADDLE HORSE

The American Saddle Horse, originally known as the Kentucky Saddler, was developed in Kentucky in the 19th century. Plantation owners needed a horse that would carry them comfortably and swiftly for many hours a day, as they travelled around their vast plantations. The American Saddle Horses of today can be traced back to 1839 when the foundation sire, a Thoroughbred called Denmark, was foaled. As the plantation life flourished, the Saddle Horses continued to be invaluable working animals, but today they are primarily bred for the show ring. The Saddle Horse also contains blood from the Morgan and Narragansett Pacer and selective and controlled breeding over the years has developed an elegant show horse with great strength and stamina, easy, comfortable paces and a friendly, intelligent disposition.

In the show ring, the Saddle Horse can be seen both under saddle as a three-gaited saddler or a five-gaited saddler, and in light harness. In light harness, the Saddle Horse is required to perform at the walk and at an animated trot. When ridden under saddle as a three-gaited saddler, it is required to perform at the walk, trot and canter. The five-gaited saddler is the most popular for spectators as it demonstrates the extravagant, elevated action to the full and will in addition perform at the 'slow gait' and 'rack'. The 'slow gait' is a four-time movement that gives the impression of prancing, and the 'rack' is the same but at a much faster speed. The Saddle Horse will show off its proud head, alert eyes and long, muscular neck when performing and the showy appearance is accentuated by its high tail carriage that is artificially set by cutting the dock muscles and using a crupper. Other means adopted to accentuate the extravagant action of the Saddle Horse is growing the feet especially long and attaching weights around the coronet. Predominant colours are bay, brown, chestnut and black.

Note the prominent eyes and close-set ears of the American Saddle Horse.

CHARACTERISTICS
Height 15 hh–16 hh.
Colours Bay, brown, black and chestnut.
Conformation Small, elegant head set on a long, muscular neck. Strong muscular shoulders , strong back and powerful quarters. Very strong, muscular legs.
Temperament Very good. Bright, intelligent and proud.
Use Showing under saddle and in light harness.

THE APPALOOSA

The Appaloosa is a descendant of the horses first brought to South America by the Spanish conquistadors in the 16th century. From this stock, the Nez Percé Indians of the Palouse Valley in north-east Oregon, a tribe noted for their excellence in horse breeding, developed an animal of great quality noted for its spotted coat—the Appaloosa (or of Palouse). The Nez Percé Indians were wiped out in the 1877 during the Indian wars, but enough of their carefully bred horses survived to form the basis of the modern breed. Today it is one of the most popular breeds in America.

The spotted coat of the Appaloosa can vary. It can be an all-over spotted pattern of dark spots on a white background known as 'Leopard'; light spots on a dark background known as 'snowflakes'; or a blanket of spots on the loins and quarters known as 'spotted blanket'. Other variations include marble, white and frost blanket. With a background colour that is usually roan, any colour combination that fits one of the six categories listed above is acceptable.

Other special characteristics are the white sclera in the eye, similar to that of the human and a skin of mottled pink and grey, regardless of the colour of the coat, around the lips, nostrils, and genitalia. Another characteristic, not always present, is the vertically striped hoof.

Appaloosas are now bred in many countries, and are particularly popular in Australia where they are used for western riding. Because of its striking appearance, the Appaloosa is frequently used as a circus or parade horse, but its great agility, speed and stamina also make it popular in show-jumping, eventing and hunting.

Appaloosas are particularly popular for western riding.

CHARACTERISTICS

Height Up to 15.2 hh (a minimum of 14.2 hh in Britain).

Colour Six different forms of spotted coat as explained above.

Conformation Lean head set well on a quality neck. Long, muscular shoulders, deep chest, short straight back, smooth loins and round, powerful quarters. Well muscled limbs, long deep thighs and wide, straight hocks.

Temperament Excellent. Bright, alert and intelligent, they make ideal family horses.

Use All under-saddle activities, English and western saddle, show classes, hacking and jumping.

THE MORGAN

This American breed enjoys considerable popularity as a show horse in the UK.

In the United States one of the first local breeds to be established was the Morgan. The New England farmers were in need of a sound all-round horse which could pull a plough and haul a load of timber and at the same time be ridden or driven in harness, and the versatile Morgan provided the answer. It is unusual that a breed should be more or less established in one generation, but with the Morgan this is what happened.

The founder of the breed was a small stallion called Figure whose origin is unknown but is thought to be the offspring of a racehorse imported from England. In about 1795 Figure was handed over to a schoolmaster in Randolph, Vermont, in settlement of a debt and the horse then became known by the name of his new owner, Justin Morgan. This tough little horse was only 14.2 hands, the size of a pony, but was an amazing all-rounder. He excelled as a saddle horse, won trotting races in harness and proved valuable working in the forest clearing trees. In spite of his small size he won weight-pulling contests. He was greatly in demand as a stallion, and it was found that he had that much sought-after quality of prepotency, for he unfailingly passed on his excellent qualities to his foals. His endurance showed itself yet again when he reached the age of 32, and during his lifetime he sired so many offspring indelibly stamped with his own qualities that the foundation of the breed was assured.

The arrival of mechanization severely reduced the population of the breed although their commercial use lingered on when Morgans were used to draw the street trams of New York. Today, the fortune of the breed has been reversed and the Morgan, which is now bred to a limited extent in Britain, is enjoying a great increase in popularity. The modern Morgan is still small—usually under 15 hands—but with his thick arched neck, heavy mane and compact strength he makes a splendid show horse. Apart from competing in endurance riding, equitation events and trotting competitions, Morgans demonstrate their strength in the show ring by pulling a heavy stone boat.

CHARACTERISTICS
Height 14.2 hh–15.2 hh
Colour Bay, brown and black and occasionally chestnut.
Conformation Slightly dished face of medium size, set on a well-crested neck. Good sloping shoulders, deep, wide chest. Muscular loins and well-rounded quarters. Short, strong and squarely-set legs. Hocks wide and deep and rounded feet.
Temperament Excellent. Very elegant and proud and easy to handle.
Use Versatile under saddle and in harness. Natural jumper.

THE MUSTANG

A descendant of the horses brought over by the Spanish conquistadors in the 16th century, the Mustang is regarded as the original cow pony of America. Its ancestry can be traced back to the Arab and the Spanish Barb. When the Spanish invaded the New World from the south in the 1500s, some horses escaped or were allowed to go free. They slowly travelled north via Mexico, growing steadily in numbers. The Red Indian favoured this small, lightweight and exceedingly strong pony and began selective breeding. The Mustang was also used by the early settlers in America to infuse with other imported breeds, providing good foundation stock. Although very small, seldom exceeding 14.2 hh, the original Mustang offered endurance and a tough disposition along with a semi-wild temper. By the 19th century, large herds roamed the plains and became well established as the popular cow pony that we associate with the wild west. Today, however, the Mustang as a cow pony has largely been replaced by its larger successor, the Range horse, which was produced by introducing Thoroughbred, Quarter Horse and Morgan blood.

Although their numbers have declined over the years, the Mustang is kept protected in many areas. It is very hardy and capable of surviving on very little food.

The Mustang was the original American cow pony.

CHARACTERISTICS
Height Up to 14.2 hh.
Colour Any colour.
Conformation Very small and rough looking. Lightweight and deceptively strong.
Temperament Wilful, headstrong and fairly stubborn.
Use A very good light saddle horse.

THE PALOMINO

The Palomino is a popular choice of Western riding enthusiasts.

In most countries, including Britain, the Palomino is regarded as a colour type and not a breed. In America, however, where the Palomino Horse Society was founded in 1936, the Palomino is considered a colour breed and the Association lays down certain rules and restrictions in order to produce a clear colour breed and to record blood lines. The more

recently established British Palomino Society has helped to bring increased interest in the colour. Whereas the American Palomino Horse Society puts restrictions on the height of those registered (the minimum height allowed is 14.1 hh, thus preventing many pony breeds from registering), the British Society permits any Palomino-coloured horse or pony to register including many native breeds such as the Welsh Mountain, New Forest and Shetland who themselves accept the colour in their own registration rules.

A rich, golden-coloured Palomino with its striking white mane and tail is a beautiful sight indeed. For centuries this colour has been treasured, valued and admired in the equine world. What makes it an especially exciting challenge to breeders is that it is not possible to breed the Palomino colour with any certainty. This inconsistency is called 'incomplete dominance'.

The Palomino, especially popular in western riding, can be seen competing in many different sports all over the world. Besides the classes that are held specifically for Palominos, the wide variety of breeds that do produce this special colour has firmly marked the Palomino as a very versatile and adaptable horse with proven success both under saddle and in harness.

CHARACTERISTICS
(according to the American Palomino Horse Association)
Height 14.1 hh–16 hh.
Colour Light or dark golden colour with natural white mane and tail. Small white markings on the face and white to the knees and hocks are acceptable. There is no discrimination as to skin colour.
Conformation Good head with alert eyes and ears, short straight back, strong square legs and natural tail carriage.
Temperament Generally very good.
Use Western and English riding under saddle and in harness. General hacking, trekking and long-distance riding. Showing.

THE PINTO

The Pinto, also known as the Paint or Calico horse, is regarded as a colour breed, meaning that it is recognized for its coat colouration and not for its size, conformation or structure. The Pinto, which receives its name from the Spanish word meaning 'painted', was of special importance to the American Indian as the broken coat offered good camouflage. In fact, the Indians often used to add their own paint to accentuate the colour contrasts. The Pinto was also a favourite with the cattlemen and cowboys because of its strength, ruggedness and ability to survive the harsh demands of the countryside. Cowhands regularly paid much higher prices for 'painted' horses and extolled their virtues with great affection in tales of the American West.

This all-purpose saddle horse is characterized by two distinct colour types. The Overo type, which is considered a 'recessive' gene, is basically a dark coat with white patches and is found mostly in South America and Asia. The Tobiano type, which is considered a 'dominant' gene, is a basic white coat with dark patches, and is found mostly in North America and Europe. The head and neck of the Tobiano are usually dark, the legs white from the knees down. When the contrasting colours are white and black, the Pinto is also known as piebald and when the contrasting colours are white and any other colour *except* black, the term skewbald is used.

While 'paint' horses appear all over the world, it was comparatively recently, and only in the USA, that they were recognised as a breed under the Pinto Horse Association, established in 1956 in Ellington, Connecticut. There is also an American Paint Stock Association whose headquarters are in Amarillo, Texas.

The Pinto cannot be achieved by simply crossing a white horse with one of a darker, solid-coloured coat. A Pinto will only be produced if two mono-coloured horses are mated and one or both has specific spotting genes inherited from a Pinto ancestor. Today, since spotting has been bred out of most pure breeds such as the Thoroughbred, Stan-

The Pinto is sometimes referred to as the Paint Horse.

dardbred and Arab, the Pinto is often disregarded by those who put emphasis on pure breeding. However, besides finding fame as movie stars in many westerns, the Pinto makes an excellent all-round riding horse combining speed, endurance and versatility and its big, natural jump makes it suitable for hunting.

CHARACTERISTICS
Height Any height.
Colour Overo—dark coat with white patches.
Tobiano—white coat with dark patches.
Conformation Variable.
Temperament Generally very good.
Use Good all-round riding horse, long-distance riding and jumping. Also for Western riding and hunting.

THE QUARTER HORSE

The Quarter Horse has good conformation with massive, powerful quarters.

The largest of the native American breeds is the Quarter Horse. This breed arose to meet the demands of local racing, and it is from the length of the race-track that it derived its name. In Virginia and the Carolinas the favourite weekend sport of farmers and plantation owners was horse-racing. At first there were no organized tracks so the races were run along straight paths cleared through the forest or down the main street of the town. In either case the distance was rarely more than a quarter of a mile, so what was needed was a compact muscular horse which could explode into an all-out sprint from a standing start. The horses that proved themselves best at doing this were most in demand for breeding purposes, and in time the Quarter Horse was established as a breed.

The Quarter Horse has a docile temperament which, combined with great muscular agility, is ideal for rounding up cattle. It can instantly wheel, sprint, and skid to a halt—in fact carry out all the manoeuvres asked of it when herding cattle. Throughout the United States there are rodeos and shows in which Quarter Horses compete and they are also widely used in normal show events. At the same time it has by no means disappeared from the racing scene, for over the quarter mile sprint the Quarter Horse is outstanding. The All-American Futurity Stakes for Quarter Horses, worth about $600,000, is one of the most important racing prizes in the United States, and is the most valuable prize for a horse race anywhere in the world.

CHARACTERISTICS

Height Average about 15.2 hh
Colours Any solid colour, predominantly chestnut.
Conformation Broad head, large kind eyes and alert ears. Thick, muscular neck, strong shoulders, short muscular back and powerful quarters.
Temperament Excellent. Very kind, willing and intelligent.
Use All-purpose pleasure horse under saddle and in harness. Showing, western riding, racing and herding cattle.

THE STANDARDBRED

One of the world's finest harness race horses.

One of the factors which contributed to the earlier decline of the Morgan was the rise in interest in the 19th century in harness racing. The Morgan was a fair trotter, but there was a demand for a horse whose prime ability was trotting at high speeds, and the Standardbred arose to fill this need.

On the male line, the Standardbred can be traced back to one Thoroughbred stallion called Messenger which was imported into the United States in 1788. Messenger was a successful stallion who passed on to his offspring his racing speed. One of Messenger's great-grandsons, the famous Rysdyk's Hambletonian, was a brilliant racer who, in turn, passed on his qualities to the 1,335 offspring he sired. Today, the majority of Standardbreds, sometimes referred to as Hambletonians, can be traced back to this one horse.

The name Standardbred arose when the American Trotting Register was started in 1871. Horses were only accepted for the register if they could trot or pace a mile in the standard time which was then fixed at 2½ minutes for the trot, and 2¼ minutes for the pace (an alternative to the trot in which the legs move in a different sequence).

As the breed improved, the speed increased, and this was helped by training on tracks of baked clay which took their toll in leg ailments but increased the speed still further. In 1938, the record for the mile was set by a grey appropriately called Greyhound. This was 1 min. 55¼ secs. and it remained unbeaten for years. More recently it has been reduced to 1 min. 54¼ secs.

CHARACTERISTICS
Height 15.2 hh–16 hh.
Colour Bay, brown, black and chestnut.
Conformation Large, sometimes plain head set on a shortish, thick neck. Longish body, very deep girth and extremely powerful quarters. Short but strong legs; good feet.
Temperament Very good. Intelligent and easy to train.
Use Harness racing.

THE TENNESSEE WALKING HORSE

The Tennessee Walking Horse is another example of a breed which developed to meet a special demand, and it is also a breed which owes a great deal to the prepotency of one sire—in this case a stallion called Black Allan. The rich owners of the cotton and tobacco plantations in the South spent hours in the saddle inspecting their vast estates, and they wanted a horse which would give them a comfortable ride and satisfy their taste for elegance. The Tennessee Walking Horse fulfilled both these requirements. Standing between 15 and 16 hands he is tall and sleek and moves without any bump or jar. His slow gaits are the flat-foot walk and the slightly faster running walk. In both these gaits the head nods up and down in time with the walk, and in the running walk the hind legs reach past the position of the forelegs to give a smooth, gliding effect. His third gait is known as a 'rocking-chair canter' and is very distinctive.

This horse is claimed to be the most comfortable ride in the world.

The front legs are brought upwards and forwards in a kind of rotating motion, while the hindquarters remain more or less level. It has been said that a really good walking horse should be able to carry a glass of water on his quarters without losing a drop.

The description gives little idea of the astonishing 'feel' of the paces of a Walker. It has been described as 'a fluid, smooth, gliding gait' during which the rider is able to sit almost motionless. This is because of the use of the horse's legs from the elbow, rather than the full shoulder so much sought in most other riding horses. The gaits are natural to the breed and can be seen in foals.

At the running walk, the horse normally travels at between 6–8 mph (9.5–13 km/h), but in the showring speeds considerably in excess of this are reached, with the very real possibility of overreach injuries. As in the Saddle Horse, the tail muscles are nicked.

In 1935, the Tennessee Walking Horse became fully distinguished when the Tennessee Walking Horse Association was established in America and the registration of the breed began. Like the Saddle Horse, the Tennessee Walking Horse, developed as a working animal, has today found fame as a show performer. An exceptionally good tempered and well-mannered horse with good conformation and a powerful constitution, it has remained very much an American breed.

CHARACTERISTICS	
Height 15 hh–16 hh.	
Colour Any solid colour, particularly black. Other colours sometimes found.	
Conformation Large, plain head with sloping eyes. Strong, arched neck, sloping shoulders. Long, powerful back, broad chest and strong quarters. Clean, strong legs.	
Temperament Excellent. Kind, docile and willing.	
Use Showing under saddle, general all-purpose pleasure.	

THE AKHAL-TEKÉ

A lean, wiry horse of distinctive appearance.

The Akhal-Teké is an ancient breed that is believed to trace back to the territory of Turkmenia over 2,500 years ago and is a strain of the Turkmene or Turkoman horse which was much favoured by mounted warriors. They are believed to derive from the same strain as the Arab, though today they show no sign of Arab blood. Today, the best Akhal-Tekés are bred at the Ashkabad Stud in Turkistan.

During the middle ages, the Akhal-Teké was exported in large numbers throughout Russia and to European countries and because of its unusual and outstanding qualities it was in great demand for use at stud. The Akhal-Teké is especially noted for its powers of endurance and its ability to survive in extreme desert conditions. An endurance test, in which Akhal-Teké horses showed their remarkable stamina, covered a distance of more than 3,000 miles, part of the 84-day journey being 900 miles across pathless, waterless, sandy desert. The most famous contemporary Akhal-Teké is *Absent*, who won the Individual Olympic Gold Medal for dressage in Rome, and the Bronze Medal at the Tokyo Olympics.

These horses carry no fat, and their small bodies are made up of skin, bone and muscle. The mane is almost non-existent and therefore in cold, windy conditions they are always covered in thick rugs when not in use. They are exceedingly intelligent and have a quite extraordinary memory for locality.

The breed is of light but strong build giving a rather long and wiry impression, yet despite its rather unusual conformation it has a distinctively majestic appearance. It is a small horse, averaging 14.2 hh to 15.2 hh with a long head and neck, long legs and sloping quarters. The breed has a very sparse and fine-textured mane and tail, the tail being set quite low. The colours usually found are bay, black and chestnut, the predominant colour being a very striking gold which often has a metallic sheen. Greys and bays do also occur.

The Akhal-Teké has earned a good reputation throughout Russia for success in various equestrian activities and competitions. Although the breed can have a rather uncertain and obstinate temper, most probably due to its environment, it is an extremely good, all-purpose horse that has excellent racing, jumping and dressage ability. Although originally no stud books were kept, they are now prepared and issued periodically and only pure-bred are allowed to be registered.

CHARACTERISTICS
Height 14.2 hh–15.2 hh.
Colour Bay, black, chestnut and grey.
Conformation Long head and neck, long body and legs with a lean and wiry look. Sparse mane and tail.
Temperament Not very reliable; can be obstinate.
Use Good, all-round saddle horse, for racing and dressage.

THE BUDYONNY

The Budyonny is a relatively new breed of horse having been developed between 1920 and 1950 in the Rostov region of the USSR. The horse was named after a famous Russian cavalry officer, Marshal Budyonny, who instigated the breed at the army stud at Rostov at the time of the Russian Revolution. He crossed Don mares with Thoroughbred stallions to produce a good cavalry mount. Indeed, a good number were used in the former Russian cavalry divisions. Only the best progeny were selected and interbred. The horses were kept on the best quality grazing, fed the highest quality food, and only after passing certain tests on the race course and as riding horses were the best selected for breeding purposes.

Very soon it was found that Thoroughbred stallions mating with Don mares produce better offspring than Don stallions on Thoroughbred mares – and to this day the reason for this is unknown. An example of one such successful breeding was the Thoroughbred Simpatyaga, a stallion which produced quite a number of valuable horses by Don mares. Because the best of the original progeny was very carefully reared and given many tests for such things as aptitude, toughness, speed and fertility, this new breed very quickly became highly selected.

The modern Budyonny is a high quality riding horse still bred in the Rostov region where it originated, chiefly at the First Cavalry Army Studs. Averaging between 15.2 hh and 16 hh, they have superb conformation with a strong body, deep girth, good strong shoulders and quarters and strong legs with good bone. The predominant colour is chestnut, and the gold sheen so prevalent among Russian horses is often seen. Bays and greys are also common. They have a very attractive head and an elegant neck and, unlike the Akhal-Teké, they have a very calm and sensible disposition.

The Budyonny has proved itself very versatile with great stamina and endurance, enabling it to tackle successfully a variety of equestrian competitions, especially steeplechasing. It is here that this horse excels

and has won many very reputable events including the Pardubice, the marathon race held in Czechoslovakia. Budyonny horses have competed throughout Russia and all over the world in races and long-distance endurance rides for which they are ideally suited.

The Budyonny was bred as a quality cavalry horse.

CHARACTERISTICS
Height 15.2 hh–16 hh.
Colour Chestnut but also bay and grey.
Conformation Attractive head, elegant neck and good shoulders. Strong body, deep girth, powerful quarters and strong legs with plenty of bone.
Temperament Very good. Calm and sensible.
Use Good riding horse, for steeplechasing and long distance riding.

THE DON

The Don is an exceptionally tough, resilient breed.

The Don breed receives its name from the Don Cossacks who used these horses as far back as the 18th century. The breed was extensively used by the Cossacks in the raids on Napoleon's army during its long retreat during the winter of 1812. It was the best of saddle horses which survived not only the lack of fodder but also the bitter cold and was able to carry its rider to constantly harass and attack. The Cossacks made a campaign unprecedented in the annals of cavalry as they marched to Paris and back mounted on Don horses. Indeed, the Don was the favourite horse of the Cossacks and used by them as a cavalry mount. As such, it was not treated as an animal to be pampered and was used rather as a working animal. It was, and still is, herded on the central Asian Steppes where it has to forage for survival in the heavy winter snows. In earlier times, the Don Cossack rode a rather smaller type of horse which they kept in herds distributed over the vast steppe pastures. The Don contains blood from Turkmene and Karabakh stallions that were captured from the south and set free to roam with the herds. The Don inherited many characteristic features from these breeds, including the prominent golden chestnut colour that is often seen. During the 19th century, further infusions of English Thoroughbred and Arab blood were made, but since the beginning of this century, no new infusions have been made and the breed has since remained pure.

The Don herds are still kept on the steppes and centuries of surviving the harsh winter climate has meant this breed has adapted to a particularly hard way of life, capable of coping with little help from man. The Don is an extremely tough and hardy horse that has proved itself tremendously useful as a working animal.

The Don averages between 15.1 hh and 16 hh with a long, deep body that gives an almost wiry appearance, long legs and sound constitution. The breed is both ridden and driven and is noted for its tremendous endurance in all forms of work. It is still used today as a mount by the herdsmen of the semi-desert areas in the south-eastern USSR. The Don is particularly good as a working harness horse and has proved itself successful in harness races throughout Russia and in long-distance mounted races.

The best of the breed are bred in the Budyonny and Zimovnikov studs in the Rostov region. They are also bred in collective and state farms in these areas. The stud book is published periodically and only permits pure-breds to be registered.

CHARACTERISTICS
Height Average 15.1 hh—16 hh.
Colour 'Gold' chestnut, chestnut, bay and grey.
Conformation Fairly wiry appearance with long back, deep body and rather long legs.
Temperament Good disposition, rather tough and self sufficient.
Use Good all-round riding and driving horse; long-distance riding; good working horse.

THE ORLOV

The Orlov is considered one of the best trotting breeds in the world and before the development of the American Standardbred was probably the best. The Orlov dates back to 1778 when Count Alexis Orloff-Tschesmenski founded the stud at Khrenov with a silver-grey Arab stallion call Smetanka. Although Smetanka was at stud for only one year, he sired four sons and one daughter. One of his sons sired the celebrated stallion Bars 1, noted for his outstanding action especially at the trot. It was this stallion, by the Arab stallion Polkan out of a Dutch mare, who passed down the valuable qualities later developed by selective inbreeding to produce the outstanding trotter we see today, and one of Russia's most celebrated breeds. The Orlov is still bred, and a cross with the American Standardbred has produced a breed of modern trotter, the Métis, which races on all the trotting tracks in Europe.

Trotting races were held in Moscow as far back as 1799. They usually took place in the winter and the horses raced with light-weight sleighs. The sport developed rapidly during the 19th century and in 1834 the Moscow Trotting Society was formed. The Orlov improved and prospered as a racing horse and speeds up to 3.2 km in 5 minutes and 45 seconds were reached, although this has now been surpassed. The Orlov, however, has not just been used as a racehorse. Count Orlov also formed a breed of Orlov Saddle Horses, mainly by crossbreeding Arabs with English Thoroughbreds, and also by using Danish and Dutch blood with a touch of native strains.

The breed has also proved very popular as a carriage horse and for a long time has been used to improve agricultural animals. Horses for breeding have been chosen for quality as well as speed. The Orlov is valued for its soundness, longevity, high fertility, power, endurance and ability to acclimatize to different environmental conditions. Over the years, the breed has experienced infusions from other breeds, notably the Thoroughbred and the Mecklenburg.

The modern Orlov is a horse of good conformation standing between 15.2 hh and

17 hh. It possesses straight, though powerful, shoulders, a long back, deep girth and strong legs. It has a rather common head and the usual colours found are chestnut, bay, black and grey.

The Orlov is principally used for racing in harness.

CHARACTERISTICS
Height 15.2 hh–17 hh.
Colour Chestnut, bay, black and grey.
Conformation Rather common head, good, strong neck and straight but powerful shoulders. Long back, deep girth and strong legs.
Temperament Good.
Use Trotting races. Good, general riding horse.

HORSE CARE

This covers the care of the horse in its widest
sense. It begins by helping you to understand
your horse, with information on the anatomy of
the horse and its mental and physical makeup.
The section goes on to describe feeding and
stable management, grass-kept horses and
saddlery. There is comprehensive information
on veterinary care and a checklist of possible
ailments. Finally, the section gives sensible
advice on buying and selling horses.

Right: A fine, healthy young horse.

ANATOMY OF THE HORSE

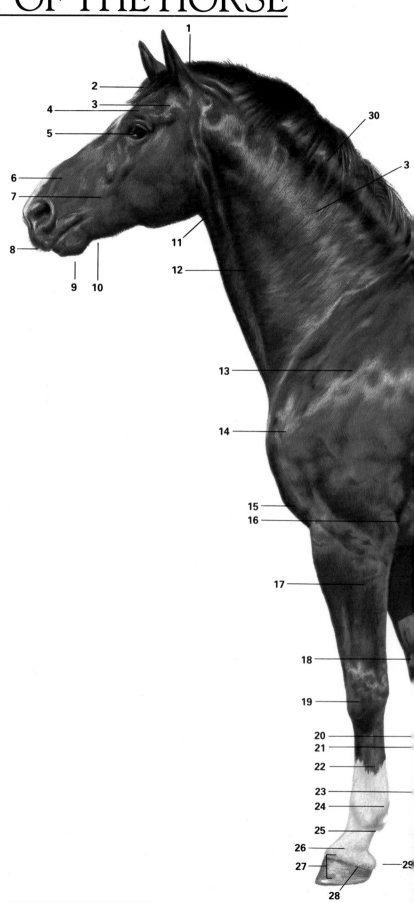

Conformation is the term used to describe the physical structure of the horse, its general 'make and shape'. Both heredity and environment contribute to a good conformation, a symmetry and balance when the parts of the horse are well proportioned in relation to one another. When both stallion and dam have sound conformation, they are more likely to produce a sound foal. Good nutrition and the prevention of disease also play their part.

Sound conformation is closely related to sound movement so that the horse not only looks better but performs better, with less risk of stress and injury. A poor head and neck carriage, for instance, make it hard for a horse to balance, upright pasterns predispose to lameness, and a pigeon-toed stance puts a strain on the knees and causes the horse to stumble. Few horses have perfect conformation but too many faults make a horse a poor prospect for riding.

Points of the horse

1. The forehand: the head, neck, withers, shoulders and forelegs

The head should be well set on and in proportion to the horse's size, with a broad, flat forehead, wide nostrils and a straight profile. Large, calm-looking eyes are an indication of a good temperament; too much white showing is a sign of a nervous disposition. A bump between the eyes often denotes a stubborn temperament.

The neck should be gently arched, well-muscled and tapered towards the head. The head and neck together should look properly balanced in relation to the rest of the body. Common faults in neck conformation are the 'bull neck', when the crest is too thick-set, making the horse too heavy in the forehand and the 'ewe-neck', concave like the neck of a sheep, with no crest, resulting in bad head carriage.

The withers are the point where the neck joins the body. They should be highest at the top of the shoulder and then slope gently into the back. They should be fairly prominent but not too high, because that makes fitting a

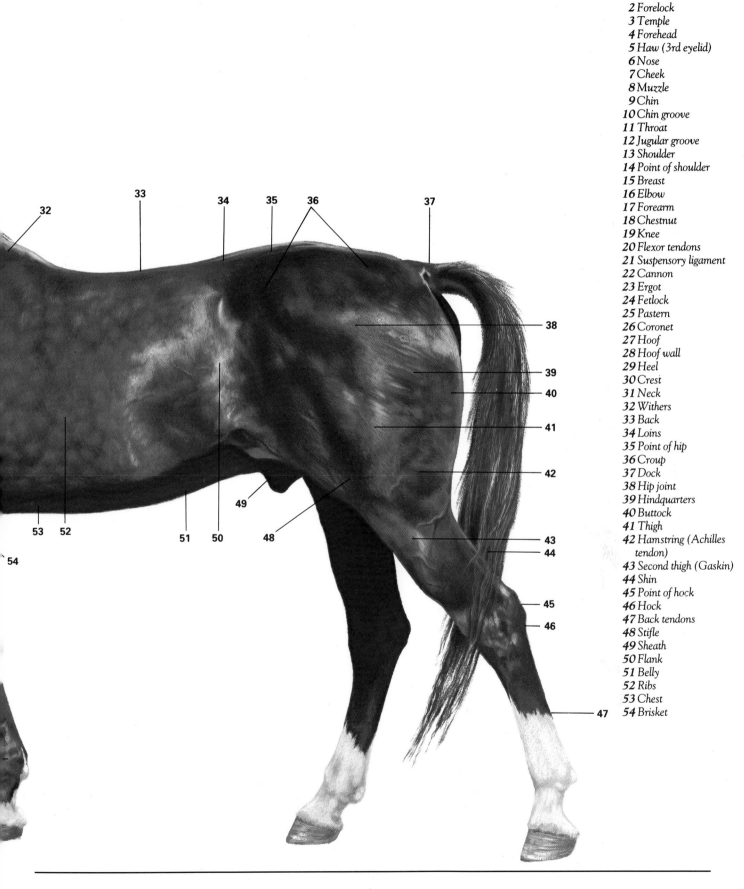

The main points of the
horse.

1 Poll
2 Forelock
3 Temple
4 Forehead
5 Haw (3rd eyelid)
6 Nose
7 Cheek
8 Muzzle
9 Chin
10 Chin groove
11 Throat
12 Jugular groove
13 Shoulder
14 Point of shoulder
15 Breast
16 Elbow
17 Forearm
18 Chestnut
19 Knee
20 Flexor tendons
21 Suspensory ligament
22 Cannon
23 Ergot
24 Fetlock
25 Pastern
26 Coronet
27 Hoof
28 Hoof wall
29 Heel
30 Crest
31 Neck
32 Withers
33 Back
34 Loins
35 Point of hip
36 Croup
37 Dock
38 Hip joint
39 Hindquarters
40 Buttock
41 Thigh
42 Hamstring (Achilles
   tendon)
43 Second thigh (Gaskin)
44 Shin
45 Point of hock
46 Hock
47 Back tendons
48 Stifle
49 Sheath
50 Flank
51 Belly
52 Ribs
53 Chest
54 Brisket

131

'Bone', which describes the build of the horse, is measured around the leg at the widest point below the knee. The greater the measurement the more weight the horse is capable of carrying.

saddle more difficult, or too low, because that makes the action of the shoulder less efficient. **The shoulders** are are their best when deep and sloping evenly from the withers to the base of the neck, as this indicates a good range of movement. Too straight a shoulder will affect the horse's movement and makes for a jarring action.

The forelegs should be long and straight from the shoulders through the knees to the feet. The elbows should be well-developed and well clear of the body for free movement and the knees large and flat in front. Possible signs of weakness are 'calf knees', when the knees seem to bend backwards, a forward bend referred to as 'over at the knee', knock-knees or bandy knees, both of which can lead to poor action.

The circumference of the cannon bones, when measured immediately below the knee, should be wide, otherwise the legs may not be strong enough for the weight of the body. If the cannon measurement on a hunter is less than 21.75 cm (8½ in) he is judged to be 'lacking bone'.

Pasterns that are long and sloping are liable to strain; if they are too short and straight, they make for an uncomfortable ride.

The feet must be a matching pair as odd-sized feet may be an indication of disease. They should point straight forward and slope at an angle of about 50 degrees to the ground. The foot as a whole absorbs concussion, and by its continuous growth it is able to replace the surface as this is lost by everyday wear and tear. Small, boxy or contracted feet do not provide sufficient shock absorption. Flat feet are associated with weakness of the general structure. 'Pigeon' toes, turning inwards, and splayed feet, turning outwards, will both result in poor action. The horn should be free from cracks or grooves. Good feet are vital; hence the old saying 'no foot, no horse'.

2. The body: the back, the chest, the flanks and belly

The back needs to be on the short side, though a horse with an over-short back will probably lack speed. A long or noticeably hollow back indicates weakness. Too straight a back restricts movement and the horse will probably lack power.

The chest must be deep enough to give the lungs and heart room to work and the depth of girth should be below the elbow at its lowest point. A shallow body indicates lack of staying power. However a 'barrel chest' makes

for an uncomfortable ride and difficulty in fitting a saddle.

The loins should be short, strong and well-muscled.

The belly should be much the same breadth as the chest but taper gradually towards the flank. A fairly straight lower line on the body can be an indication of good staying power.

3. The hindquarters

The croup is thought to give an indication of jumping or hunting ability. A straight croup denotes little flexibility and less jumping power but a 'goose rumped' horse, with quarters that slope sharply from croup to dock, is often a useful jumper.

The buttocks should be long, well-rounded and show a good swell of muscle on either side. In a horse with good conformation the point of the buttock, the point of the hock and the rear of the fetlock joint are in straight vertical alignment.

The hocks need to be large and well-developed with a prominent point. The foot should not be too far forward causing straight hocks, which will restrict movement, or too far back causing 'sickle' hocks, which are liable to result in strained ligaments. One of the common strains is a curb, which can cause lameness. It can be seen as a thickening of the ligament, below the point of the hock.

When viewed from behind, the legs should stand straight. Hocks that are turned outwards, resulting in bow legs, put an extra strain on the hock bones and ligaments. Hocks that turn inwards, 'cow' hocks, cause the legs to move outwards rather than forwards in a straight line.

Hocks should also be viewed from alongside the horse's head and compared with one another. A bony enlargement on the inside of the lower part of the hock is a bone spavin, caused by strain. This is a permanent point of weakness.

Measuring height

Horses are measured in hands, a term which originates from the time when a clenched fist was used as the instrument of measurement, with one hand equivalent to 10 cm (4 in).

The measurement is taken from the ground to the animal's withers, using a special measuring stick which has a spirit level and cross-bar. It is important to make sure that the horse is standing squarely on level ground.

Telling the horse's age

The age of a horse is determined by an examination of the front or incisor teeth: in a young horse by which teeth have erupted

By looking at the shape, wear and colour of a horse's teeth a prospective owner can get some idea of its age. The six pairs of incisors (front teeth) of a yearling (1), which are temporary, or milk, teeth, are distinctively white and are straight. By the age of three (2) the central incisors are permanent and show a little wear on the biting surfaces. The incisors of a six-year-old (3) are all permanent and show definite signs of wear with dark cavities or 'cups' on the biting surfaces. The corner incisors touch evenly, and the male has developed the tushes, or canines.
The corner teeth of a seven-year-old (4) have developed an obvious hook and the cups are less distinct.
By the eight years of age (5) the hooks have worn away and a dark line has appeared under the cups of the central teeth.
A ten-year-old (6) has developed a dark hollow, known as Galvayne's groove, on the corner teeth and the central teeth have become triangular. The cups on the biting surfaces are starting to disappear and the teeth have a definite slope. The teeth of a 20-year-old (7) noticeably protrude. The Galvayne's groove now appears down the whole of the corner teeth and the biting surfaces have worn completely smooth and have lost the cavities.

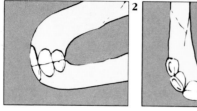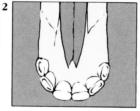
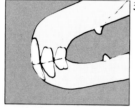
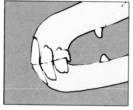
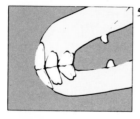
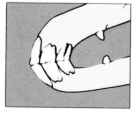
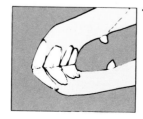

and, in a mature horse, by the wear, shape and angle of growth of the teeth. In a lifetime a horse has two sets of teeth. The temporary, or milk, teeth are gradually replaced by the permanent teeth. The 24 milk teeth are made up of six upper and six lower front teeth and three upper and three lower molars on each side. These are replaced by 36 permanent teeth: six upper and six lower incisors and six upper and lower molars on each side. In addition, the male develops tushes, or canines, between the incisors and the molars; one upper and one lower on each side. Wolf teeth are small, rudimentary teeth which sometimes appear just in front of the normal molars.

By the time the horse is a year old he has six pairs of straight, white incisor teeth which will develop signs of wear over the next year. These temporary teeth have a distinct neck, the crown being much wider than the rest.

Two central permanent incisors replace the milk teeth in each jaw at the age of two and a half. The permanent teeth are larger and more yellow in colour than the milk teeth and have no distinct neck. The temporary lateral incisors have been replaced by the age of four, when the tushes of the male erupt. By five, the corner milk teeth have erupted and have a shell-like appearance. A six year old has a 'full mouth' and the teeth, which only come into contact with their opposite numbers about six months after eruption, are beginning to show signs of wear, with dark hollows or 'cups' on the biting surfaces. The shell-like sheen of the corner teeth has disappeared.

A distinct hook develops on the top corner tooth when the horse reaches the age of seven and this wears away by the age of eight. By this time the teeth have worn down so that the hollow cups are far less obvious and a dark line has appeared below them.

After the age of eight horses are said to be 'past the mark of mouth' as it is far more difficult to read the signs of aging from the teeth. However, a 10 year old develops the beginnings of a depression in the middle of the upper corner teeth, known as 'Galvayne's groove'. By about 15 the groove will reach halfway down the tooth, by 20 it will have reached all the way down, though these ages can only be taken as a rough guideline.

From 10 onwards the central teeth begin to look triangular and develop a noticeable slope. In old horses the teeth protrude and the biting surfaces have lost their cavities and worn completely smooth.

UNDERSTANDING THE HORSE

The horse's behaviour is governed by instinct rather than reason. His brain is very small in relation to his size and his natural intelligence is rated rather lower than that of a sheep. In the wild, the horse's survival depends on the ability to sense and run from danger and this strong instinct for self-preservation explains his highly-strung, excitable nature. The herd instinct is another inheritance from the horses's wild ancestors. Being with others of his own kind gives a sense of security and can be exploited in sports like racing or hunting, where the desire to remain with the herd will spur him on to feats of speed or high jumps that he would never attempt when training alone. Fortunately for us, the horse also has a strong instinct for submission. In the wild, a herd has a single leader who exerts authority over the rest, so horses have a natural tendency to look for leadership and will accept the dominance of the owner or trainer, provided that person exerts the necessary combination of firmness and calm.

Influences on behaviour

The horse's sense of sight and hearing, and the way in which they have developed, have a strong influence on his temperament and behaviour. The eyes, set wide apart on either side of the head, give a good deal of sideways vision, a useful early warning system in the wild, and this may mean that the horse will shy at some movement glimpsed out of the corner of the eye, when the rider has noticed nothing. The set of the eyes makes it difficult

A bold outlook over the stable door—your first meeting with a horse will tell volumes. Alert, pricked ears and a large, generous eye indicate good character.

for the horse to focus on anything directly ahead and this can cause problems in jumping for, unless the horse has sufficient freedom to tilt his head, he is being asked to take off virtually blind. The hearing is acute, so the horse can be easily upset or frightened by sudden or loud noises like the bang of a car door, a tin can rattling in the gutter or the rustle of a garbage bag. On the other hand he responds well to gentle, calm tones of voice.

An excellent memory is characteristic of the horse and while this means that a good trainer can achieve first-class results it also means that a novice can easily set up bad habits in a horse by bungling the instructions. Horses, like other animals, are trained by a system of repetition, reward and correction but, because they have no reasoning power, they are unable to connect a reward or correction given several minutes after the action. If the rider is quick to reward a job well done with an encouraging word, a pat or caress behind the ears, the horse will associate that action with an enjoyable sensation and be all the more ready to perform properly next time. If it is necessary to correct, with a firmer application of the aids or even the whip, this must follow the action immediately, so that it is clear to the horse that the rider is punishing him for disobedience.

Horses are quick to sense fear or hesitation in humans; the ears pick up the slightest tremor of the voice, the nose picks up the scent of the human being's fear. Even a placid animal can react adversely if the rider is nervy and uncertain. Horses respond best to confidence and consistency. An indecisive rider is constantly sending different signals to the horse, who may become awkward or unwilling to answer any commands at all. Even worse results are caused by a bad-tempered rider whose horse constantly fears being kicked or hurt by the bit for reasons he cannot understand. Such memories stay with the horse, who is likely to react badly when the same rider next approaches, even after some time has elapsed.

Handling the nervous horse

Variations in temperament are just as common in horses as in people but any observant rider will be able to identify the outward signs of a horse's moods. The ears are often a good barometer: ears upright and alert show a receptive frame of mind; ears flicking back and forth mean uncertainty; ears laid back, accompanied by a swishing tail, indicate bad temper and possibly the will to kick. Signs of nervousness are rolling or showing the whites of the eyes, snorting, tossing the head or sidling along.

Many of the problems of nervousness can be overcome with patience and confidence. A rider should always be thinking ahead to forestall any problems that might arise. Prevention is always better than cure. A horse that is likely to shy at an unfamiliar object will probably tense and start flicking his ears; this is the moment when a sensitive rider will manage to turn the horse's head away from the offending object, while giving reassurance with firm seat and encouraging voice. If the horse does shy, he should be given time to examine and smell the object that has startled him, before being urged gently forward again. He should never be punished for shying; this will only cause more fright the next time he encounters a similar object. A nervous or young horse will gain confidence if exercised with an older, steadier animal; the herd instinct comes into play, convincing him that there is safety in numbers.

Rearing or bolting are more extreme reactions from a nervous horse and both can be alarming. The most sensible way to handle a bolting horse with the bit between his teeth is to let him go, if it is safe to do so, then, when he eventually tires and slows down, keep him going, preferably uphill, so that he learns that it is not desirable thing to do. If you have to find a way to stop him, let him have his head suddenly so that he lets go of the bit, give a determined pull on the reins, then slacken them and repeat with a second short, sharp pull if necessary. If a horse rears, the best technique is to give him his head while throwing your weight forward on to his neck. Hauling on the reins will only make things worse and could cause the horse to fall. As soon as he comes down to earth, turn him in a tight circle, as he cannot rear again while his head and neck are bent.

When faced with unusually nervous behaviour on the part of the horse, the rider should always look for possible causes. Perhaps the horse is excitable because he is overfed and underworked, or perhaps some physical abnormality is causing discomfort. Horses run away from pain, so check whether the tack is pinching. Consider, too, whether the problem is due to any human error, such as an over-heavy hand on the reins or lack of attention to local conditions.

FEEDING

Feeding time for mares and foals on a German stud farm.

Careful, balanced feeding is essential to keep a horse in good condition and allow him to reach his full potential. Underfeeding and overfeeding are both injurious to health but a well-balanced diet will keep him fit for the work required of him.

The natural food of the horse is grass and, for stabled horses, this is replaced by hay to provide bulk. A horse in work will need, in addition, concentrate foods like oats, barley and maize. This 'hard food' gives him the stamina to withstand strenuous work without damage to his health.

Do's and don'ts of good feeding

Do feed little and often. A horse's natural way of feeding is leisurely and almost continuous grazing, so allow him plenty of time to eat.

Don't make sudden changes in feeding routines or the type and amount of feed. Any variations should be phased in gradually over a period of days so that the digestive system has time to adapt.

Do make sure that fresh water is always available. Horses can safely be left to drink as and when they please but they will avoid stale, dusty water and tend to prefer fresh rainwater collected in water butts or tanks to chlorinated tap water. In very cold weather it is advisable to take the chill off the water by allowing the full buckets to stand for a while in a warm place. If for some reason the horse does not have constant access to water, and always water before feeding, then it is less likely that undigested food particles will be washed from the stomach into the intestines. A horse needs 27–54 litres (6–12 gallons) of water a day, depending on the weather and the amount of daily exercise.

Don't expect a horse to work hard immediately after a feed. The stomach expands when full of food and can cause pressure on the lungs, causing breathing difficulties. Allow an hour for digestion before light work, two hours for anything really strenuous.

Do weigh the feed and keep an accurate check on the amount given so that you can adjust the feed according to the condition of the horse and the work he is required to do.

Don't feed cheap, poor quality grain and hay. It is a false economy as it will never produce good condition. It should always be clean and smell fresh, otherwise the horse will be reluctant to eat. Clean any uneaten food from the manger before putting in the next ration. Never feed hay that looks or smells mouldy.

Do make sure your horse has enough hay to see him through the night. If he is hungry or bored he may resort to eating his bedding or acquire bad habits such as windsucking or crib-biting. Provided he is not overweight an extra full haynet at the end of the day will do him no harm.

Feeding routines

Stabled horses are totally dependent on their owners for food and need several feeds a day at regular intervals. (For details of feed for horses turned out to grass, see page 00.) A good working timetable is 7.30 am, mid-day, 4.30 pm and 7.30 pm but choose times that can be maintained fairly consistently.

The amount of food needed by an individual horse will depend on its age, size, work and the time of the year and it is impossible to lay down hard and fast rules. An observant owner will be able to gauge when to vary the amount or content of the feed by the look and reactions of the horse: by whether he is putting on weight or losing it, whether he seems excitable or lethargic, whether he appears eager for food or fails to finish his rations.

A rough guide is that the weight of food given to a horse should equal the amount he would eat if he were grazing in the wild. For a 15 hh horse, that weight is 11.5 kg (26 lbs). For larger or smaller horses, add or subtract 1 kg (2 lbs) for every 5 cm (2 in) of height. A working horse must be fed a balance of bulk food (hay and/or grass) and concentrates, or energy producing foods such as oats or barley. The following is a broad guideline to the ratio of bulk to concentrate needed by various types of horses:

	Hay	Concentrate
16 hh stabled hunter, regular hard work	6½ kg (13 lb)	7½ kg (17 lb)
15 hh horse, stabled, regular work	6½ kg (13 lb)	5½ kg (12 lb)
15 hh horse, stabled, very light work	8 kg (18 lb)	3½ kg (8 lbs)
14.2 hh horse, stabled very light work	5½ kg (12 lb)	4½ kg (10 lb)
12.2—13.2 hh pony, stabled at night, grass by day (winter)	2¼ kg (5 lb)	2¼ kg (5 lb)

If a horse has insufficient food to cope with the work demanded of him, the body will use its reserves and the horse will lose weight. If this process is allowed to continue, the body tissues will be affected and the horse will become emaciated. At the other end of the scale, if the horse is regularly fed more than his body needs, he becomes fat and is more likely to fall victim to strained ligaments and tendons, laminitis and respiratory disorders.

Older horses need special care, especially as their teeth and digestion may not be as good as they were previously. Meadow hay often suits older horses best and they need extra food in relation to their size, particularly oats, bran, linseed and carrots and boiled barley on winter evenings.

Different types of food

Hay: The digestive system of the horse needs plenty of bulky roughage to work effectively

137

and hay provides the bulk food necessary for stabled horses. It should not be fed to horses before they are six months old and should be checked for weeds; avoid hay containing thistles, docks and barley grass and discard any containing ragwort. Good quality hay is crisp, sweet-smelling and slightly greenish in colour, not washed-out yellow. There are several types of hay:

Mixed hay is grown from seed as a rotation crop and contains grasses such as clover, timothy and rye. It makes good; nutritious food for horses.

Meadow hay is grown on permanent pasture and is usually softer and less chewy than seed hay. Its nutritional content varies according to the type of grass it contains and it is not always substantial enough for horses in full work. It can be coarse if it comes from waterside meadows.

Hay-age is grass matured to a stage halfway between hay and silage and is fed in much the same quantities as hay to horses allergic to hay.

Grass A horse kept on its own at grass will require at least 2–3 acres (0.8–1.2 ha) of pasture, and at least one acre must be added for each additional horse. During the spring and summer it is not usually necessary to supplement the horse's diet unless the grass is brown and dry because of drought or if the field is over-grazed. However, the horse will need extra food during the autumn and winter.

Rich grass of the type sown for dairy cattle is unsuitable for horses as it causes severe health disorders such as laminitis, azoturia, lymphangitis and colic. It is best to choose a field with poorer quality grass, although fields containing many weeds and poisonous plants such as ragwort, yew, laurel and laburnum must be avoided.

Ideally, any ponds or streams should be cordoned off since they may well be polluted. It is safer to provide a fresh supply of water using a combination of pipes (or hosepipe) and a trough or similar large container.

Guide to concentrated foods

Oats

Dietary value: High energy food which contains all the necessary dietary elements in good balance.

How to feed: Feed bruised rather than whole or completely crushed. Once the husk is broken they should not be stored for long as they soon go stale and lose their nutritional value.

When to feed: Only according to the horse's requirements and measured with care as oats can have the effect of over exciting some horses. They are not normally considered suitable food for ponies ridden by children.

Barley

Dietary value: Similar dietary value to oats, containing rather more fat and starch, slightly less fibre and salt.

How to feed: Crushed, flaked or boiled, when it may be mixed with bran. Feed in somewhat smaller quantities than oats.

When to feed: Useful for young horses or to vary the diet of an overworked horse. Boiled barley is particularly good for condition.

Salt should always be made available in the form of a lick block.

Maize

Dietary value: High protein food rich in starches, fats and sugars but containing less fibre than barley or oats.

How to feed: Crushed or flaked, as it is inclined to be indigestible.

When to feed: When fed with other grains it is a good high energy food for winter or for tempting reluctant feeders.

Bran

Dietary value: Contains vitamins B and E, and though modern milling methods remove much of its nutritional content it is a useful dietary additive.

How to feed: Use as a mash made with boiling water and a handful of oats or boiled barley. The mixture should be crumbly rather than soggy.

When to feed: Aids digestion and prevents horses from bolting their food. Bran mash acts as a mild laxative and makes a good, filling feed for hardworking horses.

Peas and beans

Dietary value: Very nutritious, high in protein.

How to feed: Feed sparingly, as they are very 'heating'. Use split or bruised to make them digestible and add to other feed.

When to feed: Especially useful for horses living out in winter or for putting on condition.

Linseed

Dietary value: Large proportion of fat-forming elements.

How to feed: Prepare by boiling the grains, then simmering overnight in a slow oven until a jelly is formed. Mix the jelly with bran or cereal.

When to feed: Excellent for putting a shine on the coat or for fattening a horse. No more than 225 g (8 oz) should be fed per day and then only if a horse is in poor condition.

Sugar beet pulp

Dietary value: Useful extra source of energy and roughage when included in a concentrated diet.

How to feed: Soak in cold water for 24 hours before using and feed immediately, otherwise it will ferment. It should be used in conjunction with other feed, not on its own.

When to feed: Can be used to provide heat and bulk but is not suitable for horses in hard work.

Cubes or nuts

Dietary value: Formulated to provide a balanced diet of protein, roughage, carbohydrates, minerals and vitamins for various types of horses: racehorse, brood mare, horse and pony, etc.

How to feed: Must be fed in accordance with the manufacturer's instructions. Mix with a little bran or other fibrous feed to help digestion. Horses fed on cubes will need to drink more.

When to feed: Provided the right grade of cube is chosen for the type of horse, they ensure a consistent standard of nutrition but as an unvaried diet they can become boring.

Extras in the diet:

Fruit and vegetables: Horses, like people, enjoy variety in their diet. Carrots are particularly popular and other possibilities are swedes, turnips, mangels and parsnips. They should be sliced, not chopped into round pieces, which can cause a horse to choke.

Gruel is a good booster for tired horses when they return to stable. It is made by pouring boiling water onto two handfuls of oatmeal and mixing well. The gruel should be of a drinking consistency and is served once it has cooled down.

Sugar: In the form of molasses, sugar may be given sparingly. Two tablespoons diluted and mixed with the feed can be useful in tempting shy feeders but should not be used if the horse is already fat.

Salt: A salt lick should be provided in the stable. This is especially important for hardworking horses who lose a great deal of salt through sweating.

Vitamin and mineral supplements: These are expensive and should not normally be necessary for horses on a properly balanced diet. They should be used only on the advice of a veterinary surgeon.

Feeding methods

Feed should be measured and mixed in a bucket or bowl, then transferred to the manger or feed tin, which should be cleaned out and washed each day.

The most convenient method of feeding hay is from a haynet hung at about eye level so that the horse will be able to reach it comfortably but cannot catch his feet in it. It should never be hung on a hook, which might injure the horse. The best method is to tie it securely to a ring in the stable or, if outside, on a rail or tree.

If you are competing, take a feed for your horse when it is relaxing after the event, and provide hay for the journey home.

STABLE MANAGEMENT

There are many advantages in stabling horses rather than keeping them at grass: they are more accessible, easier to keep clean and can be kept at a higher peak of fitness than creatures who spend their lives out of doors. However, stabling a horse is expensive both in time and money. It must be remembered that such confinement is an unnatural state, so it is not sufficient simply to feed, water and groom. Ensuring that the horse is contented in this man-made environment takes a great deal of care, forward planning and understanding of the horse's temperament.

The stable

Today, most stables consist of individual loose boxes, either free-standing or housed within a barn. This is more satisfactory than the earlier method of keeping horses tethered in stalls, which restricted their movement, limited their access to fresh air and resulted in boredom. A box intended for a 15 hh horse should be at least 3.5 m x 3 m (12 ft x10 ft) and preferably 3.5 m (12 ft) square so that he can turn in comfort, stretch out to sleep and roll without running the risk of casting himself (becoming trapped against the wall so that he cannot get up without assistance), when he is liable to panic and injure himself. The height at the eaves should be at least 2.3 m (7 ft 6 in) but 3.5 m (12 ft) is safer as a rearing horse can easily reach this height.

Drainage: Few stables today are equipped with special stable-brick floors, grooved for drainage. Roughened concrete is the usual substitute and it should slope slightly towards a corner of the box away from the manger, hay-net and door, where a small hole leads out into a draining gully. This must be cleaned regularly to prevent blockages. The less satisfactory the drainage, the higher the bedding bills.

Ventilation: A constant circulation of fresh air is necessary to keep a horse healthy but draughts should be excluded. Free-standing boxes should have doors made in two halves, so that the bottom half is left bolted while the top half is hooked back, except when snow,

rain or bitter wind is driving straight into the box. This not only enables the horse to get all the fresh air he needs, it also means that he can watch what is going on in the yard and avoid boredom. Any windows should open in an upward direction so that the current of air is not directed straight on to the horse.

Equipment: Mangers need to be positioned at about the height of the horse's chest. Mangers at ground level get dirty easily as bedding and droppings fall into them and the feed is liable to be wasted. Removable mangers make cleaning easier.

Hay-nets are the most satisfactory and economical method of feeding hay. A ring for the hay-net should be positioned about 1.5 m (5 ft) from the ground so that when the hay is eaten the net will not drop low enough for the horse to catch his feet.

Automatic drinking bowls are labour-saving, though they must be kept scrupulously clean and checked on every visit to the stable, to make sure that they are working properly. If a bucket is used, it should be heavy enough not to be kicked over and positioned in a corner of the stable, or held by hinged rings on the wall.

An ordered modern yard. The wide overhang protects the occupants from bad weather and offers shade. The doors and surrounding areas are lined with metal to prevent horses from chewing wood.

Bedding

The horse should not be forced to stand for long periods on a bare brick or concrete floor so he will need bedding in the box day and night.

Straw bedding is the most widely used bedding material but it must be deep enough to encourage the horse to lie down, so that he will get sufficient rest, and to ensure that he does not injure himself. If the bed is too thin, he may slip as he tries to get up. Too thin a layer will also absorb less moisture, so that more of it has to be removed with each mucking out. Straw should be tossed well as it is laid and banked up round the insides of the box. Wheat straw is probably the best type, though it tends to be expensive; it is easier to handle, has good draining properties and is not readily eaten by the horse. Oat straw is rather too palatable and it tends to flatten, so horses find it less comfortable as a bed. It is wise to avoid barley straw, which can irritate the sensitive skin of some horses.

Peat Moss makes a satisfactory bed, especially for horses who are apt to eat straw. It is very absorbent and acts as a deodorant but great care is needed in removing wet and soiled patches promptly and forking over the bed thoroughly each day to ensure that it remains soft and clean. It tends to clog the feet so it is important to make sure they are picked out and clean.

Sawdust can be obtained quite cheaply from saw mills and, when laid thickly, kept clean and raked over daily, it makes a comfortable bed, but disposal may present problems. It should be used only in well-ventilated stables. As with peat, close attention must be paid to the horse's feet to make sure that no problems develop.

Wood shavings are light and easy to handle and make a warm, soft and reasonably dust-free bed, especially if they have been vacuum-cleaned before sale but they do cause allergic skin responses in some horses. Wood shavings can be combined with sawdust; a top layer of shavings, with sawdust underneath.

Shredded paper is an economical bedding material, useful for horses prone to allergies. It must be kept dry and clean or it will be heavy to muck out.

Mucking out

Whatever bedding material is used, it is essential to remove droppings as often as possible. There are three systems of managing

One of the daily chores essential in the proper care of stabled ponies and horses is mucking out the bed. All wet and soiled bedding—in this case of wood shavings—must be removed and the bed shaken and replenished for proper comfort.

bedding. Full mucking out, used for straw bedding, involves removing all soiled bedding, sweeping clean bedding to the sides to allow the floor to air, then replacing it with the addition of clean, fresh straw. The deep litter method, used for straw or shavings, involves removing the droppings and laying fresh bedding on top of the existing material. The entire bed is removed every three or four months but this is suitable only for dry, well-ventilated stables. Semi-deep litter, which can be used for any material, means removing droppings and all badly soiled bedding, adding extra bedding as necessary.

Grooming

Essential grooming kit:

1. Dandy brush, used for removing surface mud and dirt. Not to be used on sensitive parts like the face or the under-belly, or on the mane or tail, as it breaks the hairs.
2. Body brush, used for removing grease and dirt.
3. Metal curry comb, used for scraping dirt from the body brush while grooming is in progress.
4. Water brush, used wet for laying the mane and tail after brushing.
5. Hoof pick, used for removing dirt and stones.
6. Hoof oil to improve the appearance of the feet and to treat brittle feet.
7. Rubber curry comb used to remove hairs when the horse is losing his coat or for brushing sensitive parts.
8. Sweat scraper, used to remove excess sweat or water from the coat.
9. Small sponges, one for cleaning the eyes and nostrils, another for the dock.
10. Stable rubber, used to give the coat a final polish.

Quartering: One of the first tasks in the morning is to remove stable stains. This is done by turning back the horse's rug and giving the front of the body a quick brush down, then throwing it forwards and brushing the quarters.

Full grooming: The best time for full grooming is after exercise, when the horse is warm and the pores are opened. Any dried mud can be removed first with the dandy brush and, on the most sensitive parts of the body, with the rubber curry comb. Then begin work with the body brush, using a sweeping circular motion, following the direction of the hair, working

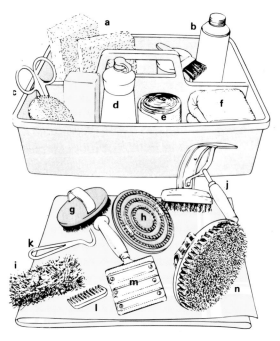

A basic grooming kit should include sponges (a), hoof oil and brush (b), scissors and sponge (c) for trimming legs and under the jaw, shampoo (d), a tail bandage (e) to set the tail temporarily after grooming, stable rubbers (f) for a final polish, a water brush (g) for dampening, a rubber curry comb (h), which is interchangeable with a dandy brush (i) for removing mud and sweat, a sweat scraper (j) to clear away excess moisture when sponging down, a hoofpick (k), a mane comb (l) for pulling the mane and tail, a metal curry comb (m) for cleaning brushes, and a body brush (n) to clean the coat thoroughly.

from front to back and from top to bottom. Every few strokes, run the brush across the teeth of the curry comb to dislodge the dirt. Pay particular attention to areas where dirt can easily lodge unseen: under the mane and tail, between the legs and on the inside of the pasterns. Brush out the mane and tail with the body brush.

Use a sponge dampened with tepid water on the muzzle, around the eyes, the lips and inside and outside the nostrils. Use a separate sponge on the dock area.

Pick out the hooves with the hoof pick, removing any dirt and stones, working from the heel to the toe. Then brush on the hoof oil, applying it right up to the coronet.

Go over the coat with the stable rubber, folded into a dampened pad, again working in the direction of the hair to give a final gloss. Use a damp water brush to lay the mane, working from the roots downwards; also smooth down the tail.

Shampooing: Normally a horse will only need to be washed all over if he is being taken to a special event or if he is very dirty. An animal shampoo in warm water should be used: douse him gently with a large sponge, avoiding the head. Then rinse thoroughly, taking care to remove all the soap and remove excess water with the sweat scraper. Rub the horse dry with old towels or straw, paying particular attention to the ears, heels and pasterns, then walk him round to dry off thoroughly. Avoid bathing altogether in chilly or cold weather.

Clipping

Clipping is carried out in winter to prevent the horse from sweating too much in hard work and losing condition. The length and thickness of a particular horse's winter coat will determine the frequency of clipping; horses normally need two clips, the first in October. Some need three but the last clipping should not be done later than the end of January, otherwise the emerging summer coat may be damaged.

The three standard clips are as follows:

The hunter clip leaves hair only on the legs and the saddle patch for extra protection.

The blanket clip leaves hair on the legs and in a blanket shape on the back and quarters for warmth.

The trace clip removes hair from the belly, across the chest and sometimes the underside of the neck and is used mainly for horses kept outside for much of the time.

The day after a hard day's hunting or competition, the horse should be trotted up in hand to check its soundness.

Rugging

Stabled horses normally need rugs to keep them warm in winter and this becomes essential after clipping. In the early part of the winter, a lined rug made from jute or man-made fibre is sufficient at night, with a woollen rug for daytime use. As the weather becomes colder, the horse will need one or more woollen blankets under the top rug. Once he has started wearing rugs, he should continue to do so until the spring. The under blankets can be discarded one by one as the weather warms up again. It is possible to test whether a horse is feeling cold by feeling his ears; cold ears mean a cold horse.

Daily stable routine

The exact times of routine chores in the stable will, of course, vary according to individual circumstances and needs, but once decided it should be varied as little as possible as horses thrive on regularity.

7.30 am Check over the horse for any symptoms of sickness or any injury sustained during the night.
Give the horse fresh water, first feed and a small hay-net.
Muck out the stable and lay day bed.

8.30 am Remove any droppings
Throw up rugs and quarter.
Pick out feet.
Saddle up and exercise.
On return from exercise, water horse.
Groom thoroughly and put on day rugs.

12.30 pm Provide fresh water.
Give second feed.

2 pm Tidy stable yard.
Whenever possible, turn out horse into paddock.

4.30 pm Remove droppings.
Pick out feet.
Provide fresh water and small hay-net.
Put on night rugs.
Lay night bed.
Give third feed.
Clean tack and tidy yard.

7.30 pm Check that all is well for the night, that rugs are still in place, and that the horse is not showing any signs of discomfort.
Remove droppings.
Provide fresh water.
Give fourth feed and full net of hay.

GRASS-KEPT HORSES

Horses kept at grass for all or part of the year need more care and attention than is often supposed. Horses can thrive on this system, provided it is properly managed and they are in suitable, securely fenced fields with a constant supply of water, but they cannot be left to look after themselves. They should be visited every day and checked over for possible injury or sickness. In winter, the hardiest of creatures will need supplementary feed and working horses cannot keep their condition on a wholly grass diet (see also p. 138).

Many owners favour the 'combined system', with horses spending part of their time at grass and partly stabled, so that they enjoy a more natural way of life but can be kept fitter and neater looking than those living permanently out of doors. The usual system is to stable the horse at night in winter and turn him loose to browse in the field by day. In summer the arrangement is reversed, with the horse stabled by day to avoid heat and flies and turned out at night.

A suitable field

The size of field necessary depends on the quality of grazing but, as a rough guide, each horse needs half a hectare (1 acre) and preferably twice that amount of space. It is not desirable to allow horses the free run of the entire field, as they will pick out the best grass and crop it to the soil, trampling and wasting other areas of perfectly good grazing. Wherever possible, divide the land into two, or, better still, three. Then one section can be rested while the other is eaten. In spring, one section can be used for taking up a hay crop, which will contribute towards winter feed. The more frequently droppings are collected up the better, especially in small fields, as horses will avoid lavatory areas and thus waste valuable grazing land.

Any field intended for grazing horses should be checked over for poisonous plants such as yew, deadly nightshade, ragwort, laurel and laburnum. Export soil analysis is advisable, either by a fertilizer firm or representatives of the Colleges of Agriculture, as pasture will only keep its quality if it is fertilized, limed or slagged and this will save money on suplementary feed in the long run.

Gates and fences: Field gates must be solid and swing easily on their hinges, loops of wire or string are not sufficient fastenings; a patent hook with a hinged tongue is far more reliable.

Fencing must be checked regularly to ensure that it remains secure, as horses will soon find any weak spot and make use of it. Post and rail is the best, but also the most expensive, choice. Hedges make satisfactory fencing, so long as they are tough and well-maintained, and they have the added advantage of providing wind-breaks. Wire is the most commonly used fencing and should be stretched taut between solid posts. Three strands are normally sufficient for horses, though an extra strand may be needed for fields with foals or small ponies and the lowest strand should be 30 cm (1 ft) from the ground, so that horses do not catch their feet in it.

Water: The horse must have access to a constant supply of fresh water, either from a running stream (*never* a stagnant pool) or a trough supplied with piped mains water or filled by hosepipe. If the supply is piped, the trough should be operated by a ballcock, so that it fills automatically when the water falls to a certain level. It should have no sharp edges to injure the horse's knee and the ballcock mechanism must be enclosed so that the horse cannot play with it. The trough should be positioned clear of the trees and cleaned whenever the water looks the least bit cloudy or there is any sign of slime. In winter it may be necessary to break the ice on the trough regularly.

Shelter: Driving rain or wet, cutting winds will quickly take off condition so grass-kept horses must be provided with adequate shelter from harsh weather in winter and from sun and flies in summer. The best type is a strong, three-sided shed with room for all the horses in the field, preferably facing south. It should be well bedded with deep litter.

Companionship: Horses are gregarious animals and they tend to become bored and

lonely without company. They will be happier in a field with others of their own kind or, failing that, a donkey. However, it is unwise to turn a horse loose in a field full of strangers. Introduce him to a member of the existing herd in advance, so that they become used to one another and, if possible, exercise him with the other members of the herd before he is expected to share their pasture. A little forward planning can prevent bullying.

Supplementary feeding

Horses need supplementary feeding whenever the pasture is not rich enough to provide them with sufficient nourishment. This means from autumn to spring and also in a hot, dry summer when the grass is scorched. The horse's behaviour is the best indication as to when to begin feeding hay. While there is good grazing he will prefer it; once he begins standing about near the gate for long periods, the grazing is probably poor and hay should be provided. The most satisfactory method of feeding hay is in a hay-rack in the field shelter or in hay-nets and, once again, the horse is the best guide as to the amount. If he consumes all the hay provided in a short time, it is not enough. If some still remains on your next visit, then it was too much.

In addition, a horse at grass in winter needs concentrates to generate body heat and maintain condition: in mild weather one concentrate feed a day will be sufficient; in harsh weather two will be necessary, one in the morning and one in the late afternoon. The amount will vary according to the horse's general condition but 2–2.5 kg (4–5 lb) is a rough guideline. Boiled barley, mixed with bran and fed warm, makes a good morning feed; bran and molasses mashes aid digestion and flaked maize mixed with bran and cubes makes a useful addition to winter rations.

A horse in regular work will need supplementary food both summer and winter, in proportion to the amount of energy he is expected to expend, on the same principle as the stabled horse. Horses under five years and over fifteen will need extra, so will those wintering in a small, exposed paddock rather than in a good quality, sheltered pasture.

Concentrates should be fed in solid containers—portable mangers which can hook on to a rail, or buckets set in holders, and if several horses share a field it is important to stay at feeding time, to make sure that each has a fair share of food.

Daily care

Horses at grass should be examined every day for scratches, cuts or lumps and any twigs or burrs removed from manes and tails. One advantage of catching up a horse every day, whether or not he is to be ridden, is that he will become accustomed to the routine. Otherwise he will soon learn that he is only caught up when he is expected to work and may attempt to avoid capture.

Horses may be dandy brushed and eyes, noses and docks may be damp sponged and dried once a week. Extensive grooming should be avoided as horses need the grease on their coats to protect them from the weather. After a ride, a hot, sweaty horse must be cooled off before returning to the field. A simple method is to cover his back with straw and sacking for 30 minutes or so. Feet should be picked out regularly and examined for cracks and bruises. In early spring, the roots of tails should be inspected for lice.

A New Zealand rug, which has specially designed straps to prevent it from slipping or flapping, will help to keep a horse dry and shield him from the wind, thus saving on the amount of concentrate he will require. These rugs are traditionally made from waterproof canvas lined with wool but synthetic materials are lighter and easier to care for.

Previous page: A Clydesdale mare and foal out at grass.
Above left: Shelter and amiable company are two important factors to consider for horses living at grass. A sturdy three-sided building with a wide opening facing south or away from prevailing winds allows the animals to shelter from extreme winter weather and to escape from the discomfort of heat and flies in summer.

Above right: A horse used to being kept at grass will live out quite happily all winter if provided with a well-fitting New Zealand rug. The type without a surcingle and fastened with hind-leg straps is preferable as it eliminates pressure on the horse's sensitive spine.

Right: Hard-working horses enjoying a well-earned rest at grass.

Canvas rugs must be scrubbed outside and vacuumed inside; synthetics can be washed. The straps must be cleaned regularly to keep them soft and supple. Rugs must be removed daily so that the horse can be checked for rubs and the rug changed if it is very wet or dirty.

A horse should be allowed to get used to the unaccustomed feel of the rug before he is turned out in it for the first time.

Turning out to grass

A hardworking horse will appreciate a holiday at grass but the changeover should be gradual. A mild spell in spring or autumn is the best time to choose, not the height of summer when the ground is hard and the flies are at their worst. Prepare the stabled horse by gradually reducing his concentrates, cutting down on exercise and allowing him to graze for a short time each day. For the first two weeks, turn him out into the field by day and return him to the stable by night. By the third week it should be possible to leave him out all the time, albeit with a rug if necessary.

The horse should be watched carefully to make sure that he is acclimatized. If he spends most of his time standing at the gate, or is obviously cold or losing weight, he should be brought back inside.

SADDLERY

Good quality, well-maintained saddlery, or 'tack', is part of the essential equipment of the riding horse. Though horses have been employed for a wide variety of purposes over the centuries, leading to an enormous variety of bits, bridles and saddles, the purpose of tack has changed little: to facilitate training and ensure a comfortable, controlled ride.

The saddle

All saddles are built on the basic framework of the 'tree', usually made from light wood or fibre-glass. Bands of webbing stretch along the tree to carry the stuffing and leather of the seat. Stirrup bars are attached to the tree and are equipped with safety catches which will release the leather and irons automatically when under pressure. A spring tree saddle has a strip of flexible steel inserted on either side of the tree to give extra resilience to the seat.

The purpose of the saddle is to ensure that the rider keeps the correct position and balance and to distribute the rider's weight evenly over the stronger parts of the horse's back. Saddles differ in design to allow for the weight distribution required for each different type of equestrian activity:

The dressage saddle, with deeper seat and long, straight saddle flaps, helps the rider to keep a well-centred seat without forward movement.

The jumping saddle is deep-seated with saddle flaps set well forward and padded 'knee rolls', so that the rider can pitch his weight over his knees as he follows the action of the horse.

The racing saddle is lightweight and allows for the maximum forward position.

The slow saddle has straight cut flaps to display the horse's shoulders to better advantage.

The all-purpose saddle is the usual choice for a riding horse. It has none of the exaggerated lines associated with specialist saddles and is suitable for hacking, jumping and showing.

Hot water pipes keep the leather in this tack room warm and dry.

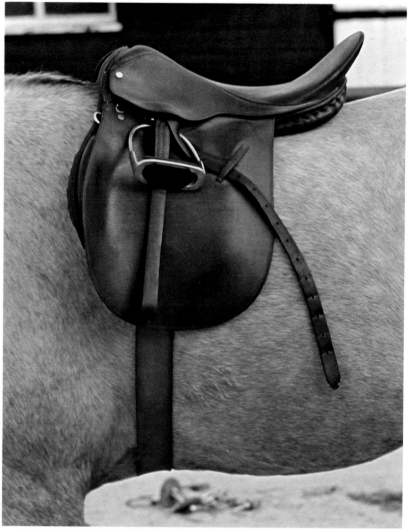

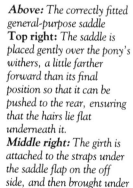

Above: *The correctly fitted general-purpose saddle*
Top right: *The saddle is placed gently over the pony's withers, a little farther forward than its final position so that it can be pushed to the rear, ensuring that the hairs lie flat underneath it.*
Middle right: *The girth is attached to the straps under the saddle flap on the off side, and then brought under the pony's belly. It is important to ensure that the girth buckles do not bang against the legs.*
Bottom right: *Fastening the girth on the near side.*

Correct fitting of the saddle is essential to protect the horse's back. It must allow free movement of the shoulders and the front arch should clear the withers when the rider is leaning forward in the saddle. The side-bars must not touch the loins, which may happen if a saddle is too long. Any pressure on the horse's spine may cause serious injury so there should always be a tunnel of daylight along the spine when the rider is mounted. A numnah, or saddle pad, made of foam, calico or sheepskin, should always be worn with a spring tree saddle to prevent sores, but it should never be used as an attempt to correct an ill-fitting saddle.

The girths are the means of securing the saddle, so they must be hard-wearing. Leather girths are efficient and long-lasting, but care is required to keep them soft and supple. Nylon is easier to keep clean, grips well and is less likely to cause galls. Webbing is less reliable and should not be worn singly; two are required for safety.

Bridles and bits

An incorrectly fitted bit causes discomfort and will lead to many problems for the rider. It is important to ensure that it protrudes 0.5 cm (¼ in) on each side of the horse's mouth so that it is not narrow enough to pinch the corners of the mouth and not wide enough to slide from side to side. When the bridle is fastened the bit should only just wrinkle the corner of the horse's mouth. The bridle itself should not rub on the cheekbones or cut into the ears and it should be possible to insert a fist between the throat and the throat lash.

The snaffle is the simplest type of bit, basically a jointed mouthpiece with a ring at each end, to which the reins are attached. This is the normal type of bit used for training a young horse not yet ready for the double bridle. The various types of snaffle include:

The egg-butt snaffle, probably the most popular, with a single joint in the middle and smooth side-joints to prevent chafing.

The cheek-snaffle which has fixed upper and lower cheekpieces to prevent the bit pulling through the horse's mouth.

The loose-ring snaffle allows greater play of the bit in the mouth, which lessens the severity of the bit.

The gag snaffle has a severe action and is only suitable for use by very experienced riders.

The double bridle is made up of the bridoon (an egg-butt or loose-ring snaffle), a curb bit with a fixed or movable mouthpiece, and a curb-chain or strap, which rests in the 'curb groove' under the horse's chin. This gives the rider more subtle control: the bridoon acts on the corners of the mouth and tongue, encouraging raising of the head, while the curb (usually a straight bar with a central port, or curve, to accommodate the tongue) operates on the bars and roof of the mouth, causing the horse to bring the head in and flex the lower jaw.

The bridoon should lie as high as possible in the horse's mouth with the curb bit immediately below it. The curb chain should be thick and flat, for comfort, and it should be possible to insert at least two fingers inside the curb chain when the reins are relaxed. It should lie flat along the chin groove, not above it, when the curb rein is tightened.

The Pelham bit attempts to combine the merits of both snaffle and curb. It has a single curb bit, both bridoon and curb reins and a curb-chain, so that a single bit acts on the

corners of the mouth when the bridoon is used and on the poll and curb groove when the curb rein is used. This type of bit has limitations for advanced forms of equitation but some horses do perform better in Pelhams than any other type of bridle and they are sometimes used for children's ponies when the ponies are considered somewhat difficult to handle.

The Hackamore or bitless bridle acts on the horse's nose, the curb groove and the poll rather than on the mouth. This does not necessarily mean that it is a less severe form of bridle, so it should not be used by inexperienced riders, but it can be useful for horses with spoilt or difficult mouths.

Nosebands

The cavesson is the most commonly used noseband, consisting of a simple strap of leather sitting fairly high over the nose, kept in place by a headstrap. This is the only

A correctly fitted Pelham bridle: the bit just wrinkles the corners of the mouth, the noseband lies comfortably below the cheekbone, the throatlatch has been buckled loosely to ensure that breathing and head movements are not restricted, and there is plenty of room for the ears between headpiece and browband.

Right: A top class show
jumper illustrating correctly
worn tack—a well-fitting
snaffle bridle, running
martingale, essential stops
on the reins, breast plate to
prevent the saddle slipping
back, skeleton knee caps,
open-fronted tendon boots,
and a comfortably-fitting
general purpose saddle and
numnah.

Far right: Exercise
bandages are seen here
properly applied on a show
jumper. They should be put
on over padding and for
competitive use should be
sewn in position to prevent
them coming dangerously
undone. Exercise bandages
normally finish above the
fetlock, but a proprietary
make of lightweight adhesive
bandage can be fitted down
over the fetlock.

noseband to which a standing martingale can be attached.

The dropped noseband sits much lower on the nose and is intended to stop the horse opening his mouth too wide and losing contact with the bit. It should lie 6–7½ cm (2½–3 in) above the nostrils and must be carefully fitted so that it is not tight enough to prevent the horse from flexing his jaw.

The Grackle noseband has two straps, crossing over the bridge of the nose. It has a similar purpose to the dropped noseband but has a stronger action.

The flash noseband is a cavesson with a drop noseband attached and can therefore be used with a standing martingale.

Martingales

Martingales are used to correct poor head carriage and increase the rider's control. They should never be used to force a horse's head into an unnaturally low position.

The standing martingale is a single strap attached to the girth at one end and the noseband at the other, passing between the forelegs and kept in place by a neck-strap. It increases control by exerting pressure on the nose, preventing the horse from tossing his head.

It should be attached to the cavesson and, when the horse's head is in the correct position, you should be able to push the strap upwards to touch the horse's gullet.

The running martingale divides into two after it has passed through the neck-strap, each end being attached to the reins by a ring. It serves a similar purpose to the standing martingale, in that it acts to correct the poor head carriage, but it acts more directly on the mouth than on the nose. Care must be taken in fitting as the action can be very severe if it is too tightly adjusted.

The Irish martingale, not strictly speaking a martingale at all, is simply a strap about 15 cm (6 in) long, with a ring at either end through which the reins run. The object is to prevent the reins being tossed over the horse's head.

Maintaining saddlery

Leather tack will become brittle and crack without proper care. It should be washed with a sponge and lukewarm water, without getting the leather too wet. Surplus water is then removed with a chamois leather before allowing the leather to dry naturally. Then, with a separate sponge, rub saddle soap into the leather, using a circular motion. The sponge should be damp but it is too wet if the soap produces a great deal of lather. If the leather has become dry and stiff, treat it with special leather preservative.

Metal parts can be cleaned with metal polish but this should not be used on the mouthpiece of the bit.

Inspect tack regularly for signs of undue wear, check the stitching on reins, girths and stirrup leathers and check the fit of the saddle.

VETERINARY CARE

An important part of any horse-owner's daily routine is to check over the horse for any signs of ill-health, and any deviation from the norm should be noted and the reason sought.

A healthy horse has an alert look, eyes bright and ears pricked, a shining coat with the skin freely movable over the underlying tissue, limbs free from swelling and cool to the touch. Droppings should be moist, firm enough to break as they hit the ground and without offensive odour. The temperature, taken from the rectum, should be 38°C (100.5°F). When the horse is at rest the pulse, felt under the lower jaw, should be 36–42 beats per minute and respiration should be even and regular at the rate of 8–12 per minute.

The digestive system

The horse's digestive system is geared towards the natural pattern of grazing, eating little and often. The stomach is small in relation to its size and passes the food almost unaltered to the caecum and the large intestine where the major process of digesting fibre takes place by bacterial fermentation. The flow of secretions available for the digestive process depends on the accustomed diet, so that strange foods can only be digested slowly at first and sudden changes in diet are likely to cause problems.

Signs of digestive disorders are reluctance to feed, trouble with swallowing, an unusual consistency or smell in the droppings, quidding or evidence of colic (abdominal pain).

The digestive and excretory systems

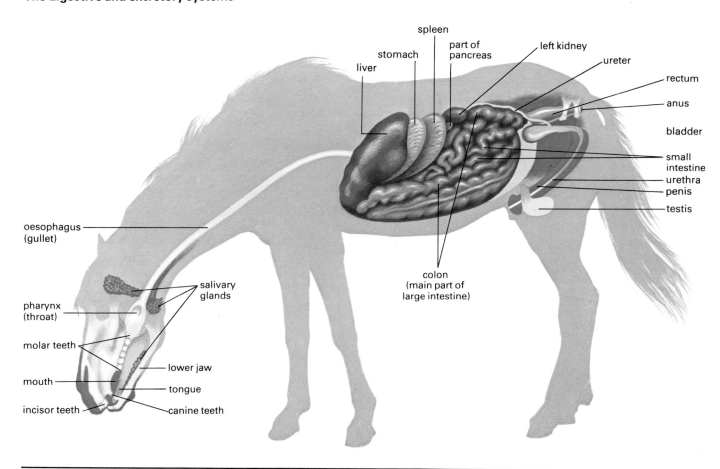

spleen
stomach
part of pancreas
left kidney
liver
ureter
rectum
anus
bladder
small intestine
urethra
penis
testis
colon (main part of large intestine)
oesophagus (gullet)
salivary glands
pharynx (throat)
molar teeth
lower jaw
mouth
tongue
incisor teeth
canine teeth

The respiratory system

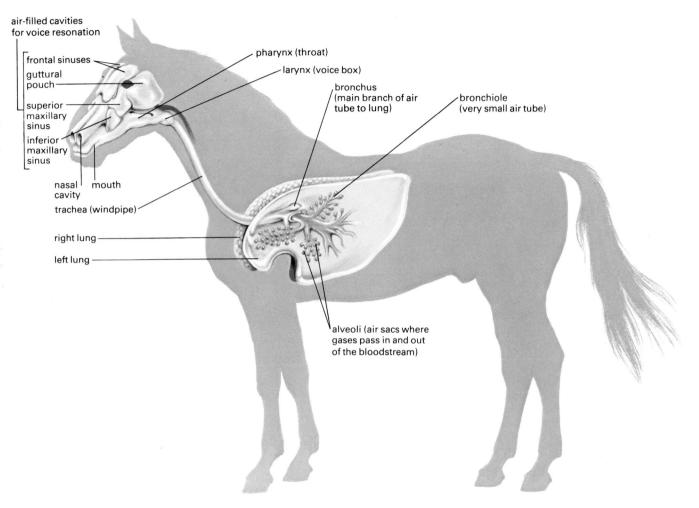

air-filled cavities for voice resonation

frontal sinuses

guttural pouch

superior maxillary sinus

inferior maxillary sinus

nasal cavity   mouth

trachea (windpipe)

right lung

left lung

pharynx (throat)

larynx (voice box)

bronchus (main branch of air tube to lung)

bronchiole (very small air tube)

alveoli (air sacs where gases pass in and out of the bloodstream)

The respiratory system

At rest the horse's breathing is slow and shallow; after exercise the increase in the respiratory rate can be seen from the horse's heaving flanks. The length of time taken for it to return to normal is a measure of the horse's fitness. Prolonged heaving flanks after a period of exercise indicates that the horse has been overstressed.

Problems in the respiratory system are indicated by increased rate and depth of breathing, noisy inspiration and sudden forced expiratory movements resulting in coughing or double movement of the flanks.

The heart

As the heart contracts it drives blood through the arteries and this can be felt as a pulse when the fingertips are pressed against the artery under the lower jaw. The normal pulse rate of 36–42 beats per minute rises as a result

of exercise, fright or excitement. As with the respiratory rate, the time taken to return to normal after work is a measure of the horse's fitness. Immediately after galloping the pulse rate will be around 100. Trainers measure the time taken for the pulse to return to around 50 beats per minute and providing this occurs within 20 minutes, the horse is fit to move on to more stressing work.

The skin

The condition of the horse's skin is one of the indications of a horse's state of health and a careful owner will learn to appreciate the normal texture and elasticity of the skin in various parts of the body. A harsh, dull or staring coat may indicate an infection or an infestation by parasites. When a horse becomes hidebound, so that the skin no longer moves freely over the underlying tissues, he may be suffering from malnutrition, worm infestation or dehydration.

GUIDE TO AILMENTS

Digestive disorders

Colic

Symptoms: Severe abdominal pain. The horse is restless, pawing the ground, kicking at the abdomen, lying down and getting up again and sweating; also increase in pulse rate.

Cause: Faulty feeding, sudden change in diet, bad teeth causing poor digestion, worm infection, twisted gut.

Treatment: Call vet if the attack lasts more than an hour. Remove food and water; keep the horse warm. If he is very restless, walk him round gently.

Worms

Symptoms: Loss of condition, bowel irregularity, dull, staring coat.

Cause: Infestation by parasites.

Treatment: Take advice from vet on worm dosing drugs. Keep up regular worm doses to prevent recurrence.

Respiratory disorders

Broken wind

Symptoms: Deep, hollow cough, heaving of the flanks and double movement when breathing out.

Cause: Overstrain when unfit, causing damage to the lung vesicles, after effects of pneumonia or bronchitic condition.

Treatment: Incurable but relief can be obtained by careful feeding and avoiding hard or fast work.

Cold in the head

Symptoms: Discharge from both nostrils, coughing, staring coat.

Cause: Infection or exposure.

Treatment: Rest the horse and keep him well-rugged, keep the stables well-ventilated, take temperature regularly and if in any doubt, call the vet.

Equine influenza

Symptoms: Loss of appetite, exhaustion, shallow cough, high temperature.

Cause: Virus infection.

Treatment: Call the vet immediately. Isolate and keep the horse warm, take temperature regularly. Prevent by immunization and regular booster injections.

Whistling and roaring

Symptoms: Whistling and roaring noises when the horse is breathing hard.

Cause: Paralysis of one of the nerves leading to the vocal cord, restricting air flow.

Treatment: surgery.

Skin problems:

Lice

Symptoms: Itching, bare patches of skin, loss of condition.

Cause: Parasites, likely to affect grass-fed horses or those in poor condition.

Treatment: Apply delousing powder to affected areas, repeat after 10 days.

Warbles

Symptoms: Hard nodules on the back, becoming larger swellings.

Cause: Hatching of the warble fly.

Treatment: Hot fomentations until the maggot has emerged. The horse should not be ridden if the swelling is in the saddle area.

Ringworm

Symptoms: Small circles of hair become raised then fall out, leaving a small bare patch.

Cause: Fungus infection.

Treatment: Isolate the horse and stop grooming. Apply proprietary ointment or powder as directed by the vet.

Sweet itch

Symptoms: Severe irritation around the mane and neck, withers and tail, causing the horse to rub himself raw. Appears in early summer.

Cause: Possibly allergy or insect bite.

Treatment: Consult vet for diagnosis. The area should be kept scrupulously clean and calamine lotion may be soothing.

Galls

Symptoms: Soreness, lumps or lacerations of the skin behind the elbows or on the back.

Causes: Illfitting girths or saddle.

Treatment: Wash with weak saline solution, dry with cotton wool and apply sulphonamide powder. Do not use saddle or girths again until the galls have healed.

Bacterial diseases

Strangles

Symptoms: Sharp rise in temperature, loss of appetite, hot, tender swelling of glands in the throat region.

Cause: Bacteria *streptococcus equi*, highly contagious.
Treatment: Call the vet immediately, isolate and keep the horse warm.

Tetanus
Symptoms: Stiffness, membranes of the eye covering part of the eyeball, raised temperature.
Cause: Bacteria entering the body through a wound.
Treatment: Call vet immediately. Prevention is essential by means of immunization and regular booster injections.

Locomotor system

The work required of the horse by man has imposed stresses not experienced by horses in the wild. Jumping, eventing, hunting, riding on hard surfaces and long distance work all increase the risk of injury and traumatic disease.

When at rest the horse carries 60 per cent of his weight on the forelimbs but during fast work and especially jumping, the entire weight is borne by the forelegs. It is therefore only to be expected that the causes of lameness in the forelimbs—pedal ostitis, navicular disease, splints, ringbone—are mainly caused by concussion. In the hindquarters poor conformation such as sickle hocks or cow hocks can predispose to strain, leading to bone spavin or curb. Strains and sprains of the ligaments or tendons are frequently caused by overstressing an unfit or tired horse, fast work in heavy going or awkward landings from jumps.

A sensitive rider will feel any slight change of action which could be the first indication of lameness and will know the normal gait of the horse well enough to pinpoint the problem. If one of the forelegs is lame, the horse's head will rise as the painful leg touches the ground and drop as the sound leg comes down. At rest he may be pointing a forefoot. If a hind leg is lame the horse will lean to one side, pulling his weight on the sound leg, perhaps dragging a toe on the lame side.

Jumping greatly increases the risk of injury and care must be taken not to overstrain a tired or unfit horse.

CAUSES OF LAMENESS

Foot conditions

Bruised sole
Symptoms: Soreness when pressure is applied to the sole.
Cause: Sharp stone.
Treatment: Have the shoe removed and poultice the sole until the inflammation has disappeared.

Corns
Symptoms: Heat in the heels, normally on the forefeet.
Cause: Ill-fitting shoes or shoes left on too long.
Treatment: Have the shoe removed, the corn cut out and a surgical shoe fitted to relieve the pressure.

Laminitis
Symptoms: Heat in the feet and obvious pain. The horse stands on his heels with forefeet thrust forward and resists moving.
Cause: Concussion from fast work on hard ground; too much heating food and insufficient exercise; too much lush grass.
Treatment: Call the vet immediately; appropriate treatment in the early stages can effect a complete cure.

Navicular disease
Symptoms: Lameness which, in the early stages, wears off with exercise. Pointing of the forefoot when standing.
Cause: Inflammatory condition of the bone over which the tendon passes. Possibly hereditary, otherwise caused by concussion.
Treatment: Consult the vet for advice. No known cure.

Pedal ostitis
Symptoms: Similar to navicular disease, though the onset may be sudden and acute.
Cause: Inflammatory condition of the pedal bone due to concussion.
Treatment: Consult vet. Rest and poulticing may show good results.

Sand crack
Symptoms: Crack in the wall of the foot, extending downwards from the coronet. Does not always result in lameness.
Cause: Brittle feet caused by poor condition or rasping of the wall with the hoof.
Treatment: Consult farrier who may fit a clasp over the crack or isolate it by making a groove at the base with a hot iron.

Seedy toe
Symptoms: The middle layer of horn becomes separated from the layer below and soft, cheesy horn fills the space between; noticed during shoeing. Causes lameness only in the later stages.
Cause: Difficult to determine, possibly faulty shoeing.
Treatment: Have the soft horn removed and treat with Stockholm tar. Consult the vet rather than the farrier in bad cases.

Pricked foot (nail binding)
Symptoms: Heat and pain in the hoof, probably soon after shoeing.
Cause: Nail driven too close to the sensitive area of the foot or nail picked up.
Treatment: Remove the nail or have the shoe removed. Hot poultices if necessary.

Thrush
Symptoms: The cleft of the frog is moist and smells offensive.
Cause: Standing in a badly drained stable, insufficiently mucked out.
Treatment: Wash out and disinfect the foot and apply dressings of Stockholm tar.

Leg conditions

Bone spavin
Symptoms: Bony enlargement of the hock inside and just below the hock joint. The horse may drag the toe.
Cause: Strain
Treatment: Consult the vet. Reduce inflammation by hot fomentations and cold hosing.

Capped elbow
Symptoms: Soft swelling at the point of the elbow.
Cause: Lack of bedding or rubbing the elbow with the heel of the shoe when lying down.
Treatment: Hot fomentations. A 'sausage boot' strapped above the fetlock or around the pastern will prevent pressure from the shoe.

Curb
Symptoms: Thickening of the ligament at the back of the hock. May cause lameness.
Cause: Strain, particularly in horses with sickle hocks.
Treatment: Take advice from vet. No treatment may be necessary.

Always protect a horse well against injuries when travelling.

Ringbone
Symptoms: A bony enlargement of the pastern. Heat may be felt. May cause lameness.
Cause: Concussion or injury.
Treatment: Call the vet and rest the horse in the meantime.

Splints
Symptoms: Bony enlargement of the cannon bone. Soreness and lameness while it is forming, though once set it may cease to cause trouble.
Cause: Concussion.
Treatment: Cold hosing, cold poultices. Walking exercise if lameness is not acute.

Sprains
Symptoms: Heat, swelling and pain.
Cause: Galloping over hard ground; fast work when the horse is tired.
Treatment: Rest the horse; a mild sprain can become more serious and put him out of action for six months. Cold hosing of the limb followed by cold poultices reduces inflammation.

First aid

Immediate first aid is necessary if the horse sustains any injury, however minor. The smallest cut can become infected and that means a great deal of discomfort for the horse and extra expense for the owner. A small, shallow skin wound should be bathed with a mild disinfectant or saline solution on cotton wool and dusted with antibiotic powder. If it is a bruised wound, perhaps caused by a kick, apply a poultice.

In the case of a deep wound bleeding profusely, a cold water compress should be applied to stop the bleeding, or if a spurting of bright red blood suggests arterial bleeding, then a tourniquet may be necessary. Once the bleeding has stopped, the wound should be cleaned.

The veterinary surgeon should always be called if the wound is deep and may require stitching or if the owner has not kept the horse up to date with tetanus injections. Puncture wounds, which may be deeper than they look and may result in abscesses, and wounds near joints, need particular care.

Below: a Palomino mare with her foal.

First aid kit
The basic first aid kit for any stable is as follows:
Gamgee tissue, gauze and cotton wool
Poultice dressings or kaolin paste for
 poulticing
Bandages
Surgical tape
Antiseptic
Epsom salts
Antibiotic powder
Emollient ointment (Stockholm tar)
Veterinary thermometer
Blunt-tipped scissors

Care of brood mare and foal

The gestation period for a brood mare is officially 11 months and 4 days, though the exact time varies. If she returns from stud in spring or early summer she can be kept at grass until autumn, with supplementary feeding only if grazing is insufficient. At the first sign of cold weather all but the hardy mountain and moorland ponies should be stabled at

Above: Foals need exercise to build strong muscles and, weather permitting, should be let out to graze.

night. She can be turned out to graze during the day, thus enjoying vital fresh air and exercise. If grazing is not available she should have up to two hours walking exercise daily. Gentle hacking with a light rider will not harm the unborn foal but riding should cease at the beginning of the seventh month.

The foaling box should be thoroughly cleaned and disinfected and bedded down with plenty of clean straw. It should be large enough for the mare to walk round and she should be thoroughly accustomed to the box in advance.

Shortly before foaling begins, the mare will pace round, swishing her tail and looking round at her sides and later beginning to sweat. In a normal birth, a gush of fluid will precede the emergence of the foal's forefeet, covered with membranes, and then the head. The shoulders are the slowest to emerge; after that the foal slides out comparatively easily.

The new-born foal should be left alone so that its struggles break the umbilical cord naturally. The mare will probably be on her feet within half an hour and after struggling and falling a few times the foal will normally manage to stay upright. It should be left to find the mare's udder of its own accord.

After a natural birth the vet should be asked to check over the mare and foal. They should remain in the box for a few days after the birth, though foals born outside can stay out, providing the weather is mild and settled. In good weather, mare and foal should be let out to graze for an increased time each day until, within two weeks or so, they are living in the paddock. Foals need exercise to build strong muscles and they should not be confined. Where grazing is good, mare and foal will need little else through the summer. Where grass is sparse a high protein diet of crushed oats, flaked maize and stud cubes mixed with bran, together with good hay, will keep the mother's milk supply flowing.

BUYING AND SELLING

Buying a horse is not something to be undertaken lightly and if the purchase is to be a success and the animal is to fulfil the owner's hopes and needs, it takes a good deal of forward planning. As a prospective owner, you must take into account the amount of time you can find to look after the horse, the facilities available for its keep and your level of experience.

For a stabled horse, a minimum of three hours a day must be allowed for feeding, grooming, exercising and general stable duties. The easy alternative, keeping a horse at a livery stables where experienced grooms do all the work, is very costly. Keeping a horse at grass takes less time but cuts down your choice, as the animal must be hardy enough to withstand the outdoor life.

Novice horse buyers frequently make the mistake of overrating their capabilities. Owning a horse that is beyond your powers of control is no way to improve your riding and is likely to result in disappointment, loss of confidence and possible injury. This is particularly important to remember when choosing a pony for a child. An expensive, mettlesome pony with a cupboard full of rosettes may be a good choice for a talented youngster having first-rate instruction, but he is not a suitable mount for a beginner.

Inspecting the horse

When you arrive to inspect a horse, take time to assess his surroundings. A dirty, untidy stable yard and slovenly groom suggest poor horse care and this is likely to be reflected in the horse's general condition. Notice the horse's stable manners; he should be amenable and willing to be handled, so try lifting one foot or ask him to move over in his box.

As the handler leads the horse out, he should walk out briskly and keenly, not reluctantly. Stand back and consider the horse as a whole. A detailed guide to good conformation is given on pages 130–133 but the overall picture should be of a well-proportioned, well-balanced animal with a pleasing outline.

The next step is to watch as the horse is walked and trotted in hand. Ask to see him walked away, then trotted towards and past you. From the front, the action should be long and free, with the hindfeet coming down just in front of the prints of the forefeet. When viewed from the front the forelegs should move in a straight line, not swing out sideways. At the trot the action should be lively and the feet picked up cleanly. Watch the horse being put through his paces by the handler and see how much use the handler has to make of the aids to get results. The horse's tail will give a useful indication of both the horse's attitude and the way in which he uses his back: a stiffly held tail may point to a back problem, a relaxed, swinging

See the horse ridden and put through all paces before you assess how it performs for you.

tail shows that he is using his back well and a swishing tail indicates temper or resistance.

During the trial ride you should fully test the horse's reaction to the aids and try him out in everything that is part of your normal riding routine.

A prudent buyer will test several horses before making a decision, or at least visit a likely horse on more than one occasion. It is important to take into account the temperament of both horse and rider: a calm rider may be able to soothe a nervous horse, a nervous rider will need a placid mount and an excitable rider with an excitable horse is an unwise combination. It is essential that the prospective purchaser feels comfortable and happy with the ride and that horse and rider make a good team.

When questioning the vendor, remember that the age and weight of the horse are important. A young horse may be cheaper but it is not a suitable buy for any but the most experienced rider. Any other rider should look for a horse that is both physically mature and fully trained and the optimum age is probably six to eight years old, when the horse has ten years of active work ahead. However, an older horse, steady and reliable, can be a good choice for a novice rider who needs to gain confidence. A heavily built rider will need a strong horse, but bear in mind that a big horse, in height, is not necessarily a weight carrier; a smaller, stockier horse may be a better choice. A short legged rider will not feel comfortable on a broad-backed horse, though a narrower horse of the same height may suit admirably.

Horse sales are best avoided by all but the most experienced as there may be no opportunity to ride the horse or have him vetted and there is a high risk of buying on impulse and regretting the purchase later.

Clinching the deal

Any offer made to the vendor should be conditional on examination by the buyer's veterinary surgeon. Never rely on a veterinary certificate offered along with the horse. Employ a specialist horse vet and give him a clear idea of the purpose for which the horse is required so that he can judge its suitability accordingly. A thorough examination should take about two hours, during which time the vet will check the horse for blemishes or unsoundness and test the heart, wind and limbs as well as giving an estimate of the age.

The onus is on the buyer to find out all the salient facts about a horse, not on the seller to divulge them but if, at a later date, you have reason to believe that statements made by the vendor were false or misleading, you may have recourse to legal action against him. It is wise to ask for a warranty in return for your cheque and this is essential in any case where you have been unable for some reason to examine the horse thoroughly. Check the wording of the warranty carefully and make sure it covers any major point on which you are uncertain. It should read something like this: 'Received from Mr Andrew Green the sum of £150 for bay mare, which I hereby warrant six years old, sound and free from vice.'

Selling a horse

When putting a horse up for sale it is wise to study the equestrian press to gauge a realistic price. The price you set will depend on whether you are prepared to wait as long as it takes to meet your price or need to make a quick sale, but remember to balance the cost of keeping the horse for the extra weeks or months against the eventual sale price.

It is often possible to sell through friends but remember that you are likely to receive complaints if the horse is less than perfect. The easiest way to sell is probably to take the horse to a dealer. The price may be a little lower than could be obtained in a private sale, but it avoids all the time and trouble of showing the horse to prospective purchasers. If you decide to advertise, then stick closely to the facts. Describing a run-of-the-mill horse in glowing terms will only result in hours of wasted time for both buyer and vendor. Remember that there is a buyer for any horse, so long as the price is right.

Any trial ride should take place on your premises and under your close eye. A heavy-handed or unkind rider can upset a sensitive horse and may mean that he eyes the next stranger to arrive with suspicion, thus losing a sale with another buyer.

Finally, it is important that any horse should have a certificate issued by a veterinary surgeon to say that he has found no sign of disease, injury or obvious unsoundness before you part with him, otherwise you may find the buyer returning a lame horse, claiming that he was misled at the time of sale and you will be unable to prove that his poor handling has caused the fault.

ROAD SAFETY

Horses and their riders are legitimate road users and as such are entitled to proper consideration, but most motorists are unused to horses and tend to regard them as time-wasting nuisances, so roads are not particularly safe or pleasant places for them. There are always risks: cars pass too close and too fast, pedestrians rush out unexpectedly and there are all manner of sudden noises. It is the rider's duty to keep constantly vigilant and to make sure that the horse is under control at all times, so no horse out on the highway should be allowed to meander along on a loose rein.

The pace should be a walk or a steady trot, never a canter which will jar the horse's legs and make it more difficult to keep control if something unexpected happens. Never trot round corners where the road surface may be worn smooth and slippery, or on grass verges where the horse may catch his feet in litter or stumble into a ditch. Skirt man-hole covers whenever it is safe to do so, as they can be slippery and take care not to underestimate the size of the horse when skirting stationery vehicles.

It is important that the horse's feed should be related to his work, as an over-fed and under-exercised horse is a potential danger to all concerned. If a horse is too fresh, he should be given the opportunity to run off his high spirits before he is taken on the road.

Riders should always wear proper clothing, including hard hats and boots and light, bright colours so that motorists can see them clearly. Even in summer, long sleeves that will give sufficient protection in the case of a fall should be worn.

Road rules

Any rider taking a horse on the highway must read and obey the *Highway Code* and follow these basic road rules:

★Ride on the appropriate side of the road to move with the flow of traffic, keeping near to the kerb but not so close that the horse grazes his fetlocks on it.

★Ride with both hands on the reins, except when signalling.

★Use the correct signals, as follows: *To turn left or right* extend the appropriate arm for the turn planned, giving plenty of warning to other traffic. *To halt oncoming traffic* raise the right hand and hold it, palm facing forwards, towards the oncoming traffic. Make the movement as firm and definite as possible. *To slow down traffic* extend the arm on the traffic side, raise and lower it several times. *To wave traffic on* extend the arm of the traffic side and rotate the hand several times in an anti-clockwise direction.

★When you need to cross the road at a junction position yourself where motorists can see you plainly, but not close enough to the main road for the horse to be buffeted by the wind of fast-moving vehicles. Never make a dash for it; wait until the road is clear, then set off briskly.

★When a driver stops or slows for you, always acknowledge his consideration; it will encourage him to do the same the next time there is a horse in the road.

★Avoid riding at dusk or after dark whenever possible. If it is absolutely necessary to ride out, wear a fluorescent jacket and stirrup lights on the stirrup irons.

★When you are riding one horse and leading another, make sure that the led horse is always on the inside.

★On country lanes with high hedges, listen for approaching traffic and make sure you do not meet head on, on a bend. If necessary, stop and wait, so that the car can pass you on a straight stretch of road.

★When riding in a group, keep in single file with the quietest horse at the front to set a good example and the best trained and most reliable at the rear. The group's leader should make all necessary signals. Make sure that the group stays together; a horse left behind by the rest may panic.

★If a horse takes fright and does not respond readily to your soothing tactics, dismount and lead him off the road until he calms down rather than risk an accident.

Group of riders coping with traffic in London.

Falls and accidents

All riders experience falls, most of them hurting little more than pride, but falls on a busy road are obviously more serious as there may be passing traffic and the horse may bolt into the middle of it. If possible, hold on to the reins when you fall to prevent the horse getting loose. If he does gallop off, proceed as calmly and quietly as possible. Running feet or galloping hooves in pursuit will only spur him on to greater speed. Attempt to head him off the road or corner him, talking soothingly.

If either rider or horse sustains injury in an accident involving a car, the police must be called. They should be informed that a horse is involved, as they will know where to contact the local veterinary surgeon. Never leave an injured horse; if necessary flag down another motorist to make the necessary calls. If the horse is down, make no attempt to pull him to his feet. A winded animal will rise in his own time and if he is more seriously injured he should not be moved until the vet arrives, so sit at his head and keep him as calm as possible.

Insurance

It is in the interests of any horse owner to take out third party insurance cover. This will cover any damage caused by a horse who suddenly shies into the path of an oncoming car, knocks a cyclist off a bicycle or breaks through a fence on to the road and causes an accident.

Premiums vary according to the 'class of use' to which you put your horse. Basic cover usually provides for third party liability and loss by theft or straying. The more expensive comprehensive insurance may cover, in addition, veterinary bills, permanent incapacity, personal accident and loss or damage to saddlery.

COMPETITIVE SPORTS

Horses are used in a wide range of sporting activities, from the glamour and excitement of professional racing to the more homely thrills of children's gymkhanas. This section covers them all, including show jumping, eventing, dressage, Western riding, hunting and polo. In each case it describes the history of the sport and its rules and regulations, as well as outlining the special riding skills required of both horse and rider in such demanding sports as dressage and eventing.

The show jumper's early education should prepare him for the more permanent, fixed obstacles which he will meet.

FLAT RACING

No doubt there has been horse-racing of one sort or another ever since man learnt to sit on a horse—even if it was only to outstrip his enemies. In England there is an early record of horse-racing at Wetherby under the Romans and where there was one probably there were more.

The first racecourse in England was established at Chester in the reign of Henry VIII, whose royal stud did much to improve the breed of horses. James I imported a small bay Arabian stallion, the Markham Arabian, whose progeny became the basis of the modern Thoroughbred. During James' reign race meetings were held, amongst other places, at Newmarket, Doncaster, York, Chester, Liverpool and Salisbury, all of which have racecourses today. Races of up to six miles were run under no mean weights and often consisted of matches between two horses as the result of a wager.

Under King Charles I regular meetings were held at Newmarket and the first Newmarket Gold Cup was run in 1634.

There was a momentary hiccup when Cromwell and the Puritans banned horse-racing but it was quickly revived with the Restoration; Charles II had a passion for horses as well as ladies. Newmarket became the headquarters of racing and the court spent almost as much time there as it did in the capital. Charles was able to employ the divine right of kings to arrange the races, make the rules, settle disputes and run and ride his own horses. The Rowley Mile at Newmarket is named after one of his horses, Old Rowley.

Queen Anne inherited her uncle's interest in racing and founded the racecourse at Ascot, since when the first race at Royal Ascot has been the Queen Anne stakes.

The Jockey Club

A great step forward in racing's future came with the forming of the Jockey Club in 1750—so called because most of the members rode their own horses. It acquired the freehold of Newmarket and the adjacent land and gradually extended its control to all other racecourses, making the rules and regulations, appointing officials and approving the programmes.

The history of the Jockey Club is punctuated by commanding figures, dictators, each of whom refined and improved the sport.

In the period of more than 40 years when Sir Charles Bunbury (1740–1821) dominated the club, the five classics for three-year-olds, the One Thousand Guineas, the Two Thousand Guineas, the Derby, the Oaks and the St Leger, were founded.

Sir Charles was followed by Lord George Bentinck (1802–1848) who was one of the ablest, if least attractive, administrators. Lord George introduced the parade of horses before the race, racecards, the numbering of horses to facilitate identification, the declaration of the colours in which they would run and the method of starting with a flag. He also laid out a model racecourse at Goodwood.

Racing was codified by the next great name, Admiral Rous (1795–1877), in his weighty *The Laws and Practice of the Turf*. He also made an in-depth study of racing results with reference to the horses' ages, the distances they ran and the weights they carried and produced the weight-for-age handicap scale, still used today, which gives allowances to immature horses. He continued the task of cleaning up the turf. Stewards were given power to suspend jockeys instead of just fining them, which was not a great deterrent to pulling a horse if the reward was big enough. Not the least of his achievements was to take the Jockey Club's finances from the red into a healthy state. He had a great sense of fair play and firmly believed that racing should be enjoyed by all classes.

At the turn of this century, starting gates replaced the flag start. Jockeys were prohibited from betting. Doping horses—a custom that had spread largely from America where the horses needed doping if they were running throughout a seven-day meeting—was made an offence.

In 1967, the Levy Board was instituted to look after the finances of racing but the Jockey Club is still the disciplinary body.

Racing as an organized sport has been popular in England since the Restoration.

Thoroughbreds

The racehorses, meanwhile, had evolved from the very mixed bunch of early days into a new breed, the Thoroughbred. Spanish, Arabian, Turkish and Barbary horses had been imported since the days of Elizabeth I to improve the breed, but all Thoroughbred racehorses in the world can trace their ancestry back through the male line to three imported stallions, the Darley Arabian, the Byerley Turk (probably another Arabian) and the Godolphin Arabian which were interbred with British mares (see pages 38–39).

The three blood lines are named after Herod (great-great-grandson of the Byerley Turk), Eclipse (great-great-grandson of the Darley Arabian) and Matchem (grandson of the Godolphin Arabian).

The General Stud Book registers all the names of the horses deemed to be Thoroughbred. To be eligible, a horse's ancestors have to have appeared in previous volumes, or it has to be the last product of eight successive Thoroughbred crosses all of whose performances on the turf warrant its assimilation. At the moment only natural breeding is recognized, and nothing such as AI or embryo implants is even contemplated.

The huge expense of keeping and racing Thoroughbreds has inclined bloodstock breeders to go for speed rather than stamina. Older horses suitable for longer distances are seldom kept in training. A three-year-old classic winner is usually retired to stud at once to make a fortune rather than be kept in training, because as a four-year-old he could not earn as much and might even decrease his value if he had not trained on well.

When the Derby was first run races were generally what we would regard as long distance, and the horses were at least five years old. Today, a racehorse is normally broken to riding as a yearling and runs as a two-year-old. The five classics are exclusive to three-year-olds.

Races are divided into weight-for-age, handicaps and selling races.

Weight-for-age races

The weight a horse carries compensates for his immaturity up to the age of five in weight-for-age races and is also in accordance with the distance to be run. There is an extra allowance for fillies. The table, originally compiled by Admiral Rous, gives weights applicable for each month of the season as the horse matures. Distances quoted vary between five furlongs and two and a half miles. Racing distances do not even nod to metric and cling to the almost extinct furlong (an eighth of a mile).

Important weight-for-age races are known as pattern races, are graded into three and have their own conditions. Other weight-for-age races are framed by individual racecourse executives who can make their own conditions and add to the variety of races to attract entries and customers.

They can, for instance, hold a race for maidens (horses which have never won, no matter what sex) or for colts or fillies of a stipulated age only.

Handicaps

Every racehorse has a handicap weight allotted to it, worked out by a team of handicappers with the aid of computers. The aim of the handicapper is to get all the horses in a handicap race to pass the finishing post at the same time. This gives chances to less talented horses and a chance of success to smaller owners and trainers. There is a minimum weight any horse can carry but this can be varied if it is ridden by an apprentice, who has a weight allowance which diminishes according to the number of races he wins.

Selling races

In selling races the winner must be sold by auction immediately the race is over. The price paid must be above a published amount depending on the value of the race. If the price paid is high enough the surplus goes to the course and the winning owner. Any of the other runners in the race can be claimed (bought) at the price given on the racecard.

There is no difference between a plate race and a stake race except in the prize money. A plate race is run for a definite sum; a stake race's prize money has various additions to the basic sum from entry fees, sponsorship money, and so on.

International racing

Racing spread naturally from Britain to her territories overseas—Australia, New Zealand, South Africa and Canada. It also gradually developed in Germany, the United States, Argentina and other South American countries. At first there was a greater exchange of breeding horses than racers because of transport, but today there is a growing number of racehorses flown all over the world to compete for the richer or more prestigious prizes.

Racing in France suffered setbacks of revolutions and wars, but it is now a premier racing country. A French-born Englishman and the Duc d'Orléans founded a Jockey Club in 1833. This turned into largely a social club and the real enthusiasts split away to form the Société d'Encouragement pour l'Amelioration des Races des Chevaux en France—mercifully shortened to the Société d'Encouragement. In 1836, the Chantilly racecourse was opened and became a training centre rather like Newmarket. Here, the five French classics, equivalent to the British ones, are run: Prix du Jockey Club, Poule d'Essai des Poulains, Poule d'Essai des Pouliches, the

Top right: Racehorses thundering round Tattenham Corner at the Derby, 1983.

Bottom right: racing in Miami. Thoroughbred racing is now a huge industry in the USA.

Below: horses parading before the start of a race.

168

Prix de Diane and the Prix Royal Oak. Twenty years after the Société d'Encouragement was formed, French horses were crossing the Channel to win important British races. The great international race, the Prix de l'Arc de Triomphe was first run at Longchamp in 1920. The only legal betting is on the pari-mutual (the Tote) from which the government takes a large amount in taxes but ploughs back a good percentage into racing. In the South of France there is a winter season of racing at Cagnes-sur-Mer for which many British horses cross the Channel. French prize money, especially for placed horses, is good.

Milan is the principal racing city in Italy, regular meetings beginning there in 1868. Their Jockey Club was formed around 1881. Italy has bred some top international horses. In Germany the equivalent of the Jockey Club, the Union Club, was founded in 1867.

Australia, New Zealand and Japan are the principal racing countries in that part of the globe. Australia is one of the few countries outside Britain where bookmakers operate.

There had been horses in North America in prehistoric times, but they were regarded as good food rather than transport, and were

extinct long before the European settlers arrived, bringing their horses with them. Early racing took place either down the main street or on quarter-mile-strips tamed from the forest, hence the breed of racehorse called Quarter Horses, crosses of English stallions with Spanish mares. Quarter horse racing, sprints over short distances, is still popular but racing with Thoroughbreds is now a huge industry in the USA. Each state has a racing commission to run it and American-bred horses raid the European classics with notable success.

Training

Training racehorses is an inexact science. Each horse has to be assessed as an individual. What will suit one will not suit another. It is a great gamble, too. Brothers of impeccable ancestry can turn out to have widely differing abilities. There's no telling if a yearling bought for a huge sum on his looks and pedigree will win valuable races or be a complete failure. On to breeding—and a Derby winner can sire a mediocre line while a good but not brilliant horse may have outstanding progeny.

Officially, racehorses all advance a year in age on January 1 no matter when foaled (foaling takes place in the first six months of the year). After January 1 they are called yearlings. Two-year-olds and upwards are

called colts or fillies. At five years old they are horses and mares. At stud they are stallions and sires or brood-mares and dams.

After a year running free, a yearling starts his training in the autumn. He will first be lunged (urged to walk in a circle on the end of a long rein), then be introduced to a saddle and after a fortnight or so he should bear the weight of a lightweight man. With the man in the saddle he is lunged until he understands the signals of voice, hands and legs, when he can come off the lunge and be walked behind a staid old horse. In the worst weather he will be exercised in an indoor school. He will also be taught to enter and jump out of racing stalls. Come January 1 he is officially a two-year-old and can be raced in the coming season which starts in March.

At the end of the year the handicapper will publish a list of handicaps (the Free Handicap) for the best two-year-olds, based on their performances. By now, owners and trainers will have entered their promising two-year-old colts and fillies for next year's classics and paid their entry fees. The large number of entries will gradually be whittled down by withdrawals for one reason or another, each paying a forfeit for doing so, the forfeit increasing as the race approaches.

Some two-year-olds will have shot their bolts and not train on as three-year-olds. After a successful three-year-old season a colt will usually be sent to stud. An unsuccessful

Top left: racing at Royal Ascot, one of the most famous race meetings in the world.

Top right: jockeys riding neck and neck. Today's photo-finish has become an indispensible aid to judges.

Above: racing at Sandown.

salls contains the paddock where the horses parade before races and costs more to enter. The members' enclosure or Club is the most expensive, less crowded and no longer just for Club members, and has access to Tattersalls.

The meeting is run by stewards who are organizers and arbitrators. If there is an objection to a runner for interfering with another's chances they can disqualify the offending horse at an immediate Stewards Enquiry, announced over the public address system. No bets are paid out until the result of the enquiry is announced.

The clerk of the course is responsible for the general arrangements and maintenance of the course.

On race day the horses taking part have their everyday shoes replaced by very light aluminium racing plates. The horses are saddled up about half an hour before their race and led out into the ring in the paddock by their lads for the spectators to see. Owners, trainers and jockeys in the owners' colours gather in the ring to discuss tactics until 'Jockeys, please get mounted' comes over the loudspeakers. Before the advent of the American jockey Tod Sloan in 1897, English jockeys rode with long stirrups; Tod's short stirrups and crouching style was so effective that the other jockeys followed suit.

Down at the start the starter oversees the loading of the horses into the starting stalls. There is a troop of experienced handlers to help and if a horse refuses to enter he is blindfolded, turned round once or twice (just like blindman's buff) to lose his sense of direction, then led and pushed in. He's usually quite happy when the blindfold is taken off. Should he cause too much trouble, the starter can order him to be withdrawn from the race.

When all the horses are in, a white flag is raised which means that the horses are under starter's orders. The starter immediately presses the button which opens all the gates simultaneously.

The judge's box is directly opposite the winning post and he gives the result of the first three horses (or four if the field is a big one) and the distances separating them. If the results are close he can call for a photograph from the automatic photographic system.

After the race the jockeys with their saddles must weigh in (they will have weighed out before the race) to make sure they have carried the right weight; the judge can then confirm the result.

one if he is lucky may be sold off or pursue another career on the racecourse as a hurdler. An unsuccessful filly will always have a future as a brood-mare—obviously many more females than males are needed for breeding.

Highly-bred racehorses are prone to sickness and injury. They are cosseted as few human beings are and their health closely monitored. Inoculations and blood counts are routine. Swimming pools in which to exercise horses with leg injuries are becoming common. The dreaded cough has yet to be conquered. This can sweep through a stable and render the horses useless—if not worse—for months.

Racecourses

There is no standard racecourse. Each is on a different plan and can run right-handed or left-handed. It is not necessarily flat. The Derby is run at Epsom over a mile and a half, which includes a right-hand curve, a sharp left-handed corner and both rising and falling ground. Racecourse amenities vary too, from the course with luxurious 'entertainment boxes' where companies can wine and dine their clients during racing, to others with more basic catering facilities.

Whatever the course it has three enclosures for paying spectators. The cheapest is the Silver Ring which has no access to the paddock but has full betting facilities. Tatter-

NATIONAL HUNT RACING

Steeplechasing by its nature is much more dramatic than flat racing. The horses are older and stay on the scene longer, too, to make memorable careers and become public favourites. On the flat a Derby winner is in the public eye for two years, then as like as not it vanishes to stud and is heard of no more except in pedigrees. An exception is the unfortunate, brilliant Shergar, notable for being kidnapped and killed in Ireland after his first season at stud. But many more people will have heard of Golden Miller, triple Gold Cup winner, than of a contemporary Derby winner, Hyperion. Steeplechasers can spend as many as eight years in the public eye. No stud duties beckon, unless they are mares; horses are mostly gelded both for their own comfort over prickly fences and to keep their minds on racing.

Steeplechases are run more slowly than flat races; the horses and riders have to be adept at jumping as well as running and there is more to hold the spectator's interest for longer. There is less money in the sport and more simple enthusiasm. The spectators are less fashionable and more hardy to be able to enjoy standing about in all weathers. The season proper starts around October and lasts until April.

Originally, steeplechasing was a race from church steeple to church steeple (the highest landmark around) and was mostly matches between two horsemen. In the early nineteenth century, steeplechases began to be organized for bigger fields over roughly marked out courses. The Grand National was first run in 1839 over a four-mile course and rough country with 29 natural obstacles—stone walls, banks, hedges and brooks into one of which Captain Becher fell, now immortalized in one of the Grand National's famous jumps.

A number of small independent meetings arose and, as there was no authority for the sport, there were no common rules or standards for fences. Inevitably there were abuses and frauds. Those who could not make a fast buck on the better-regulated flat racing scene latched on to steeplechasing.

In 1860, a steeplechase was held under the aegis of a number of hunts. It was called the Grand National Hunt Steeplechase, was well-organized and run to a set of rules drawn up by Fothergill Rowlands. Subsequently, enthusiasts formed the Grand National Hunt Steeplechase Committee in 1866, adopting Fothergill's rules with little alteration.

The Jockey Club itself ignored steeplechasing but in 1884 the reconstituted Committee included several Jockey Club members and was renamed the National Hunt Committee. Its authority was by no means universal and odd, unregulated races continued to be run for some time.

At the turn of the century the Committee drew up standards for the sizes of fences and the numbers there should be. Prize money was never munificent and up to the formation of the Levy Board the Grand National was the most valuable race. The second most prestigious was the Cheltenham Gold Cup, a level weights-for-age race for stayers of five-year-olds and upwards.

In 1968, the National Hunt Committee amalgamated with the Jockey Club. With the advent of the Levy Board and sponsorship the financial basis of National Hunt Racing was vastly improved. The Grand National is no longer the focus for the season, though it arouses most public interest thanks to television which follows it from beginning to end.

Hurdle racing grew up alongside steeplechasing. Often used as a nursery for steeplechasers it has its own classics such as the Champion Hurdle run at the great Cheltenham Festival meeting, as is the Gold Cup.

Meetings include steeplechases and hurdle races on the same card and the courses run side by side. There are three types of steeplechase fence: the plain fence not less than 1.4 m (4½ ft) high, the open ditch which has a guard rail on the take-off side in front of a 1.8 m (6 ft) wide ditch, and a water jump 3.6 m (12 ft) wide. There is a set number of obstacles to a set distance. A steeplechase is at least 2 miles long; there is no maximum but the longest is the Grand National at 4 miles 856 yards.

Right: Hurdle race at Sandown. Unlike steeplechase fences, hurdles are easily knocked down.

Below right: Racing at Cheltenham, venue for the famous Gold Cup and Champion Hurdle.

Hurdles are 1 m (3 ft 6 in) high, and unlike steeplechase fences are easily knocked over. There is a set number of hurdles to a race's length.

Races are started by a starting gate, a tape tha flies upwards, operated by the starter who stands on a platform. The starter waits until the horses are as level as possible (there are no starting positions for the horses) then pulls the starting lever, usually calling 'Come on,' at the same time. As no races are sprints a length gained or lost at the start hardly matters.

The horses

Jumping horses have to be able to carry at least 76 kg (168 lb) over two miles so they should be stouter in build than their flat race counterparts. They must be bold in temperament, intelligent and move well. Most essentially they must have good legs with strong cannon bones and pasterns to stand up to the spring of take-off and shock of landing. The bigger the horse the more strain on his legs, so in general a medium-sized horse is preferred.

Many horses with the right conformation graduate from the flat, where they may have been fairly unsuccessful, to success over hurdles. To take part in a hurdle race a horse must be three years old on the previous 1 July. Some go on to become chasers, who must be four years old on the previous 1 July. Hurdle racing is pacier than chasing, needing long, fast jumps over its low hurdles, so hurdling horses cannot always master the technique of jumping higher fences.

There is not a big breeding industry centred on steeplechasing for obvious reasons. Steeplechasers are geldings and their sires may well be dead by the time their progeny make their names around nine years old. Some horses are specially bred in Ireland and bought unbroken as three or four years olds. These will need to go through their preliminary lessons of lungeing, being saddled, having a man on their back while being lunged until they understand his signals before they are freed of the lunge. Often the buyer will send his unbroken horse to a livery stable which specializes in breaking young horses.

When the horse joins the racing stable he is allotted to a lad, a personal assistant who will look after him, his health and appearance for the rest of his career. Lads are often females, who seem especially sympathetic to

Top left: Racing in winter snow at St Moritz.

Left: Artiface, ridden by P. Scudamore clears the last fence to win at Aintree in the Parkhamper's steeple chase.

Right: Jumping horses must have good legs and strong bones to withstand the strain and shock of take-off and landing.

horses and content with the not-very-rosy career prospects. A training and feeding schedule is drawn up to fit the needs of the individual horse.

There is no one way to produce winners. What is needed is a sound and healthy horse of ability who enjoys his work. A horse that does badly in a large stable may well perk up and produce results if moved to a smaller one.

A horse will have a best distance above or below which he is not likely to win. A trainer must know his horse inside out. Some horses sulk if they are not allowed to run in front all the way; others when they get to the front stop running so the final spurt to the post has to be judged to a nicety. Some horses enjoy themselves enormously, others get nervous, others get bored after a while and sometimes a holiday hunting will restore their enthusiasm.

Professional trainers are licensed; amateur trainers with just one or two horses can get permits to train and are called permit-holders. Many of these are farmers using home-bred horses. Officially, the horses they run must be their own, or the property of their parents or their children.

Point-to-points

A truly amateur sport is point-to-pointing, which is really part of the hunting scene though it is subject to overall control by the National Hunt Committee. It arose from annual races run by Masters of Hunts at the end of the hunting season which were social get-togethers at temporary courses marked out by posts round which the horses turned, taking their own line between. Spectators clustered near the finishing post with a row of wagons for grandstands. In time, complete programmes were made up which included races with entrants from adjacent hunts, ladies' races and races open to any genuine hunters.

Today, point-to-points have made fences similar to, but slightly smaller than, steeplechase jumps and financial reasons cause some hunts to share courses. Entrance is usually by charge for a car, and the car parks are arranged so that as many as possible have a view of the course.

There is a certain amount of interplay with the professional game. In the early spring Hunter Chases are part of many steeplechasing programmes, open to horses that have been 'regularly and fairly hunted' with a pack during the previous winter.

Point-to-point prize money is very modest and none of the riders is paid or sponsored, though some of the races are sponsored. There are national sponsored championships, with qualifying rounds and finals, for both men and ladies. Essentially, point-to-points are hugely enjoyable outdoor picnic occasions where not even the most horrendous weather can dampen the enthusiasm.

SHOW JUMPING

Show jumping at Hickstead, a course well-known for its exciting obstacles.

Jumping is a fairly recent equestrian sport compared with other forms of riding. It is first mentioned in a French cavalry manual in the late eighteenth century, about the same time that the Enclosure Acts in Britain gave the hunting men more obstacles to traverse in the shape of hedges and fences. It was some hundred years before show jumping emerged at the Royal Dublin Society's 1865 show when there were classes for high and wide leaps on a horse.

Agricultural Shows were naturals for the new contests. In 1876, the first indoor show in England was recorded. The 'leaping' was judged by Masters of Foxhounds on style only.

By 1900, the Modern Olympic Games in Paris had jumping competitions for high jumps, long jumps and prize jumping, but it was not until the 1912 Games that show jumping was inaugurated on a regular basis with a set of complex rules, since modified.

The first International Horse Show in London was held at Olympia in 1907. The board and directors came from many European countries as well as the USA. The programme included high jumps and wide jumps and there was good prize money.

In abeyance during World War I, the first post-war Olympics were held at Antwerp in 1920, where Italians took the gold and silver medals for show jumping, largely owing to Federico Caprilli, an equestrian genius who had invented a new style of forward seat as opposed to the rider leaning backwards on landing. The backward seat had led to so many falls and fractures among the Italian cavalry that their government at one point proposed a rule that the military should not golds at all three equestrian events: dressage, show jumping and the three-day event.

During the war, providentially three British show jumping enthusiasts found themselves in the same prisoner of war camp, and were able to occupy their time discussing post-war possibilities for the sport. One of these men, Mike Ansell, though blind, has since become a legend in show jumping. Chairman of the BSJA for twenty years, with his committee he reorganized the sport, introduced better jumps, tightened the rules, introduced a grading system for entries on prize money won, and revolutionized show jumping into a modern mould.

In 1948 the Olympic Games were held in England with combined team and individual events, almost marred by typically English weather, very soggy indeed, which is perhaps a factor in the winning of the first British show-jumping medal, a bronze. In 1948, too, the first official FEI championships for juniors between 14 and 18 years was held.

FEI held the first Men's World Championships in 1953, which were thereafter held at first every year but subsequently every four years, interspersed with the European Championships held every other year.

A European Championship for women, won by Britain's Pat Smythe, was introduced in 1957 and amalgamated with the men's in 1975, although women were allowed to compete in the Stockholm Olympics of 1956. Since when women have taken a larger percentage of medals than the number of their entries would suggest.

A significant influence on British show-jumping took place in 1965 when Douglas Bunn founded a first-rate permanent jumping course at Hickstead, Sussex with exciting obstacles that all TV sports fans will be familiar with.

In 1975 a great furore arose over professionalism and the Olympics. There was a good deal of shamateurism going on, and the first nation to come out in the open and operate the strict redefined rules of who was a pro was Great Britain. Although this meant that British top riders were ineligible for the Montreal Olympics it did give a kick to the sport and brought in a lot more money in the way of sponsorship. Show jumping is an expensive sport and few people are rich enough to do it full-time for free.

Now there is a year-round professional circuit. Thanks to TV with its dramatic close-ups, principal show jumpers and shows are

The Italian seat with its forward position was adopted universally for show jumping after the 1920's Olympics.

be allowed to partake in hunts and jumping contests. Thereafter the Italian seat was adopted universally for show jumping. Ironically, Caprilli had been killed in a fall in 1907 when walking his horse on a slippery pavement.

Sweden and France initiated an international governing body for equestrian sports in 1921, the Fédération Equestre Internationale, (FEI) with six other founder members—Belgium, Denmark, Italy, Japan, Norway and the USA.

In 1923 the British Show Jumping Association was founded by a mixture of civilian riders and military men, and the Association joined the FEI in 1924.

The Berlin Games in 1936 were the last Olympics to be held before World War II where the host country won the individual familiar to millions of viewers. Although the two prestigious events, the Royal International Horse Show and Horse of the Year Show both have serious show jumping at their core, such things as obstacle races, pony-driving and relay races add to the entertainment, sometimes verging on opera bouffe.

The show jumping horse

The show-jumping horse has to be a good athlete with good conformation. It should be of average size between, say, 15.3 and 16.3 hands. If the horse is on the small side it may do well in lower grade competitions but will be at a disadvantage if it upgrades to big courses. A large horse is less agile, seldom matures before eight years old and in the meantime will be a difficult ride. He is rather prone to back and leg troubles, too. There are exceptions to the rules but it is wise not to start training with a potential handicap.

To be avoided is a horse that is a bad mover, has big joints, has legs or feet out of true or is over fat or thin. There could be trouble later when greater demands are made on the horse.

Hanoverian, Holstein, Irish Draught, Selle Française and Trakehner are all breeds that produce good show jumpers, and most of these have been improved by Thoroughbred blood. The Thoroughbred itself, of the more substantial type, is a favourite despite its need of careful handling. The horse is not a natural jumper. In its original state it was a herbivore, living in open spaces where its quick reactions and speed of foot enabled it to escape its predators. It will always avoid or bypass an obstacle if it can. Being a herd animal, if it loses its rider in a steeplechase it will usually continue riderless, running round the obsta-

cles and rejoining its companions on the other side. So training for jumping has to start literally on the ground.

Training

Training a show-jumper starts when it is four or five years old, is well broken in and has been around a bit. Initially the training is much the same as for elementary dressage, to develop its suppleness, power and balance and its understanding with its rider. In addition it is walked and trotted over ten or so brightly-painted poles laid on the ground about 120 cm (4 ft) apart. This makes it both careful in placing its feet and pay attention. In time the poles are replaced 300 cm (10 ft) apart, then alternate poles are slightly raised (bricks are convenient supports). Then they are slightly raised again, with the horse popping over them on a loose rein. Everything is done gradually so that the horse never feels intimidated and he is given a suitable reward—sugar or his favourite mint—after his exertions. The daily routine is varied, pole trotting interspersed with normal training of trotting and walking in wide circles, changing direction and pace and gradually narrowing the circle. The use of equidistant poles gives the horse an even stride and the small jumps lower the horse's head and rounds his back.

In due course one or two poles can be made to imitate small spreads, first placing an extra pole across the base, then moving it a little forward from the raised one, then raising it a little—each stage being walked, trotted and cantered over for several days. If a pole should be knocked off no notice is taken and with luck the horse will pick up its legs a little higher at the next obstacle.

Training should not be hurried as these

Right: Robert Smith riding Alabama.

Below: a horse and rider tackle a double combination fence of an upright followed by a parallel, and depict the correct ways and some faults of show jumping.

1. The rider keeps a good seat as the horse lands, to ride it forward to the parallel.

2. The strain of landing is taken by the fore-foot and tendons and ligaments below the knee.

3. The rider prepares the horse for take-off, maintaining an even contact with its mouth.

insignificant jumps are not only training the horse to look where it is going and judge distances but also developing muscles it does not naturally exert.

When the horse can no longer clear the jumps from a slow trot it will spontaneously put in one or two gallop strides. The rider must be careful to keep his balance and not jerk the reins or the horse may get into the bad habit of raising its head when jumping to avoid hurting its mouth.

A variety of small fences and combinations can be gradually introduced and increased in height, but never too abruptly and always decreasing the frequency of jumping days.

The novice show

After some months of jumping training the horse should be ready for his first novice show, preferably not too far away. It will help with both horse and rider's education and give some idea of progression.

Early arrival at the show is a must to give time to get used to the area and atmosphere. After the journey the horse will need to be walked around a bit to release tension caused by travelling. Then the rider should try to leave it in good hands while he or she walks the course. Any slope in the ground should be noted, as well as any doubles and combinations which will probably need to be ridden at a bit more strongly as a novice horse will probably take a good look at them.

Then the rider can return to his box and dress for the competition. Apart from his own kit and normal riding, grooming, watering and feeding equipment, it is wise to take spare reins, stirrup leathers, and an extra girth.

Horse and rider should be in the collecting ring in good time and jump the practice fence

4. As the horse takes off, the rider has shifted too much weight to one side.

5. The rider's weight is still unbalanced. He should look straight between the horse's ears.

6. The rider allows with his hands so that the horse can stretch to make the parallel.

J. McVean riding Furst 2 in the World Show Jumping Championships held at Aachen in 1986.

gently six or seven times. Throughout the test the rider should remain as calm as possible so that the horse does not think the occasion is too exciting or out of the ordinary, no matter how the test goes.

Subsequent training depends on the proficiency shown by horse and rider, also on the individual horse; some horses need much less work than others to reach their peak.

Show-jumping shows

There is a great number and variety of competitions at different levels. Obstacles to negotiate include spread fences, high fences, combination fences, water jumps and Derby banks. Courses for major competitions are built by recognized course designers. Organizers can devise their own competitions so long as they comply with Fédération Equestre International rules.

The obstacles and all their parts are constructed so that although they can be knocked down they are not so light that they fall down at the slightest touch. The poles are supported in cups not exceeding half the diameter of the poles and shallow and flat cups are used to support planks and the gates.

Major events are Nations' Cups (with the team with the best record of the season winning the President's Cup), the World Championships and, of course, the Olympic Games, all with individual and team entries allowed except for the Nations' Cup which is teams only.

Show-jumping at the Olympic Games is a two-round competition. The best eight teams and 20 individuals go forward to the second round on a different course where their marks are added to those of their first round. Obstacle limits are 1.30–1.60 m (4–5 ft) high for straight fences, 1.50–2.20 m (5–7 ft) for spreads, and the water jump must be at least 4.5 m (14 ft 8 in) wide, with a total of 12–15 obstacles. In the second round straight fences are 1.40–1.70 m (4½–5½ ft) high, spreads not more than 2 m (6½ ft) wide and the water jump as for the first round.

Horse and rider negotiating the Derby bank at Hickstead.

finishing lines, obstacles and turning points. Riders keep red flags to the right and white to the left. Each obstacle is numbered in the order in which it should be jumped. Before the competition a detailed plan is given showing the positions and types of obstacles, starting, turning and finishing lines and the track to be followed, and giving the time limits and penalties. Before the event riders can walk the course. Starting order is always by a draw.

Rules

Riders can wear riding club or hunting uniform with white shirt, white, fawn or pale yellow breeches, a hunting cap or top hat (or bowler for women) and black boots (at smaller shows hacking jackets are often worn with a choice of shirt and tie and either brown, fawn or pale yellow breeches). Those in the services can wear their uniform.

Whips must not exceed 75 cm (30 ins) in length or be weighted at the end. Blinkers and hoods are not allowed. Only an unrestricted running martingale may be used.

A standing martingale may only be attached to the cavesson part of a noseband fitted above the bit. A gag snaffle may be used; a Market Harborough rein may be used, but only with a snaffle. All other running or check reins and reins acting through sheaves or pulleys are prohibited in the arena.

Time allowed varies with the course and starts when a rider crosses the starting line, finishing when he crosses the finishing line. The clock is stopped for rebuilding knocked down obstacles but not for falls or course deviations. The time allowed is twice the time given.

In most scoring systems penalties are expressed in terms of points for faults—3 for first disobedience, 4 for knocking down an obstacle or putting a foot in the water, 8 points for a fall, 6 for a second disobedience, elimination for a third and a quarter fault for each second over the time allowed.

In a time penalty system, seconds are added to the total time taken according to the fault.

Where there is a tie for first place there may be a jump-off which may be against the clock. Obstacles may not be changed, though some may be left out. The height and/or spread of obstacles may be increased if those taking part in the jump-off went clear in the previous round. There is usually a limit of two jumps-off.

The Nations' Cup is an international team one-day competition with two rounds on the same course. Teams consist of four riders with their three best scores counting. There are 13–14 obstacles.

The World Championship has three preliminary competitions and a final. Teams can consist of three or four riders, with the three best scores counting in the first two rounds. Four individual riders with the best scores go into the final in which each competitor rides each of the four horses in turn.

Puissance (French for power) competitions are horses' high jumps with 6 to 8 straight fences at least 1.40 m (4½ ft) high. If there is a first place tie, the jump-off is held over at least two jumps, if necessary going progressively higher to a total of four jumps-off. Competitions have a president and at least one other judge.

An indoor arena for a major event has a minimum area of 2500 sq m (2990 sq yds) and is completely enclosed.

Red and white flags mark starting and

DRESSAGE

The pedigree of classical riding stretches back to the ancient Greeks who needed well-trained cavalry, men who could control their horses with one hand, to win battles. Through the ages, cavalry schools have been centres of equitation excellence.

Owning and riding horses was also the privilege of the aristocracy. They had the time and leisure needed to develop their own and their horses' skills, so dressage flourished in the courts of Europe. In renaissance Italy dressage began to assume the form in which we know it today.

In World War I there were still cavalry regiments in action, but they were ousted by the machine and now military horses are kept mainly for ceremonial occasions.

In the meantime, civilian interest in competitive sports had been growing, and dressage was first included in the Olympic Games of 1912. In continental Europe, climate and terrain combined to keep riders in indoor riding schools for much of the year, whereas in Great Britain outdoor riding was reasonably pleasant even in winter. As a result, dressage competitions were practically unknown in Britain until comparatively recently, though common in Europe. Since then, with better travelling facilities and publicity, our riders have caught up with their Continental cousins.

With the spread of the sport to civilian life has come the entry of women riders who have proved themselves particularly gifted at dressage.

The dressage horse

Physically a dressage horse should be athletic, strong, speedy and light in the hand, with good natural paces and rhythm. It should have a fine head, long sloping shoulders with a well set neck, prominent withers, a good back and strong quarters and loins.

Temperamentally the horse should be calm but eager to go forward, obedient and ready to change paces promptly without resistance.

Europe has for centuries specialized in breeding horses suitable for dressage, such as Hanoverians, Holsteins, Swedish and Danish Warm-Bloods, Trakehners, Selle Français, and so on. The Thoroughbred is not truly ideal for dressage, though a few have excelled at the sport. Thoroughbreds are bred for racing and their sensitivity demands great sympathy in handling; half crosses or three quarter crosses are preferred.

Training

The training of a young horse starts with the lunge, ie the horse is attached to one end of the lunge rein while the trainer holds the other. Free of a rider's weight on its back the horse will be able to develop its paces freely and rhythmically and be brought to the bit more easily under the mild persuasion of the whip. Horses have little natural ability to bend the section of the spine between withers and croup, so lungeing is often used in training throughout a dressage horse's career. To enable the horse to trot and walk with long strides a lunge circle should be as large as 20 yds (18 m) in diameter.

When the horse has accepted a rider on his back and learnt to be reasonably obedient to controls, the next stage is to develop his strength and to get his confidence so that he obeys the aids without resistance, and to encourage his desire to go forwards. The latter is especially important in dressage. In about another three months schooling sessions begin. Daily work consists of three phases: first, a loosening up and relaxing session; then the actual work; then a winding down phase, with the horse taken from the school and given about ten minutes' walk or gentle hack.

The amount of relaxation needed by a horse at the beginning of a schooling session depends on the horse. Normally, about ten to fifteen minutes walking, then a rising trot, varied with a little cantering with changes of direction or circling to improve his balance will put the horse in the right frame of mind to start work and loosen his back muscles. The rider can feel through his seat when the horse's back muscles are no longer taut, as the horse becomes more comfortable to sit on.

Riders' aids must be almost imperceptible, so that the horse appears to be moving of its own accord.

Previous page:
Training for dressage takes years and even at Grand Prix level, the dressage rider must continue to practise and learn.

Early schooling concentrates on impulsion, rhythm, suppleness, development of paces and acceptance of the bit. Most horses are naturally crooked, moving their hindquarters not quite in line with their forehand; this can be countered by riding in curves and circles with the opposite tendency. As training proceeds, the horse attains a suitable degree of collection for longer periods, bringing his hind legs under his body and making him more compact. This makes him lighter in hand and more mobile. He practises large circles and serpentines with changes of pace effected smoothly. He learns to move sideways as well as forwards.

The novice test

When the horse can remain on the bit throughout, can change paces smoothly, lengthen his stride in the trot and maintain a correct bend on curved lines, he is ready to compete in a novice test. The chosen event should not be too big, to ensure a peaceful atmosphere, and with good going, the ground not slippery or hard.

The rider learns the test in advance, with the movements and their order, and can practise it on the horse in sections; it is not advisable to run it through completely too many times or the horse may start to anticipate rather than respond.

The rules should be digested and the tack collected in good time: saddle, snaffle bridle, brushing boots, studs for a grass arena, travelling equipment, lungeing tack if required, and the correct dress for the rider—hunt cap or bowler, hacking jacket, breeches, tie or stock, boots and gloves.

On the day with a young horse it is best to arrive well before his event to get him settled and used to the atmosphere. He can be walked around or given a lunge. Serious warming up for the arena should start about a quarter of an hour before the test. After the test the horse should be rewarded no matter what the performance was like—it is important to preserve his enthusiasm.

The test will have shown up any deficiencies in training and indicated what area needs to be improved. When this has been worked on, new movements can be introduced.

As the horse progresses with a growing degree of collection and a bigger repertoire of movements to medium and major events, he is ridden with a double bridle which includes a curb bit that gives a greater degree of control.

Official dressage tests

There are different tests laid down for various grades of accomplishment. Each test includes variety of pace, movements and figures to be performed at specified places in the arena. For scoring, the test is divided into sections each of which is marked up to 10, and marks are also given for general impression, paces and impulsion, the rider's position and correct application of aids.

The National Federations are responsible for publishing sets of tests for each level of national competition—these are known as the National Tests.

Official tests for international events are laid down by the Fédération Equestre Internationale, the international governing body of equestrian sports. Their grades are: Prix St Georges, medium standard (time allowed, 9 minutes 30 seconds); Intermediate Com petition No. 1, relatively advanced (time allowed, 10 minutes); Intermediate Competition No. 2, advanced standard (time allowed 11 minutes 30 seconds); Grand Prix, the highest standard (time allowed, 10 minutes); Grand Prix Special, the same standard as Grand Prix but slightly shorter and more concentrated, limited to the highest placed competitors in a previous Grand Prix (time allowed, 8 minutes 45 seconds).

There is a draw for the competitors' starting order. Competitors must enter the arena within 90 seconds of their starting bell. If the competitor deviates from the test sheet the

President may order a warning bell, and can indicate at what point the competitor should resume.

Each test starts with a halt and salute, then the timing starts from when the horse moves forward. It ends at the final halt when the competitor salutes. The clock is not stopped for errors. Exceeding the time allowed is penalized at half a point for each extra second or half second.

The horse and rider should give the impression that the horse is moving on his own accord and the rider's aids should be almost imperceptible. Marks are awarded for the freedom and regularity of the horse's paces, its impulsion, its eagerness to move forward, elasticity of step, suppleness of back and engagement of hindquarters. The rider should be well-balanced, supple, hips and legs

Immaculate turnout of both horse and rider is most important in dressage events.

stretched well down. The upper body should be erect, arms close to body, hands low and close together with thumbs uppermost.

The rider executes the test from memory. Exactitude of position is important and each movement should be executed when the rider's body is at the point indicated in the arena. *The dress* for major events is a black jacket and top hat or dark coat and bowler hat, white breeches, hunting stock, black boots and spurs. Service dress is also allowed. A whip can be carried only by a lady riding side saddle. An English saddle and double bridle are compulsory. Prohibited are horses' boots, bandages, blinkers and any unusual devices such as special reins.

Horses must be registered with the National Federation, conform with its general rules and be at least four years old. Riders may compete as individuals or members of a team. In major competitions teams consist of three riders, all of whose scores count.

At an official international championship a horse may not be schooled by a mounted person other than its rider during the four preceding days or at any time during the event except by a fellow team member.

The judges and arena

At major international events there are five judges including the president. Each judge is assisted by a secretary and the president has an assistant to ring the bell, inform him of competitors' errors and record times. Three judges, with the president in the centre, stand 5 m (5½ yds) behind the fence on the short side opposite the entrance. The other two judges stand at the centre of each long line about 5–10 m (5½–11 yds) behind the fence.

The arena is a flat and level rectangle 60 × 20 m (66 × 22 yds) enclosed by a fence, in the centre of one short side of which is an easily replaceable section for the competitors' entrance. The centre line which runs the length of the arena is marked by mowing if the surface is grass, or rolling or raking if it is sand (specified for the Olympics). Points along the centre line are likewise marked stretching for 1 m (3 ft 4 in) each side. Points near the arena side are indicated by lettered markers 50 cm (20 in) outside the fence and, if possible, marked on the fence also.

A practice area of the same dimensions as the arena for use of competitors in the event must be provided.

Competition paces, figures and movements

Paces

The *walk* has four variations—collected, medium, extended and free. In a collected walk the horse takes higher, shorter steps than medium, and an extended walk covers as much ground as possible. A free walk is a relaxed pace in which the horse is allowed complete freedom of neck and head.

The *trot* is a regular two-time pace on diagonally opposite legs with a moment of suspension between.

The *canter* is a three-time pace with either the right or left foreleg leading.

The *counter canter* is when the horse is made to lead with the less natural foreleg in its work, ie to lead with the right leg when circling left.

To *change legs* at the canter the horse is brought to a walk for two or three steps, then cantered on the opposite leading leg. All changes of pace should be smoothly made.

Movements

The *halt*—the horse should be quite still with its weight evenly distributed.

The *half halt*—is a very slight action to prepare the horse for a transition of pace or execution of a new movement.

The *rein back*—the horse walks backwards with its diagonal legs moving almost simultaneously. It should move directly into its next pace without any hesitation or intermediate step.

The *passage* is a sprightly, measured and elevated trot. Little ground is gained. There is a slightly prolonged suspension between the raising and putting to the ground of diagonal pairs of legs.

The *piaffe* is an elevated trot on the spot.

Change of direction—the horse should bend its body to the curve of the line being followed without change of pace, speed or rhythm. When traversing a right angle the horse should follow the circumference of an imaginary 6 m (6½ yds) diameter circle if at a collected or working pace, or a 10 m (11 yds) diameter at medium or extended pace, until on the new line.

Lateral movements or work on two tracks

In these the horse's forequarters and hindquarters proceed on different parallel tracks. The horse should bend uniformly from poll to

The canter pirouette requires great collection: the horse has to keep a three-time rhythm while moving on its quarters.

Changing leg every stride the horse appears to skip, remaining light, calm and straight.

In half-pass the horse moves sideways but always forward and parallel to the arena edges, its outside legs passing in front of the inside legs.

For piaffe the horse must trot on the spot. Each diagonal is raised alternately with even rhythm and slightly prolonged suspension.

tail except in leg-yielding, when it should bend only at the poll.

Leg yielding: The horse's inside legs pass and cross in front of its outside legs. It looks away from the direction in which it is proceeding. If it is going along the straight side of the arena the horse should be at an angle of about 35° to its direction; if it is moving across the arena on a diagonal its body should be nearly parallel to the long sides of the arena with its forequarters slightly ahead of its hindquarters.

Shoulder in: The horse bends slightly round the rider's inside leg. Its inside legs pass and cross in front of the outside pair, with the head bent away from the direction of movement and the outer shoulder on the same track as the inner hip. Shoulder in is performed along the arena wall at about 30° from the direction of movement.

Travers: This is performed along the side of the arena or its centre line. The horse is

Official tests and marks for international events are laid down by the Fédération Equestre Internationale.

slightly bent around the rider's inside leg. Its quarters are brought inwards; the track of the outer hind leg is about half a pace inside that of the outer foreleg. The outside legs step forwards and sideways over the inside pair. The horse's body is at an angle of 30° to the direction of movement, its head parallel to the direction of movement.

Renvers: The opposite of travers, with the horse's tail, instead of its head, to the side of the arena.

Half pass: A variation of travers but performed along the diagonal of the arena. The horse should be as nearly parallel as possible to the long side of the arena with the forequarters slightly in advance of the hindquarters.

Figures

The volte is a circle of 6 m (6½ yds) diameter.
The circle has a diameter of designated size larger than 6 m (6½ yds).

The figure of eight is two touching voltes or circles. The horse should be kept straight for an instant before changing direction at the centre of the eight.

The pirouette: The horse turns in a circle with the radius of its own length. The inside hind foot is the pivot round which it turns while its hindquarters remain on the same spot. The rhythm and correct sequence of steps is retained. The pivot foot should return to the same spot, or just in front of it, each time it returns to the ground.

The serpentine starts in the middle of one short side of the arena and ends in the middle of the opposite short side, proceeding in loops which change direction at the quarter, half and three quarter marks and reach across the width.

Scoring and penalties

Each section is given a mark from 0 to 10 by each judge. The Fédération Equestre Internationale designates the marks as follow: O Not Performed; 1 Very Bad; 2 Bad; 3 Fairly Bad; 4 Insufficient; 5 Sufficient; 6 Satisfactory; 7 Fairly Good; 8 Good; 9 Very Good; 10 Excellent. Ten marks are also given for impulsion, paces, submission and the rider's aids.

Penalties are imposed (even if the error is corrected) for errors of course or of the test (such as rising instead of sitting at the trot, taking the wrong turn, starting the wrong movement); for the first error 2 marks are subtracted, for the second 4 marks, for the third 8 marks, and for the fourth the rider is eliminated but may complete the test without classification. Also subject to elimination are: wearing a forbidden article of saddlery, carrying a whip (unless riding side saddle), starting the test early, failing to start within 90 seconds of the signal, if the horse's four feet leave the arena during the test, or if the horse is lame.

The individual judges' marks are added together and penalties subtracted. Collective marks may be adjusted to coefficients laid down by the FEI. No horse may get a prize if he has not earned more than 50% of the marks.

If there is a tie (except in a Grand Prix Special) equal placings are given. In a Grand Prix Special there is a ride-off for ties in the first, second and/or third places, using the same test and starting order.

EVENTING

Eventing is the supreme test of horsemanship and the horse. It combines the control of dressage, the endurance of cross country and the suppleness of show-jumping.

Cross-country tests were originally designed for the cavalry. A military mount had to be able to cover long distances over rough country, keeping up a fair pace, and still be fit enough to work the next day. Its rider had to be fit, too, as well as a good judge of country, and able to push his mount without over-exerting it and to pick out the quickest and safest route which often meant tackling fairly formidable obstacles. These very long distance tests were held by the military of mainland European countries from time to time.

Equestrian events were introduced into the Olympic Games in Stockholm in 1912 and consisted of 'prize riding' (dressage), show-jumping and a pentathlon on horseback. The latter was open to serving officers riding military horses and the minimum weight was 80 kg (176 lbs). The pentathlon consisted of a long-distance ride of 55 km (34 miles) which included cross-country on the first day, a steeplechase (speed test) on the second, jumping on the third and dressage on the fourth. Out of 24 starters only 15 finished the test.

The form of the competition gradually evolved and in 1924 it assumed much the same form as we know it today—dressage on the first day, speed and endurance on the second, and jumping on the third. Although civilians were now allowed in teams none actually competed.

The continental European tradition of classical riding stood them in good stead and Sweden and Holland dominated the first few equestrian Olympics. When the games were held in Los Angeles in 1932 the home country took the team gold but in those days both travelling time and expense were great and there were not too many entries.

In 1948, the Equestrian Games were staged in England and helped raise the public's enthusiasm for horses and riding. Watching the event was the Duke of Beaufort, who

conceived the idea of building an eventing course on his estate at Badminton. With the support of the British Horse Society the first Badminton Three-Day Event took place in 1949, open to both services and civilians, including women. The idea behind it was to find competitors for the next Olympic Games in Helsinki in 1952, but what was meant as a short-term project turned into a long-term success, and the Badminton Horse Trials are the most prestigious and well-known both in the horse world and to the general public.

Since then, with the growing interest in eventing there have been a number of permanent park courses built. Television has brought the sport to millions with its coverage of the spectacular middle-day cross-country stage and the breathtaking final day's show jumping, when one fence down can sometimes make all the difference between the medal winners.

The Badminton Horse Trials, which started in 1949, are the most famous and prestigious in the world.

Eventing requires great courage, versatility and fitness on the part of both horse and rider.

successful but they are the exceptions rather than the rule, and 16 hands is a better height for a prospective eventer. He needs to have hard bone, good conformation and feet, be deep through the girth and have strong hindquarters. Favoured for training are Thoroughbreds and Three-quarterbreds, although a number of horses with different ancestry have made good. When it comes to the crunch a horse with heart and intelligence will get himself out of trouble where a lesser horse will land in it. Physical toughness is vital; such a demanding sport finds out weaknesses, and eventing is littered with might-have-beens had no injury intervened.

The rider has to be a special sort of person too, very physically fit, matching his/her partner's boldness over cross-country, be a first rate horseman/woman and be able to keep cool in competition.

Eventing is expensive. Riders can take part in commercial advertising without becoming professionals which would bar them from European and World Championships. A rider may not be paid to ride but the horse can be sponsored and expenses paid by a private or commercial sponsor without the rider losing amateur status.

Equipment

As well as taking horses and helpers to a three-day event, the eventer will need to take a load of clothing and equipment for the three disciplines, for example: dark jacket for show-jumping and dressage (or a tweed jacket for novice events); at least two pairs of breeches; tail coat, stock or tie; shirt and pullover for cross-country; three types of headgear; boots and spurs; whip; dressage saddle and normal saddle; numnahs (saddle pads); bridles; surcingle; irons and leathers; weights and weight cloth; girths; horse boots; headcollar and rope; lungeing equipment; side reins; grooming kit; horse blanket; feed and water bucket; hay-net; bandages; towels; set of spare shoes; studs; and perhaps extras such as food and drink for personnel, insect repellent and first aid kit.

The one-day event

The idea of a one-day event as a sort of taster for the Badminton Horse Trials was around for some time before it finally took off in 1950 in Oxfordshire over the Woodland Hunter Trial course. It was the forerunner of many one-day events, which are useful training for the three-day and cheaper and easier to organize and attend.

Horse and rider

A very versatile type of horse is required for the exacting disciplines of eventing. He needs speed and stamina, intelligence, boldness as well as ability in jumping and the temperament to remain calm in dressage but fiery over fences. Above all he must be tough. He must by international rules be at least 15 hands for adult eventing. Horses this size have been

The three-day event

Horses competing in Three-Day Events must be at least five years old and their riders at least 18. The marks are expressed in penalties and weighted so that values are in a ratio of 3 for dressage, 12 for speed and endurance and

1 for jumping. The competitor with the lowest total of penalties is the winner.

As the event is held in the countryside all courses—except for the dressage arena—are different. Teams (normally of four with the marks of the best three counted) can be entered; all team members are automatically considered as individuals though they may compete only once. An individual may enter more than one horse. Minimum weight carried for endurance is 75 kg (165 lb); dressage and jumping have no minimum.

The starting order is determined by a draw and that order is kept throughout the competition, except for the final day's show-jumping when the order may be in the reverse of marks to that point so that the likely winners jump last.

Day 1 is devoted to dressage (plus a further day if the entry is very large). The rules, dress and saddlery are as for any other dressage competition and the arena is of normal size and markings. The standard asked is not above medium, with the more difficult movements left out, and generally conforms with the standard of the particular event. The aim is to produce an accurate performance of fluency and rhythm, with the horse showing good impulsion, suppleness and balance, the rider a good seat and almost imperceptible application of aids.

Day 2 is the speed and endurance test. The object is to prove the true cross-country horse's speed, endurance and jumping ability and the rider's knowledge of pace and judgment of line of country. It is a test of the rider's endurance as well, as it consists of four phases: (a) Road and Tracks (to be ridden at a trot or slow canter); (b) Steeplechase; (c) Road and Tracks; (d) Cross-Country. Each phase is timed. Phases (a) and (c) total around 10–12 km (6–7½ miles) and riders may walk or run beside their horses providing they are mounted at the finishing post. The steeplechase course has between 20 and 32 quite easy fences and is between 5–8 km (3–5 miles), ridden at a gallop. After this the horse has a compulsory rest and a veterinary inspection before embarking on the crucial cross-country course.

The competitor will have been given a plan of the course and been able to walk it the day before. Besides deciding the best line to take and getting familiar with the obstacles, the rider can envisage the horse's likely reaction when it comes into his view.

Above: The first day of Eventing competitions is devoted to dressage.

Many of the obstacles have alternative but more time-consuming ways of being jumped.

The course will have been built by a recognized course designer and any new and ingenious jumps may well be copied by other designers. Some of the now familiar obstacles are: the Irish bank, which the horse has to 'bank' (ie touch down briefly in the middle while jumping over it); Helsinki steps (giant steps preceded by a small rail); a zigzag arrangement of posts and rails which can be jumped into and out of or taken boldly at one leap across a corner; a Trakehner (a tall post and rails in the centre of a wide ditch); and the water jump, a great favourite with spectators as they may expect to see at least one rider ducked—it usually consists of a fence with a stretch of water at a lower level in which to land.

Though the course may look horrific to a layman, the skilled course-builder will make it just intimidating enough to test the nerve of horse and rider without causing undue grief to a less experienced competitor.

Time penalties can be incurred for each of the phases (taken separately) with further penalties for refusals, falls or taking the wrong course. Elimination follows for such things as three disobediences in phases (b) or (d), two falls in (b), three falls in (d), an uncorrected course error, omission of an obstacle, excessive use of whip or spurs. Elimination in one of the events means total elimination.

There are fairly generous bonus points given for time taken below that allowed (within limits) on both the steeplechase and cross-country phases.

Dress for endurance day comprises choice of lightweight clothing plus compulsory protective headgear and boots.

Show jumping on the final day of Eventing is designed to test whether the horse is still fit and supple after the previous day's exertions.

Day 3 And so to the final show jumping on Day 3, which is preceded by a veterinary inspection. The show jumping course is not severe, as the object of this exercise is to test whether the horse is still supple and obedient despite his previous day's exertions. Various direction changes test his handiness. Penalties are given for exceeding the time allowed and for the usual show jumping faults— disobedience, fall, foot in water. A third disobedience eliminates the competitor as does an uncorrected course deviation or an obstacle taken in the wrong order.

The penalty points for all three stages are added and should produce a worthy winner. If there should be a tie the cross-country speed is the deciding factor.

Taking up eventing

By the time a horse is chosen for eventing he will usually be about four or five years old, reasonably experienced and have done a little jumping and dressage.

The first and most important thing is to get both horse and rider fit, as eventing is a most demanding sport on both. Fitness cannot be rushed, either for horse or rider, as strain and injury may result.

If the horse has been out to grass the process of getting it fit to begin special training will take at least six weeks, beginning with walking out. After two weeks he can be trotted for short periods until after about five weeks he can happily do ten-minute trots on the bridle. While he is gaining condition his back is checked carefully for any rubbing from the unaccustomed saddle which could cause sores. Now he can start to canter a little and soon he should be able to take about two hours' varied work without strain.

The work should be diversified, with some easy jumping and schooling exercises to keep him from getting bored, and he should have the odd day off to relax. Three months should see the horse approaching full fitness, ready for more specialized training for his new career.

Elementary dressage will improve his suppleness and test his obedience. Eventing dressage is not so demanding as dressage per se, but a good dressage test at the beginning of an event will give a great psychological boost. Dressage requires great concentration from the horse and after a session he should be allowed to wind down in different surroundings well away from the arena.

The right equipment

Always remember that safety and prevention of accidents must be your number one priority. A crash hat of the right size, correctly adjusted for cross-country riding, is a common-sense precaution, as is a back protector. Your horse should wear a breastgirth (or breastplate) and surcingle (or overgirth) to hold the saddle in place. Your horse's legs should be protected, especially if he tends to knock himself when jumping.

Cross-country jumps need different skills from show jumping. The horse will need to be able to shorten or lengthen his strides. Grid work over poles or *cavaletti* will help him (see the section on show jumping). Jumping sessions should not be taken too often—perhaps two or three times a week. Between, gentle hacking over rough ground and up and down hills will help the horse's balance and accustom him to various different states of going.

To give him confidence in cross-country he should not be presented with difficult fences until he is quite happy over easy ones. If his jumping becomes a little sticky a lead by an experienced horse may restore fluency, but he will need to go on his own in competitions so he should not be allowed to get used to being a follower.

Obstacles should be as varied as possible and include low banks he can jump on and off, jumping brooks and walking through water so that he can get used to the sight and feel of it.

Different horses progress at different rates and require different amounts of nourishment. The event horse needs to be fed a diet that will keep him a little frisky and on his toes, but not so frisky that he cannot calm down for dressage. A horse should never work on a full stomach, so before any fast work his hay-net should be taken away an hour or so before saddling.

Special care should be taken of his feet with regular shoeing. Experience will tell if he needs to wear protective boots or bandages to stop him knocking himself.

The horse can be introduced gently to competition with a novice dressage or show-jumping event or a hunter trial. This will accustom him to the bustle and atmosphere before he tries a one-day event and gives his rider bench marks for further training.

What of the rider? He or she needs to be as fit as the horse. The rider needs an upright, supple back, relaxed shoulders, strong flat

thighs and strong legs. Like the horse, good configuration counts; this cannot be altered but the use of it can be improved. Sports that help develop the right muscles in the right way are swimming, running, cycling and tennis. Regular loosening exercises—bending and stretching, swinging legs and circling arms, trunk bending from a cross-legged position—are beneficial. A good healthy diet should be followed.

The first event

The horse's first event should be an undemanding one-day one. This is the moment of truth for both horse and rider. Early arrival at the course will enable horse and rider to settle before the event. When the rider walks the cross-country course he will need to plan his attack with his horse's ability in mind, noting the easiest route, the best place to jump each obstacle and the state of the going. Often there will be water to jump into. If the horse is familiar with such an obstacle it should present no problems but his pace should be carefully regulated so that he will not think of refusing or become unsteady through entering the water too fast. A second walk round the course with the plan in mind is a good idea if time is available, but the rider will also have to find time to examine the show-jumping course in the same way.

Three Day Eventing at Badminton is the supreme test for both horse and rider. **Left:** *Diana Claphom on Jet Set III.*

During the day the rider should make sure his horse is never chilled after exertion. The horse can be given short drinks and small feeds, if there is time, at least a couple hours before galloping. Horses in their natural state graze most of the time so require to be fed little and often.

In the cross-country the aim should be to allow the horse to go at its own pace so long as it is steady. Speed can be added later. If the horse is excited and starts off at great speed the rider should go with him as he'll probably be able to exert control more easily after a fence or so.

Before entering the arena for the show-jumping, warming up need be minimal; one or two practice jumps, following another horse's lead, should be enough to give him confidence. In the arena the rider should look for the next fence immediately one is jumped and try to give the horse a good view of it.

After the event the horse will need a few weeks' recovery period during which he is kept in training. He may need several more

one-day events before he can tackle a three-day one. Training should end about ten days before this with only gentle exercise in the interval—a little dressage work, easy jumping and cross-country to keep the horse in condition.

As the horse progresses to bigger events his home performance should be of a slightly higher standard than that of the event. The rider will have to learn to time his speed accurately with a stop-watch. To get some idea of the speed required for roads and tracks a kilometer (5/8 mile) can be measured out over which the horse should take about four minutes, roughly the time required in the competition. The steeplechase timing is quite fast and a slightly different technique from the cross-country is needed, something similar to a jockey's in a hurdle race. Timing is crucial in all three phases of eventing.

If the rider and saddle weigh under 75 kg (165 lb), weights will have to be carried. Practice is needed in placing the weight cloth in the best position and to get the horse used to the dead weight which is quite different from the feel of a rider's.

Interval training

Interval training is a scientific concept whereby the body is harnessed to condition itself and gradually improve its effectiveness. Normally, any period of intense activity is followed by a necessary rest during which the body restores itself. To put it rather oversimply, in interval training the rhythm is adjusted so that the time for recovery is just a little less than that required, and this stimulates the lungs and heart to work a little harder and increase their capacity, with the effort required never straining the horse. This requires strict monitoring of the horse's pulse, respiration rate and temperature. The trainer notes the horse's normal pulse, respiration and temperature at rest then records them at short intervals after a work-out to assess the horse's rate of recovery. The programme is planned for the horse, taking into account the speed and distance of each period of effort followed by the extent of the recuperative period needed. This could be three periods of cantering followed by walking, the first relaxation period allowing the horse almost fully to recover, the second being slightly shorter. Because each horse's capacity is carefully measured throughout training this method claims never to overstrain the horse.

Below: *Diana Claphom on Windsomer.*

HUNTING

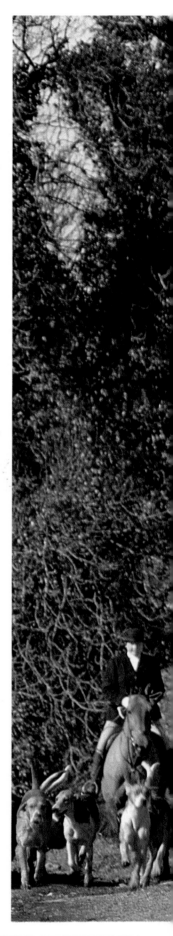

The history of hunting on horseback goes back to the original partnership of man and horse. Stag, boar and fallow deer were the main European quarry for centuries until they became rare or the country they inhabited was no longer suitable for hunting, when the fox became the main quarry. The nature of the hunt changed with the nature of the ground and with the 18th-century enclosures the hunting horse had to be speedy in the open as well as be able to jump more formidable obstacles than were met in a forest. England and Ireland were foremost in this type of hunting and so in breeding suitable horses. It was from this stock that horses for the newer sports of steeplechasing, horse trials and show-jumping came.

Although there are harriers and stag hunting packs in Britain today they are a small minority. There are over 200 registered foxhound packs, so when talking of hunting it is fox hunting that is referred to generally.

The British Isles are divided for fox hunting into geographical areas called countries and each country is hunted by a pack of hounds run by a Master of Foxhounds with the help of his committee. The pack will hunt a given number of days per week.

Freedom of running and jumping over rough country rather than on an artificial course makes hunting the most exhilarating of equine sports.

The foxhunting year runs from May 1 to April 30, leaving the summer free for any hunt employees who have changed jobs at the season's end to get to know their new country.

Cub-hunting starts in early August or when the harvest is completed and there can be no damage to crops. The hunting season proper starts on November 1.

Dress for hunting is strictly traditional. For cubbing all wear ratcatcher—that is, a tweed coat, shirt and tie or stock, buff breeches with hunting cap or bowler hat and black or brown boots (a royal, perceiving a hunt follower inappropriately dressed, is said to have asked if that fellow was a ratcatcher, and the definition has stuck).

Come November 1 and huntsmen and followers burst into 'full fig', that is, a red or black hunting coat worn with top hat, white collarless shirt, white stock, white breeches with light or brown tops and white garter straps, or black coat with hunting cap or bowler, white collarless shirt and white stock, black butcher boots and black garter straps. Women can wear dark blue or black coats with bowler hats or hunting caps, white collarless shirt and stock, fawn or yellow breeches, black boots with garter straps.

There are many details of cut and buttons of hunting coats, some of which tradition rather than utility dictates. The stock is unique to equestrians and has a special method of being fastened. The correct dress for a lady riding sidesaddle (fairly rare these days) includes hair in a bun—false if necessary.

There is a lot of standing and waiting for things to happen in the hunting field in winter weather so the wise hunt follower augments the uniform with warm waistcoat (beige or check), tights and other comforts.

Having got a suitable horse (which can be hired) and acquired the proper dress the prospective hunter will need to get in touch with the hunt secretary to find out about the subscription, though as a casual hunter he may pay a fee, the 'cap', on the day. He must arrive at the meet well on time and if his horse has come on wheels he should be walked to get him supple. The horsebox should not clutter up the vicinity of the meet so it should be left in some suitable parking place some distance away. At the meet he should pinpoint the Field Master and keep his horse's feet away from that important element of a meet, the hounds.

At two to three months a hound puppy is handed over to a puppy walker, a friend of the hunt, who endures his puppyhood escapades. Before the puppy leaves the kennels he will have been named, the initial of which indicates his family. He must learn to answer to this name which will be used by the Huntsman when he joins the pack. The Huntsman knows and calls every hound by name. The

young hound returns to the kennels in the spring of the following year. Cubbing is used to educate the young hound and it usually takes two seasons before he is of use to the pack.

All sorts and shapes of horse make hunters. Most favoured are three-quarter or half-breeds. Many contain the blood of tough, native pony breeds. The horse should have the same training as for other demanding equine sports and not be taken on to the hunting field until he is quite mature. He should have got used to dogs and ideally his owner should puppy-walk a hound. He should also be accustomed to the close presence of other horses and of people. He must learn to be patient while his rider opens and shuts gates while other horses are cantering around him.

The night before a hunt, while the fox himself hunts, the earthstoppers get to work stopping up earths in the area of the meet with sacking or faggots.

The hunt and followers meet at a specified place and it is usual for the host there to hand round drinks, the stirrup cup, before the hounds move off.

Two hundred and fifty years of tradition have produced an etiquette and code of conduct that covers both actions and clothing of the hunt.

In overall charge is the Master of Fox-hounds. In charge of the hounds is the Huntsman (whose role may be filled by the

Below: Hunting in Germany is confined to drag lines with the emphasis on jumping. A small pack of hounds hunt an aniseed trail laid by a runner over a pre-arranged route.

Master) assisted by two Whippers-in. In charge of the followers, the field, is the Field Master.

The Huntsman's horn is used to signal to hounds and hunt what is happening. A single note tells the hounds where he is when they are looking for a fox in a thicket, a warbling note means that a fox is found and a five-note sequence, 'gone away', means the fox is running and it is time for the field (which has been standing round at a little distance so as not to interfere with operations) to pick up the reins and follow.

Foxes do not run straight, often making sudden turns of direction so that the hounds, running nose to ground, may overrun the scent. Followers have to be careful not to cross the running line and mask the fox's scent. They should never get in front of either the Master, huntsmen or hounds and never find themselves amongst the hounds when they are casting around for the scent. Gates

should never be left open. Open and close them with the aid of the hooked handle of the hunting crop.

Not for nothing has the fox a reputation for cunning. He has been known to run through a flock of sheep or across a newly fertilized field which kills his scent. He may jink back into covert and, while the hounds are casting around inside, take off in another direction. If he does, and is seen by anyone in the field, the horseman turns his horse to point in the direction the fox is running, rises in his stirrups, takes off his hat and points it too, hallooing if necessary to get the Huntsman's attention.

If the fox finds an earth open, a terrier is sent in to keep the fox at bay in one spot while it is dug out.

An experienced fox that has been hunted before may have learnt one or two tricks and get clean away once more. Should the hounds catch the fox it will be despatched very quickly by them and eaten. The squeamish should remember that few animals are vegetarian and most animals (including the fox) live by eating others and are in turn liable to be eaten. Those at the top of the food chain become pests unless controlled.

After the hunt, when everyone has gone home, the earthstoppers get to work unstopping the earths and a whipper-in has to round up any miscreant hounds that have gone astray during the day's hunt.

Above: *Coyote hunting in California.*

Right: *it is once again fashionable for ladies to ride side-saddle to hounds.*

POLO

The far east was the cradle of polo some 2000 years ago. From there it travelled with the marauding Muslims and Chinese into India which is still a pre-eminent polo country. In Victorian times in the days of the British Raj the British Army took it up with enthusiasm. The first polo club was formed at Silchar in 1859 and rules drawn up. The ponies were nippy little Manipuris of about 12 hands. Teams were up to nine a side. Gradually the size of the team came down to the four it is today and the size of the pony increased to 13.2 hands in India and 14 in England. In 1919, the height limit was abolished.

The army brought the game to England and the Hurlingham Club became its headquarters. The English rules were framed in 1875. Meanwhile, the game spread by way of the army to other British possessions and their neighbours, notably the United States.

Between the two world wars the game flourished but it was not surprising that after World War II the international champion was Argentina, the biggest breeder of polo ponies. By then Argentina had some 3000 active players compared with 1000 Americans and 500 British.

In the early fifties the English game was revived by the efforts of Lord Cowdray on whose ground at Cowdray Park Prince Charles plays.

Polo ponies

The polo pony has to be very agile and fast. The game is played at the gallop and at this speed the pony must be able to stop within his own length, turn on the spot and gallop off without hesitation. He needs exceptionally strong quarters, a short, strong back and a long neck with good shoulders. Indian teams are reckoned the best mounted with stock bred from English, Argentine and Australian thoroughbreds. A man needs at least three ponies for a match. The horse needs two years of training before it is fit to play.

The rider must be able to move his body freely from the waist and able to control his pony with the reins in his left hand. He must

practise turning his pony on its hocks, making it change its leading legs, and riding-off an opposing pony. A good exercise is to put down a series of marks and ride close to them, imagining the marks to be balls, controlling his pony with one hand and his legs. This helps him to judge the positioning of the pony. Before the rider graduates to making his strokes on a horse he practises his shots without a ball on a wooden horse in a pit where he can do no damage; failing a pit, he can use a wall or balustrade.

Basic shots are the offside forehander—a straightforward right hand forward swing; the offside backhander—hitting the ball straight back on the right side; the nearside forehander—leaning over the horse and hitting the ball forward on the left hand side of the horse; the nearside backhander, hitting it backwards on the left-hand side of the horse; and two under-the-horse's neck strokes from nearside or offside. After this the rider can try the shots mounted, first moving slowly without a ball, then at a canter, then taking the ball and making half-swings at it and so on, in short sessions so as not to tire his horse.

The rules

The polo ground is a rectangle with a maximum size of 300 by 200 yards. The goals at each end are 8 yards wide and light enough to break if collided with. There is a line across 30 yards from each goal and another at 60 yards. In the centre is a T facing one long side where at the start of play the horses line up each side of the down stroke facing the cross stroke. Normally there are two mounted umpires on the field and a referee off it.

For matches and tournaments the rider wears a polo helmet with chinstrap, white breeches, brown boots with no buckles, knee guards, team shirt with number on and gloves. The pony must wear protective boots or bandages on all legs and a tail bandage.

The game is divided into 7½-minute periods called chukkas. A game consists of 4 to 6 chukkas. There is a 3-minute interval between chukkas and a 5-minute break at half time. A goal is scored when the ball passes between the posts or an imaginary extension above.

There are four players on each side and each player has an official handicap between -2 (for beginners) and 10. In handicap games the team's handicaps are added and the lower score subtracted from the higher; the weaker

Left: a mounted umpire, wearing a striped shirt, controls the match.

Below: a top class polo pony will not just be obedient but will anticipate the rider's commands.

side is given this number of goals start, unless the game is not full-length, in which case the handicap is proportionately reduced.

The teams change ends each time a goal is scored (other than a penalty) and also at half-time if no goal has been scored.

Play starts at the timekeeper's bell. After he sounds his bell to signal the end of the period, play continues until the ball goes out of play or there is a goal or 30 seconds have elapsed, when the bell is rung again.

To start the game the umpire bowls the ball underarm between the two lines of players at the centre T mark. When the ball goes over the sidelines it is bowled back by the umpire from where it left the pitch between the teams lined up parallel to the goal line, as in a Rugby lineout. If the attackers send the ball over the goal line a defender hits it back with the attacking team positioned behind the 30-yard line. If a defender sent it off the opponents are awarded a penalty hit from the 60-yard line with the defending team 30 yards away.

Positionally the players numbered 1 and 2 are forwards, 3 is a half-back and 4 is a back.

To avoid collisions there is a right of way rule. A player following behind the ball on exactly the line it has taken has right of way; if another player is approaching on the same line from the opposite direction he shares right of way as both must keep to the left. When there is no player riding on the line of the ball but two players are foreclosing, the one at the smallest angle to it has right of way. It takes fine judgement to decide if one can reach the ball ahead of the player who has right of way without impeding him.

A player may ride off another by riding in the same direction and pushing him sideways with pony and shoulder so long as he keeps his elbow in. It is allowable to hook another's stick to prevent him playing the ball if he is in the act of striking it and one is directly behind or on the same side as the ball, and the stick is below the shoulder.

There are various penalties, varying from the extreme of being sent off or having a goal awarded to the other side, to free hits from various positions. Penalties are awarded for infringement of rules, dangerous riding, misuse of stick and rough handling. At the end of the final period play stops at the bell.

A pony is good for only two successive chukkas so a player must have at least three ponies, allowing one in reserve in case of lameness or injury.

MOUNTED GAMES

The only full-length international mounted game played with a ball and hitting implement is polo (see page 198).

Other mounted games divide into the arena competitions played to international or British Show Jumping Association rules, and gymkhanas where almost anything goes.

Arena competitions

Arena competitions under the bright lights of the Horse of the Year Show at Wembley with top show-jumping personalities are annually televised. Games they compete in include the following: *Accumulator*—points are gained for jumping each obstacle of progressive difficulty, gaining one point for the first jumped successfully, two points added for the second, and so on. A joker fence is sometimes tacked on at the end of the course which the rider may choose to jump, gaining another 10 points if successful but losing 10 if not. *Double Accumulator* is a two-round competition like Accumulator in scoring in the first round, but with penalty points instead of plus ones in the second, starting at 10 and reducing. The second round is against the clock. *Power and Speed*—the power section is jumped to an Accumulator score with a two minute time limit. If successful the rider proceeds to the second, speed section which is timed. In *Take Your Own Line* the competitor must jump all the obstacles once, in whatever order he chooses. *Fault and Out* explains itself. *Six Bars* comprises six identical obstacles in a row (or two rows) with two strides between, to take in a two-minute time limit. *Knock Out* is played with pairs of riders competing against each other on identical jumping courses, the winner going through to the next round. *Baton Relay* is a team relay of two or more competitors and is run like any relay race. Usually the team most adroit at passing the baton wins—excited show jumping horses are not easy to manoeuvre. These games are generally ancillary to show jumping competitions with riders so kitted out and no special training is required.

Gymkhanas

Gymkhanas, like polo, travelled to the west from India, where the British army ran jollies to entertain themselves and their families. Gymkhanas are essentially fun affairs in which all ages and mounts of any size or shape can compete. Favoured mounts are ponies, more manoeuverable because of their compact size. They must be fairly placid and very obedient.

A prospective gymkhana pony should answer promptly to aids and neck-reining. The rider should practise mounting and dismounting in a hurry which he'll need to do in such things at the Egg and Spoon race when a dropped egg will have to be picked up or Supermarket Dash where various objects have to be picked up from various heights. The rider may have to ride bareback as in the Unsaddling Race or in Apple Ducking, which is competed in pairs on one pony and the

A well-coordinated handover of the baton in a relay race. Split-second timing, the result of hours of practice is required if the baton is to be quickly and safely exchanged during these team events.

The potato-in-the-bucket race is always popular.

For pairs races practising with a partner to ride with a piece of rope held between or holding hands as in the Gretna Green Race will help both ponies and riders.

The rider may also be presented with some out of the way tests of skill or agility—crawling through motor-tyres, making a paper hat, threading a needle, throwing balls at a target, or walking on upended flower pots.

Practice should be without the aid of whip or spurs, which are not allowed.

The pony will have to get used to the turmoil and unexpected noises of a gymkhana. Many of the games are played to loud music, some games include bursting balloons and there will be loudspeaker announcements and a lot of rattling and waving around of cloths, flags or garments. The rider should also remain cool (a horse quickly senses panic). It goes without saying that both horse and rider should be physically fit.

The gymkhana arena is usually marked out in a level field and is about 55 m (60 yards) long by 73 m (80 yards) wide, with a whitened start and finish line and a turn-round line at the opposite end. Officials will vary according to the scope of the gymkhana but will include a secretary, a starter, judges, stewards, and an arena party to set the scene for each race.

The entrant will have got a schedule in advance and filled in an entry form with the events he wishes to compete in. On the day the pony is fed and watered early enough to digest by the time he competes. Riding clothes are casual if clean and smart—the compulsory hard hat, jodhpurs or breeches, shirt and jersey or jacket according to the weather. At the field the entrant will collect his tie-on number and check the order of events so that he can be ready in the collecting ring in good time. Between events the pony should be kept warm and watered. After the prize-giving and the thanks, all can return home looking forward to a rest day.

The British Pony Club organizes a large number of gymkhanas each year and has competed against American and Canadian teams.

The great event of the Pony Club year is the final of the Prince Philip Mounted Games Championship which takes place at the Horse of the Year Show in London. Six teams of youngsters under the age of 15 will have won their way through various area meetings and zone finals to give a spectacle as thrilling and popular as any provided by their elders.

ability to vault on to the pony behind one's partner is an asset. Many of the possible games include cantering in and out of a row of poles at about six or eight yard intervals; this can be practised with ground markers or canes. Some games involve changing paces, one pace to one line then a neat change to another pace which should cause a well-trained pony no trouble. Many of the games involve placing objects in pots or baskets while mounted, with galloping between pick-up and placement; positioned halts can be practised. A race may involve carrying an object across the pony's withers as in a rescue race. Often the pony may require to be led and an easily led pony will gain time in the Sack Race, for example, when the competitor has galloped to and donned the sack and has to lead the pony back while thus encumbered. A pony should be prepared to stand patiently while the rider puts on a shirt or other clothes for the Shirt Race or a dressing up race.

WESTERN RIDING

Western riding derives from the cowboys and vaqueros of the American west where huge herds of cattle roamed the ranges. Nowadays a cowboy has a pick-up for leisure as well as a horse for work and a ranger rides in a chopper, but western riding is pursued for pleasure by a wide public and professionally by the rodeo riders.

The western horse has to be intelligent and very agile, with a good bone structure. The American Quarter Horse is favoured, but almost any of the light breeds can be used.

The stock saddle is robust as it has to be to carry a cowboy's equipment and be used as an anchor for roping. The pommel is extended into a horn and sweeps back to hold the rider's thighs in place; the cantle and seat are well padded for comfort and security. The stirrup leathers are worn long giving the rider an upright profile. The stirrups are broad to hold a cowboy's foot in comfort.

There are two styles of western riding, Californian and Texan, the latter being the most popular. The Californian vaqueros had a tradition of horsemanship and took pride in breaking and training their mounts. The Californian horse carries his head in a vertical position with a pronounced arched poll. The rider pushes the horse forward with his legs to get the hindquarters under the body in a collected position. The horse is initially trained in a hackamore, a bitless bridle which acts on the nose rather than the mouth. After ten months it is replaced by a bosal (braided noseband) and bit, but the bit reins are kept loose and the horse still controlled by the bosal. After another year the bosal is replaced by a lighter model without nose pressure reins and the horse is ridden on the bit. The horse is ridden controlled very lightly by the reins, and the rider rings the changes between bosal and bit through the horse's career.

The Texas cowboys were as new to riding as their horses. The horses were crudely broken and ridden in a day. The cowboy's duties at first would be riding very slowly behind the herd until he was promoted to riding alongside and rounding up strays. He and his horse were partners, together day and night. In Texan style riding the horse moves naturally, neck straight out, poll slightly flexed. The reins are held in either hand, taken up palm down between thumb and index finger, then the hand slightly tilted,

Left: The Texas style has always been the most popular amongst Western enthusiasts.

Below: The reins, held in either hand, are taken in the palm, the fingers are closed and the hand turned over so that the wrist is straight and the thumb up.

Above: *A working cow horse is the epitome of the Western Horse.*

Left: *The Californian style was developed by the immigrant Spanish ranch owners.*

Below: *The reins can be held in either hand. They are held principally between the thumb and the index finger. The free hand grasps the romal, the integral whip.*

thumb up, elbow slightly bent. There is no steady pressure on the bit, the horse responding to the rider's leg and weight shift and indirect reining.

The Californian rider holds the reins in either hand, passing between thumb and forefinger, with the knuckle to the horse's head and thumb up, elbow bent. The free hand grasps the integral whip, the romal, and rests naturally on the thigh.

Western horses today usually have the normal training of lungeing, backing and schooling. They are trained to three gaits, the walk, a long stride in which the hind foot should well overstride the front hoof print, the jog, which is a slow trot that the horse is able to keep up for hours, and the lope which is a slow canter that covers ground but would not stampede a herd.

The western working horse is trained to work calmly amongst cows. When his rider wants him to hold a cow in a small area he should be able to do it without prompting. When asked to run a cow down he should be able to cut in front of it and turn it back. The king of the western horses is the cutting horse who can move quietly into a herd, lock on to the animal to be separated, separate it out and hold it there—just as a sheepdog would with a sheep.

The western pleasure horse is asked to show all these skills in competition. There is a variety of events: a kind of dressage in the ring performing his three gaits; trial classes where horse and rider negotiate obstacles they might expect to find on a ranch in a day's work; classes demonstrating speed and agility with flying changes of leg, abrupt slide stops and pirouettes; pole bending; a sort of slalom race; and barrel races, clover-leaf courses round three barrels, traditionally the cowgirl's timed race.

The slide-stop is peculiar to western horses. It originates in the halt required when a steer is roped. The horse sits back on his hind feet and slides them while moving his front feet as necessary to keep his balance. The stop is practised first from the walk, the horse learning to stop dead on cue and stay still. After several months of training more speed can be used, when the horse is worked in skid boots and shod with special plates. The western figure of a rollback is similar to the dressage half-pirouette. The horse makes a 180° turn over its inside hock, crossing one foreleg over the other as he does so. He immediately resumes the gait he was in—if it was a jog he

now jogs in the opposite direction. An offset is a quarter-turn of 90° performed from a standstill. In a competition these two movements can be linked with only a slight hesitation between. The horse can also perform a sidepass, which is a sort of half-pass, the horse crossing both front and back legs as he proceeds sideways.

The slide stop is a dramatic extension of the hard, fast stop required of the cow pony when roping, but should be practised in moderation. Form and style should be practised, not speed and distance.

Rodeos

The rodeo was the original wild party, the letting off of steam after days and monotonous days of driving cattle in the round-up or to the railhead.

The first rodeos were impromptu, showing off events in the main street or stockyard with riding and roping contests and wagers. In the 1870s they began to get organized and in 1883 Buffalo Bill (who got his name from slaughtering 5000 buffalo) started touring with his famous Wild West Show.

Today, there are some thousand or so rodeos held annually in the Western United States, major Eastern and Southern states and Canada. There is a Rodeo Cowboys' Association and an All-round Championship which goes to the rodeo rider earning most in prizes during the year.

Above: The spin, a full 360° turn, is a complete turn on the haunches and is practised slowly at first by making a series of quarter turns, or 'off sets'.

Above right: The roll back is a half-turn, pivoting on the inside hind leg. At whatever pace the horse starts the movement it must continue without hesitation on completion.

The rodeos vary in size and scope from the inter-collegiate or small town fixtures to the big ones which have all the razmatazz of the circus, with a rodeo queen, a chuck wagon race, trick riding, musical rides and clowns. But every rodeo has six standard events—bareback riding, saddled bronco riding, bull riding, calf roping, steer dogging and the women's barrel racing.

Bareback riding: the horse has a strap set behind its shoulders to which the cowboy is allowed to cling with one hand only. The horse is put in a chute. It wears an uncomfortable strap round its flank which makes it buck. The cowboy lowers himself on to its back and the chute door is opened. The cowboy must pass the judges with both spurs in contact with the horse's shoulders, which qualifies the ride. The judges score 50 points for how well the horse bucks and 50 points for riding style during an 8 to 10 second period. The rider must not touch the horse or strap with his free hand. If he is thrown during the timed period he is disqualified. If he is still on the horse a second rider comes alongside and helps him dismount.

Saddled bronco riding is similar except that the horse wears a light saddle and a rope attached to its halter.

Bull-riding follows the same pattern except that the rider is allowed to use both hands on a strap round the barrel of the bull. If the cowboy is thrown the bull is liable to pursue him and will attempt to toss him.

Calf-roping imitates the everyday ranch job of catching and branding a calf. The calf is released into the arena followed by the mounted cowboy wielding a lasso. The event is timed. The cowboy swings his lasso over the calf's head and secures the rope round the pommel horn and leaps off. His horse keeps the rope taut by stepping back. The cowboy throws the calf and ties three of its legs securely with a small length of rope.

Steer dogging is another timed event. The cowboy is helped by a second man, called a hazer, who rides on the other side of the released steer to keep it running straight. The contestant dives from his horse and grasps the steer by the horns, bringing it to a stop by digging in his high boot heels. He now has to throw the steer over so that all four feet leave the ground.

Barrel racing: the cowgirls race in turn round three oil barrels, taking a clover-leaf route, the one with the fastest time winning.

Professional rodeo riders are not paid for appearing and have to pay their own and their horses' expenses. They make their living out of prize money, which can be substantial, and sponsorship.

Western-style holidays are popular in the States and Canada. They can consist of staying on a ranch and joining in the ranching activities with such things as barbecues and square dancing laid on in the evenings, or long-distance rides, camping at night or more likely staying in cabins specially built along the route. Western saddles are ideal for this sort of riding because they evolved for slow pace comfort.

RIDING FOR THE DISABLED

Above left: *Riding for the disabled is of enormous benefit, both physically and mentally.*

Above right: *The movement of the horse stimulates muscle and joint movements in the rider and helps to improve balance.*

Only those who have attended sessions of Riding for the Disabled can conceive what a joy it is for the participants and how therapeutic the riding can be, both mentally and physically.

The riders can be of any age and suffering from almost any disablement—those with cerebal palsy, spina bifida, disseminated sclerosis, muscular dystrophy, multiple injuries, the limbless, the mentally handicapped, blind and deaf, emotionally disturbed and those with various neuropathies and skeletal deformities are all accepted.

In 1965 the Advisory Council on Riding for the Disabled was placing its skills at the service of nine groups. Four years later it became the Riding for the Disabled Association with 80 groups. There are now well over 600 groups in Great Britain and the Channel Islands, with affiliated associations in Australia, Hong Kong, New Zealand, the Republic of Ireland and the United States, and associated groups in Australia, Bahamas,

Bermuda, Canada, Cyprus, Malta, Portugal, South Africa, West Germany and Zimbabwe.

The disabled riders are referred by their doctors. Some come as individuals, others from schools. Qualified physiotherapists, occupational therapists and experienced riding instructors are all involved in the programmes.

Horses are carefully selected for their good temperaments. There is an annual Lloyds Bank National RDA Championship for the best behaved mount. Ponies have to pass such items as goats, barking dogs, cross a level crossing and go through a noisy crowd shaking and waving all sorts of objects and enter and leave horse boxes serenely, taking no notice of the human antics.

For safety, each disabled rider has someone to lead the pony and one or two helpers at the side, according to need. In time, some riders go solo.

The movement of the horse, even at a walk, stimulates muscle and joint movements in the rider. Riding improves the sense of balance which some disabled are unable otherwise to practice. It gives the rider a new outlook; it gives a very different view of the world from a horse's back than from looking up at it from a wheelchair. And there is a great sense of freedom in being able to proceed with hardly any effort.

Riding is taken seriously—the aim of the Association is to make its riders as proficient as possible. Riders are encouraged to take the special RDA proficiency tests of which there are seven grades, the top three being bronze, silver and gold. There is a separate test for those too severely disabled to proceed further in which candidates record their work with the group over six months and also do a project connected with it.

Riding sessions take place in commercial riding schools, on fields and farms and in privately owned covered and outdoor arenas. Riding for the Disabled Association is, of course, a charity, and groups and the riders themselves help to raise funds.

Regions and groups arrange extra activities for their riders—gymkhanas, jumping and dressage competitions, barbecues and picnics. National and regional holidays are organized and there is an annual national dressage competition.

Riding for the Disabled is personnel intensive with three people to one rider at first, at any rate, and helpers who volunteer stay on to get the enormous satisfaction of seeing their charges improve their skills and their health.

Driving for the Disabled is an offshoot of the Association. It was started over ten years ago and has over seventy groups. With the encouragement of the carriage driving world the disabled drivers have been given the opportunity of competing in classes for the wheelchair bound in major driving shows all over the country.

For wheelchairs, specially designed carriages are used, with ramps that can be lowered at the back. Some are fitted with hydraulic mechanisms for fast loading. Donkeys as well as ponies or horses are used and all have to be very calm, with extremely good temperaments.

Riding sessions for the disabled take place not only in commercial schools, but also in privately owned arenas and on farms.

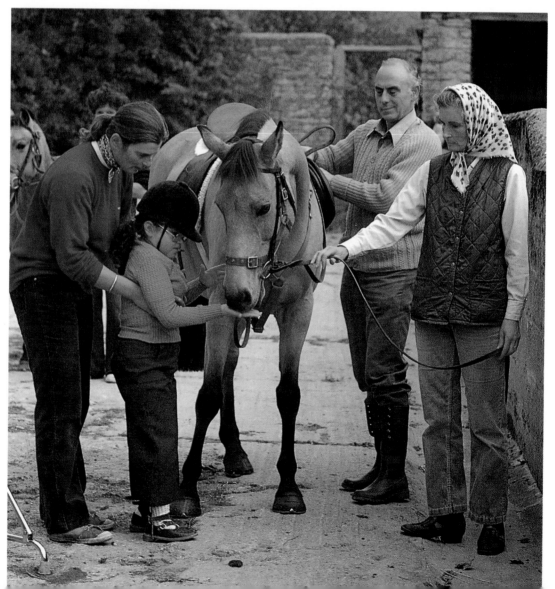

GLOSSARY OF EQUESTRIAN TERMS

Account for to kill a fox.

Acey Deucey riding with one stirrup leather longer than the other, a style sometimes adopted by jockeys in the U.S.A. to help them keep their balance on sharp bends.

Acting Master a person appointed temporarily to organize a hunt, either for a day, or for a longer period pending the appointment of a permanent master.

Against the Clock in show-jumping—a competition or jump-off decided by time, the winner being the competitor with the least number of faults in the fastest time.

Aged a horse which is seven years old or more.

Aid any of the signals used by a rider to give instructions to his horse. See also ARTIFICIAL AIDS, NATURAL AIDS.

Air Above the Ground any of the various high school movements performed either with the forelegs or with the fore and hind legs off the ground. See also BALLOTADE, CAPRIOLE, COURBETTE, CROUPADE, LEVADE.

Albino a colour type, rather than a breed, comprising pure white hair, pale skin and pale translucent eyes.

All On a hunting term normally used by the whipper-in to let the huntsman know all hounds are up with the pack.

All-Round Cow Horse a horse which is skilled at carrying out all the duties required of it by a cowboy.

Also-Ran any unplaced horse in a race.

Alter to castrate a horse or colt, thus rendering it sterile.

Amble a slow gait in two time in which the horse's hind and foreleg on the same side are moved forward together.

Ante-Post Betting the placing of bets on a race, at an agreed price prior to the day of the race.

Anvil (a) a heavy iron block with a smooth flat face, usually of steel, on which horseshoes are shaped. (b) (Western U.S.) a horse, particularly one which is shod, which strikes the forefeet with the hind feet.

Appointment Card a card sent out to interested parties by the hunt secretary informing them of the time, date and place of forthcoming meets.

Apprentice a youth who is being trained as a jockey and serves an indentured apprenticeship of five to seven years.

Apron a covering made of strong horse-hide worn by farriers to protect the front of the body whilst shoeing a horse.

Arena the area in which a horseshow or show-jumping competition is held.

Artificial Aids items such as whips, spurs and martingales which are used by the rider to help convey instructions to the horse.

As Hounds Ran the distance covered in a hunt by hounds.

Asking the Question asking a horse to make a supreme effort when it is being pushed to its limit in competitive events, such as racing, show-jumping or combined training.

At Bay the position of hounds when kept off the quarry.

Automatic Timing an electrical apparatus used for show-jumping events. The horse breaks an electronic ray as it goes through the start, triggering off the mechanism which starts the clock. As it goes through the finish it breaks a similar device which stops the clock.

Autorisation Spéciale a pink card issued to a rider by his national equestrian federation permitting him to compete in an international dressage, show jumping or combined training event.

Autumn Double the Cesarewitch Stakes and the Cambridgeshire Stakes—two racing events held annually at Newmarket, England in the autumn.

Back to place a bet on a horse.

Backer a person who places a bet on a horse.

Back Hander a polo stroke in which the player travelling forwards hits the ball backwards in the opposite direction.

Back Jockey the stop skirt of a Western saddle.

Badge of Honour an award presented by the F.E.I. to riders competing in Prix des Nations competitions with points given as follows: Bronze-five, Silver–25, Gold–50. Competing in an Olympic Games is counted as competing in five Prix des Nations.

Bag Fox a fox kept temporarily in captivity until it is required for a hunt.

Ballotade an air above the ground in which the horse half rears, then jumps forward, drawing the hind legs up below the quarters, before landing on all four legs.

Band a group of horses.

Bang-Tail a horse.

Bareme any of the three tables of rules set by the F.E.I. under which show jumping competitions are judged.

Barrage a jump-off.

Bareback Riding riding a horse without a saddle or blanket on its back.

Barrel the part of the horse's body between the forearms and the loins.

Barrier (a) the point at which a race starts. (b) in a rodeo arena the barrier behind which the roper or steer wrestler's horse wait until the stock is far enough out of the chute.

Bay (a) a dark skinned horse with a dark brown to a bright reddish- or yellowish-brown coat, with a black mane and tail and normally black markings on the legs. (b) the noise made by a hound.

Bayo Coyote a dun horse with a black dorsal stripe.

Beaning disguising an unsoundness in a horse.

Bed Down to put down a bed for a horse in a stable or loose box.

Bell as rung in show-jumping competitions to signal competitors to start, restart or stop, or to indicate elimination.

Bet (a) a wager placed on a horse in a race. (b) to make a wager.

Betting (a) the quotation of the wager prices of horses in a certain race. (b) to place a bet on a horse.

Betting Shop a licensed bookmaker's establishment, not on a racecourse, which takes bets on horseraces, etc.

Big Race the principal race of the day at any race meeting.

Bit a device, normally made of metal or rubber, attached to the bridle and placed in the horse's mouth so as to regulate the position of the horse's head and to help control the pace and direction of the horse. It is manipulated by use of the reins.

Bitch Fox the name given to a female fox.

Bitch Hound a female hound.

Bitless Bridle any of a variety of bridles used without bits, pressure being exerted on the nose and the curb groove instead of the mouth.

Black a horse with a black coat, mane and

tail with no other colour present, except possibly white markings on the face and/or legs.

Black Saddler a saddler who specializes in making items of saddlery for riding horses.

Blacksmith an artisan whose medium is iron and who, amongst other things, makes horse shoes.

Blemish any scar left by an injury or wound.

Blind Bucker a horse which bucks indiscriminately, heading into anything when ridden.

Blinkers a pair of leather eye-shields fixed to the bridle or on a head covering used to prevent a horse from looking anywhere other than in front of it.

Blood the amount of blood in a horse's body is made up of approximately one-eighteenth of its total body weight.

Blood Horse the English Thoroughbred.

Bloodstock Thoroughbred horses, particularly race and stud animals.

Blow a Stirrup to lose a stirrup iron. If this happens in a rodeo contest the rider is disqualified.

Blow Away to send hounds after a fox by blowing a given signal on the hunting horn.

Blow Up (a) a term used in the dressage arena or the show ring when a horse either breaks from the pace at which it is meant to be going or misbehaves generally. (b) (U.S.) to start bucking.

Body Brush a tightly-packed, short bristled brush used to remove dust and scurf from a horse's coat.

Bog Rider a cowboy whose job is to rescue cattle which have got trapped in mud or marshland.

Boil Over to start bucking.

Bookie an abbreviated term for a bookmaker.

Bookmaker a professional betting man who is licensed to accept the bets placed by others on horses, etc.

Boundary Rider station (ranch) worker whose task it is to ride round all the fencing on the huge Australian cattle and sheep properties, to find holes in the fences and to repair them.

Bran a by-product of grain milling, which, when freshly ground and dampened, acts as a mild laxative and aids digestion.

Break the initial training of a horse for whatever purpose it may be required.

Break Down to lacerate the suspensory ligament or fracture a sesamoid bone, so that the back of the horse's fetlock drops to the ground.

Breastplate a device usually of leather, attached to the saddle to prevent it from slipping back on the horse.

Breeder (a) the owner of a mare which gives birth to a foal. (b) the owner of a stud farm where horses are bred.

Breeze In to win a race very easily.

Bridle the part of a horse's saddlery or harness which is placed about the head.

Bronco an unbroken or imperfectly broken wild horse.

Bronco-Buster a person who breaks and trains broncos.

Bronc Riding one of the standard rodeo events. The only piece of tack worn by the horse is a wide leather band round its middle, from which a leather handhold protrudes.

Bronc Saddle a saddle used in breaking broncos.

Browband the part of the bridle which lies across the horse's forehead below the ears.

Brumby Australian wild horse.

Brumby Runner Australian bush horseman who captures wild horses.

Brush the tail of a fox.

Buck a leap into the air by a horse keeping its back arched, and coming down with its forelegs stiff and its head held low.

Buckaroo (a) a cowboy. (b) a bronco-buster.

Bulldogging see STEER WRESTLING.

Bulldogging Horse a horse which is used for steer wrestling.

Bull Riding one of the standard events in a rodeo, in which the contestant has to ride a bull equipped only with a rope round its middle, which the rider may hold with only one hand.

Bumper (a) an amateur race rider. (b) an amateur race.

Bush Track an unofficial race meeting in the United States.

By sired by.

Bye-Day an extra meet held by a hunt, usually during the Christmas school holidays or to compensate for days lost through bad weather.

Calf Horse a specially trained horse used for calf roping.

Calf-Roping one of the standard events in a rodeo in which the rider ropes a calf and then swiftly dismounts in order to tie the calf by three legs.

Call Over the naming of the horses in a race, when the latest betting odds on each horse are given.

Camera Patrol equipment for the filming of a race while it is in progress.

Camp Drafting a uniquely Australian rodeo contest in which a rider separates a large bullock from a group of cattle and drives it at the gallop around a course marked with upright poles.

Canter a pace of three time in which the hoofs strike the ground in the following order: near hind, near fore and off hind together, off fore (leading leg): or off hind, off fore and near hind together, near fore (leading leg).

Cap the fee payable by a visitor for a day's hunting.

Capriole an air above the ground in which the horse half rears with the hocks drawn under, then jumps forward and high into the air, at the same time kicking out the hind legs with the soles of the feet turned upwards, before landing collectedly on all four legs.

Catchweight the random or optional weight carried by a horse when the conditions of a race do not specify a weight. Except in matches, this does not occur now.

Cavalletti a series of small wooden jumps used in the basic training of a riding horse in order to encourage it to lengthen its stride, improve its balance and loosen up and strengthen its muscles.

Cayuse an Indian horse or pony.

Certainty a horse regarded as certain to win a particular race (may or may not be the official favourite).

Chaff meadow hay or green oat straw cut into short lengths for use as a feedstuff.

Charley a fox.

Check a halt in hunting when hounds lose the scent.

Cheekpiece (a) the leather part of the bridle

to which the bit is attached at one end and the headpiece at the other. (b) side pieces of a bit to which the reins are attached.

Chef d'Equipe the manager of an equestrian team responsible for making all the arrangements, both on and off the field for a national team competing abroad.

Chestnut a horse with a gold to dark reddish-brown coat, usually having a matching or slightly lighter or darker mane and tail, or with a flaxen-coloured mane and tail.

Chime hounds giving tongue in unison when on the line of the quarry.

Chukka a period of play in polo lasting seven and a half or eight minutes, depending on which country the game is being played in.

Classic any one of the five chief English flat races for three-year-old horses: that is, the Derby, the Oaks, the St. Leger, the 1,000 Guineas and the 2,000 Guineas.

Clear Round a show-jumping or cross-country round which is completed without jumping or time faults.

Cob a type rather than a breed. A short legged animal with a maximum height of 15.1 hh with the bone and substance of a heavyweight hunter and capable of carrying a substantial weight.

Co-Favourite one of two or more horses equally favoured to win a race and given the same shortest price in the betting odds.

Colic sharp abdominal pains often the symptom of flatulence, an obstruction created by a mass of hard food, or faeces in the bowel, and which can lead to a twisted gut.

Collection shortening the pace by a light contact from the rider's hands and a steady pressure with the legs to make the horse flex its neck, relax its jaw and bring its hocks well under it so that it is properly balanced.

Colt an ungelded male horse less than four years old.

Combination Obstacle in show-jumping, an obstacle consisting of two or more separate jumps which are numbered and judged as one obstacle.

Combined Training Competition a comprehensive test of both horse and rider, consisting of the following three phases: dressage, cross-country and show-jumping, held over a period of one, two or three days depending on the type of competition.

Contact the link between the rider's hands and the horse's mouth made through the reins.

Corn bruising of the sole in the angle between the wall of the hoof and the heel.

Corral a pen or enclosure for animals, usually made of wood and always circular in shape, so that the animals cannot injure themselves.

Country the area over which a certain pack of hounds may hunt.

Couple two hounds.

Courbette an air above the ground in which the horse rears to an almost upright position, and then leaps forwards several times on its hind legs.

Course (a) a racecourse. (b) in show-jumping and cross-country a circuit consisting of a number of obstacles to be jumped in a particular order within a specified time limit. (c) for hounds to hunt by sight rather than by scent.

Course Builder the person responsible for designing and building a show-jumping or cross-country course.

Course Designer (a) a person who designs a show-jumping or cross-country course and may or may not actually build it as well. (b) (U.S.) a course builder.

Covert a hunting term for a thicket or small area of woodland.

Cowboy a man who herds and tends cattle on ranches, doing his work mainly on horseback.

Cow Horse the horse which a cowboy rides while working cattle.

Croupade an air above the ground in which the horse rears, and then jumps vertically with the hind legs drawn up towards the belly.

Cry the noise made by hounds when they are hunting their quarry.

Cub a young fox.

Curb Bit type of bit used in conjunction with a snaffle bit in a double bridle. This consists of two metal cheekpieces and a mouthpiece with a central indented section (called the port).

Curb Chain a metal chain which is fitted to the eyes of a curb or pelham bit and lies in the curb groove of the horse's jaw.

Curb Groove the groove of the lower jaw just behind the lower lip.

Curry Comb a piece of grooming equipment used to remove dirt and scurf from a body brush. It has a flat back, while the front consists of several rows of small metal teeth.

Cut to geld or castrate a colt or stallion.

Cutting Horse a horse especially trained for separating selected cattle from a herd.

Dam the female parent of a foal.

Dandy Brush the long-bristled brush for removing the surface dirt from a horse's coat.

Dark Horse in racing, a horse whose form is little known outside its own stable.

Dead Heat in racing, a tie for first, second or third places.

Declaration a statement made in writing by an owner, trainer or his representative, a specified time before a race or competition, declaring that a horse will take part.

Dirt Track a race track, the surface of which is a combination of sand and soil.

Dividend the amount paid to a person who has backed a winner or a placed horse on the totalizator. In the U.S. called the pay-off.

Dog Fox a male fox.

Dog Hound a male hound.

Dope to administer drugs to a horse, either to improve or hinder its performance in a race or competition. It is an illegal practice and carries heavy penalties in all forms of equestrian sport.

Double (a) the backing of two horses to win in separate races, the winnings of one race being carried as a stake on to the second. If either horse fails to win the bet is lost. In the U.S. known as the DAILY DOUBLE. (b) in show-jumping a combination obstacle consisting of two separate jumps.

Double Bridle a bridle consisting of two bits, a curb and a snaffle which are attached by means of two cheekpieces and may be operated independently.

Drag an artificial scent for a hunt made by trailing a strong smelling material such as a piece of sacking impregnated with aniseed or a fox's droppings over the ground.

Draghound a hound trained to follow a drag.

Draghunt a hunt with a drag or artificial scent.

Drain an underground pipe, ditch or watercourse in which a fox may hide.

Dressage the art of training horses to perform all movements in a balanced, supple, obedient and keen manner.

Drover Australian horseman who herds cattle or sheep over long distances.

Each Way in racing, to back a horse to win and to finish in the first three.

Earth the lair of a fox which it digs below ground level or in the side of a bank.

Elimination the excluding of a competitor from taking further part in a particular competition.

Engaged a term applied to a horse entered in a particular race.

Enteritis inflammation of the intestinal or bowel lining which may be set up by bacteria, chemical or vegetable poisons, or mouldy or damaged food containing harmful fungi.

Equestrian (a) of, or pertaining to, horsemen or horsemanship. (b) a rider or performer on horseback.

Equestrienne a female rider or performer on horseback.

Equine (a) of, or pertaining to, the horse. (b) a horse.

Evens in racing, the betting odds given on a horse when the person who places the bet stands to win the same amount as his stake. In the U.S.A. known as even money.

Event Horse a horse which competes or is capable of competing in a combined training competition.

Exacta a type of wagering in which the better must select the first and second place finishers in exact order.

Fall a horse is considered to have fallen when the shoulders and quarters on the same side touch the ground. A rider is considered to have fallen when there is separation between him and his horse which necessitates his remounting.

Fancied said of a horse likely to win a particular race. In the U.S. called favourite.

Farrier a person who makes horseshoes and shoes horses.

Fault in show-jumping, a scoring unit used to record any knockdown, refusal or other offence committed by a competitor during his round.

Favourite the horse in a race having the shortest odds offered against it.

F.E.I. the Fédération Equestre Internationale (International Equestrian Federation) which is the governing body of international equestrian sport and was founded in 1921 by Commandant G. Hector of France. It has its headquarters in Brussels. The F.E.I. makes the rules and regulations for the conduct of the three equestrian sports which comprise the Olympic Equestrian Games; show-jumping, three-day event and dressage, as well as international driving competitions. All national federations are required to comply with these regulations in any international event.

Fence (a) any obstacle to be jumped in steeplechasing, cross-country, show-jumping or hunting. (b) in racing, to jump over an obstacle.

Field (a) the mounted followers of a hunt. (b) in racing, (i) all the horses running in a particular race; (ii) all the horses not individually favoured in the betting.

Filly a female horse less than four years old.

Finish a horse is said to finish a race when it passes the winning post mounted, providing, in the case of a steeplechase or hurdle race, it has jumped all the obstacles with its rider.

First Jockey the principal person engaged by an owner or trainer to ride for him.

Flapper a horse which runs at an unauthorized race meeting.

Flapping an unofficial race meeting which is not held under the rules of racing.

Flat Racing racing in which there are no obstacles for the horses to jump.

Foal a young horse up to the age of 12 months.

Forehand the part of the horse which is in front of the rider: that is, the head, neck, shoulders, withers and forelegs.

Form the past performances of a horse in racing.

Fox a carnivorous animal of the canine family.

Fox Dog a foxhound.

Foxhound one of a breed of swift, keen-scented hounds trained for hunting foxes.

Foxhunting the hunting of the fox in its natural state by a pack of foxhounds, followed by people on horses or on foot.

Full ungelded.

Full Mouth the mouth of a horse at six years old, when it has grown all its teeth.

Furniture any item of harness or saddlery put on a horse.

Fuzztail Running the act of herding and catching wild horses.

Gad a spur.

Gag Bridle a severe form of bridle: cheek-pieces are made of rounded leather and pass through holes at the top and bottom of the bit rings, before being attached directly to the reins.

Gall a skin sore usually occurring under the saddle or girth.

Galloway an Australian show ring category based upon an animal's height: a Galloway measures from 14 to 15 hh (in Australia ponies are under 14 hh).

Garron any native pony of Scotland or Ireland.

Gate frequently used as an upright obstacle in show-jumping competitions.

Gelding a male horse which has been castrated.

Gestation the period between conception and foaling, normally about eleven months.

Get the offspring of a stallion.

Girth (a) the circumference of a horse, measured behind the withers round the deepest part of the body. (b) a band, usually of leather, webbing or nylon, passed under the belly of the horse to hold the saddle in place.

Give Tongue for hounds to bark or bay when in full cry after a quarry.

Going the condition of a race track or other ground over which a horse travels; variously classified as soft, good etc.

Gone to Ground a fox having taken refuge in an earth or a drain.

Good Mouth a horse with a soft, sensitive mouth.

Go Short said of a horse which is lame or restricted in its action.

Green (a) a horse which is broken but not fully trained, an inexperienced horse. (b) a trotter or pacer which has not been raced against the clock.

Grey a dark skinned horse with a coat of black and white hairs mixed together; the whiter ones becoming more predominant with each change of coat.

Groom (a) any person who is responsible for looking after a horse. (b) to clean the coat and feet of a horse.

Grooming Kit collectively, the brushes and other items of equipment used to groom a horse.

Ground to let the reins touch the ground after dismounting so that the horse will stand without having to be tied up.

Ground Money in a rodeo the entry fee and purse money split equally among all the contestants in an event when there is no outright winner.

Gymkhana mounted games, most frequently for children under sixteen, many of which are adaptations of children's party games.

Habit the dress worn by a woman riding side-saddle consisting of a jacket and matching long skirt or shaped panel which is worn over the breeches and boots.

Hack (a) a riding horse for hire. (b) a pleasure ride.

Halter a hemp rope headpiece with lead rope attached, used for leading a horse when not wearing a bridle, or for tying up in the stable.

Hand a linear measurement equalling 4 in (10 cm) used in giving the height of a horse, the fractions being expressed in inches.

Handicap (a) the weight allocated to a horse in a race. (b) a race in which the weights to be carried by the horse are estimated so as to give each horse an equal chance of winning.

Haunches the hips and buttocks of a horse.

Haute École the classical art of equitation.

Hay grass cut and dried at a particular time of the year for use as fodder.

Head one of the measurements of distance by which a horse may be said to have won a race: the length of a horse's head.

Head Collar a bitless headpiece and noseband, usually of leather, for leading a horse which is not wearing a bridle, or for tying up a horse in a stable.

Heavy Horse any horse belonging to one of the breeds of large draught horses, such as Clydesdale, Percheron, Shire or Suffolk Punch.

Height the height of a horse is measured in a perpendicular line from the highest part of the withers to the ground.

High School the classical art of equitation.

Hitch Up to harness a horse or horses to be driven.

Hit the Line for hounds to pick up the scent of the quarry.

Hog's Back in show-jumping, a spread obstacle in which there are three sets of poles, the first close to the ground, the second at the highest point of the obstacle and the third slightly lower than the second.

Holloa the cry given by a person out hunting to indicate that he has seen the fox.

Hood (a) a fabric covering which goes over the horse's head and ears and part of its neck, and is used when travelling, most usually in cold weather. (b) blinkers.

Hoof (a) the insensitive horny covering which protects the sensitive parts of a horse's foot. (b) a term used to describe the entire foot.

Hoof Pick a hooked metal instrument used for removing stones and dirt from a horse's foot.

Horse (a) the general term for an equine animal, whether it be a stallion, mare or gelding. (b) a stallion or uncastrated horse. (c) to provide a person with a horse to ride. (d) to ride on horseback.

Horseman (a) a rider on horseback. (b) a person skilled in the training and management of horses. (c) a farm labourer who works with horses.

Horse Race a competition for horses ridden by jockeys which takes place on the flat or over obstacles within a given area and over a prescribed distance, under the control of appointed officials.

Horseshoe a shaped metal band nailed to the base of riding and harness horses' hoofs to protect them and prevent them from splitting.

Horse Show a meeting at which competitions are held to test or display the qualities and capabilities of horses and their riders.

Horse-tailing taking charge of the band of horses used by drovers when herding cattle or sheep over long distances.

Hull a term for a saddle.

Hunt Button a button with the symbol or lettering of a particular hunt on it.

Hunter a horse bred and trained to be ridden for hunting.

Hunter Trials a type of competitive event held by most hunts, and other organizing bodies during the hunting season, in which horses are ridden over a course of obstacles built to look as natural and similar to those encountered out hunting.

Hunting the sport of following different types of hound, either mounted or on foot, in pursuit of the fox, the stag or the hare or an artificially laid drag line.

Hunting Cap a velvet-covered protective riding hat.

Hunting Horn a cylindrical instrument, usually 23–25 cm (9–10 in) long, made of copper with a nickel or silver mouthpiece, used by huntsmen to give signals, both to hounds and to the field.

Hunt Livery the distinctive coat of a particular hunt worn by the staff of the hunt.

Hunt Secretary a person who carries out the normal duties of a secretary in connection with the hunt; is also responsible for keeping close contact with farmers and landowners within the area of the hunt, and collects the cap money at the meet.

Hunt Servant any salaried employee of a hunt, such as the huntsman, kennel huntsman or whippers-in.

Huntsman the person in charge of hounds during a hunt, whether the master or someone employed by the master.

Hunt Subscription the fee payable by a person who is a member of a hunt.

Hunt Terrier a small, short-legged terrier kept by a hunt and used to bolt foxes from earths, drains or other places whch are inaccessible to hounds.

Hurdle one of a series of wattle fences over which a horse must jump in hurdle racing. In the U.S. the fences are made of brush.

Hurdle Racing horse races over a course of hurdles.

In Blood said of hounds having made a kill.

Inbreeding the mating of related individuals, such as brother and sister, sire and daughter or son and dam.

Independent Seat the ability to maintain a firm, balanced position on a horse's back, without relying on the reins or stirrups.

In Foal pregnant.

In Full Cry a pack of hounds in strong pursuit of the quarry and giving tongue.

In-Hand Class any of various show classes in which the animals are led, usually in a show bridle or head collar, but otherwise without saddlery (except for draught horses which are often shown in their harness), and are judged chiefly for conformation and/or condition.

In the Book accepted for, or entered in, the General Stud Book.

Irons stirrup irons.

Jiggle the ordinary gait of a cow horse averaging about 8 km/h (5 mph).

Jockey (a) a person engaged to ride a horse in a race. (b) formerly a dealer in horses, especially a disreputable one.

Jog a short-paced trot.

Joint-master one of two or more people who share the mastership of a pack of hounds.

Jumper any horse trained to compete over jumps, such as a steeplechaser or showjumper.

Jump Jockey a jockey who races horses over hurdles or steeplechase fences.

Jump-off in show-jumping, a round held to decide the winner of the competition from competitors who have tied for first place in the previous round.

Keep a grass field which is used for grazing. Known as pastures in the U.S.

Kennel Huntsman a person employed by a hunt which has an amateur huntsman to manage the hounds and to act as first whipper-in on hunting days.

Kennel Man a person who works in hunt kennels under the supervision of a huntsman or kennel huntsman.

Kennels the buildings and yards where a pack of hounds is housed.

Lad (a) a boy or stableman who works in a stables of any kind. (b) a girl who works in racing stables. Known as a groom in the U.S.

Laminitis inflammation of the sensitive laminae which lie between the horny wall of the hoof and the pedal bone. It is a very painful condition.

Lawn Meet any meet of a hunt held at a private house by invitation of the owner.

Length one of the measurements of distance by which a horse may be said to win a race; the length of a horse's head and body.

Levade a high-school movement in which the horse rears, drawing its forefeet in, while the hindquarters are deeply bent at the haunches and carry the full weight.

Light a term meaning to dismount.

Light Horse any horse, except a Thoroughbred, used or suitable for riding such as a hack or hunter.

Line the direction in which a fox is travelling with hounds in pursuit.

Linseed the seed of flax generally used in the form of linseed jelly, oil or tea, both as a laxative and to improve the condition and gloss of the coat.

Livery Stable an establishment where privately owned horses are kept, exercised and generally looked after, for an agreed fee. Called Livery in the U.S.

Loriner a person who makes the metal parts of saddlery and harness such as bits, curb chains and stirrup irons.

Lunge Rein a piece of cotton or nylon webbing, usually about 2.5 cm (1 in) wide and 7.5 m (25 ft) long, which is attached by a buckle and leather strap to one of the side rings on a breaking cavesson and is used in training horses.

Maiden a horse of either sex which to date has not won a race of any distance.

Maiden Mare a mare which has not had a foal, though she may be carrying one.

Maiden Race a race in which only horses which have never previously won a race may be entered.

Mane the long hair growing on the top of a horse's head and down the neck.

Mane and Tail Comb small long-toothed metal combs used for cleaning or pulling the mane and tail.

Mare a female horse aged four years or over.

Martingale a device used to help in keeping a horse's head in the correct position. It generally consists of a strap, or arrangement of straps, fastened to the girth at one end, passed between the forelegs and, depending on the type, attached at the other end to the reins, noseband or directly to the bit.

Mask the head of a fox.

Master the person appointed by a hunt committee to have overall responsibility for the running and organization of all aspects of the hunt.

Match a race between two horses, on terms agreed by their owners. There is no prize awarded.

Meet (a) the place where the hunt servants, hounds, followers, etc. assemble before a hunt. (b) the hunt meeting itself.

Mixed Meeting a race meeting at which both flat and steeplechase or hurdle races are held on the same day.

Mixed Stable a racing stable where both flat race and National Hunt horses are kept.

Montura (a) a riding horse. (b) a saddle.

Mount (a) a horse used for riding. (b) to get up on to the back of a horse.

Mount Money the money paid in a rodeo to a performer, who is riding, roping or bulldogging in exhibition but not in competition.

Muck Out to clean out a box or stall in which a horse has been stabled removing the droppings and soiled bedding.

Mudder a racehorse which performs well on a muddy track.

Mud Fever an inflammation of the upper layer of skin, caused by subjection to muddy and wet conditions.

Music the cry made by hounds when they are hunting.

Mustang a wild horse. The original American cow pony.

Nap (a) a horse is said to nap if it fails to obey properly applied aids, as in refusing to go forward or to pass a certain point. (b) in racing a good tip.

National Federation the governing body of equestrian affairs in any country affiliated to the F.E.I.

Natural Aids the body, hands, legs and voice as used by the rider to give instructions to the horse.

Near Side the left-hand side of a horse. This is the side from which it is usual to mount a horse.

Neck one of the measurements of distance by which a horse may be said to win a race; the length of a horse's head and neck.

Nose the shortest measurement of distance by which it is possible for a horse to win a race.

Noseband the part of a bridle which lies across the horse's nose consisting of a leather band on an independent headpiece which is worn below the cheeks and above the bit. Also known as a cavesson in the U.S.

Numnah a pad placed under the saddle to prevent undue pressure on the horse's back. Cut to the shape of the saddle, only slightly larger, it may be made of felt, sheepskin or cloth-covered foam rubber.

Oats cereal used as part of a horse's feed. May be whole, bruised or boiled.

Objection in racing, an objection may be made against any of the placed horses, and must be heard by the stewards at the meeting where it was raised.

Odds the betting quotation on a horse in a particular race.

Odds On betting odds of less than even money.

Off Side the right-hand side of a horse.

On its Toes said of a horse eager and keen to move on.

On Terms said of hounds able to keep hunting steadily because there is a strong scent.

One-Day Event a combined training competition consisting of dressage, show-jumping and cross-country phases and completed in one day.

Opening Meet the first meet of the regular hunting season.

Outfit (a) a ranch with all its equipment and employees. (b) the personal equipment of a cowboy.

Outlaw a horse which is particularly vicious and untameable.

Outsider a racehorse which is given long odds in the betting as it is thought to have little chance of winning the race.

Owlhead a horse which is impossible to train.

Owner the person in whose name a racehorse runs, irrespective of whether that person is the sole owner of the horse or is a member of a syndicate.

Pace a lateral gait in two time, in which the hind leg and the foreleg on the same side move forward together.

Pacemaker in racing, a horse which takes the lead and sets the speed for the race.

Pad the foot of a fox.

Paddock (a) a grassy enclosure near a stable or house in which horses can be turned out. (b) the enclosure at a racecourse in which the horses are paraded before a race.

Pancake an English riding saddle.

Parabola the arc made by a horse from the point of take-off to the point of landing as it jumps an obstacle.

Parallel Bars a type of spread fence used in both show-jumping and cross-country courses, consisting of two sets of posts and rails.

Parimutuel the U.S. and continental equivalent of the totalizator; a form of betting in which the total amount wagered, after a deduction of a percentage for costs, etc., is divided among the holders of the winning and place tickets. An electro-mechanical apparatus is used for recording the number and amount of bets staked by this method.

Passage one of the classical high school airs, comprising a spectacular elevated trot in slow motion. There is a definite period of suspension as one pair of legs remains on the ground with the diagonal opposites raised in the air.

Pelham Bit a bit designed to produce with only one mouthpiece the combined effects of the snaffle bit and the curb bit. Normally made of metal, vulcanite or rubber and used either with two reins, or one rein, in which case a leather couplet is used to link the two rings of the bit.

Penalty in racing, an additional weight handicap carried by a horse, usually imposed when it has won a race since the weights for the race in which the penalty is given were published.

Perfecta a type of wagering in which the better must select the first and second place finishers without regard to the actual order in which they pass the post.

Photo-Finish the result of a race photographed by a camera with a very narrow field of vision situated at the winning post on a race-course. A camera was first used for recording a photo-finish in 1890 by John Hemment at Sheepshead Bay in the U.S.

Piaffe a classical high school air, comprising a spectacular trot with great elevation and cadence performed on the spot.

Picnic Races meetings held in Australia's Outback, when amateur riders and their grass-fed mounts compete against each other for small prizes on primitive bushland racetracks.

Piebald a horse whose coat consists of large irregular and clearly defined patches of black and white hairs.

Pinto a piebald or skewbald horse.

Pirouette in dressage, a turn within the horse's length, that is, the shortest turn it is possible to make. There are three kinds of pirouette—the turn on the centre, the turn on the forehand and the turn on the haunches.

Place to finish second in a horserace.

Planks a show-jumping obstacle made up of painted planks about 30 cm (1 ft) wide.

Plug any slow or broken down horse.

Polo a mounted game, bearing a resemblance to hockey played between two teams of four a side. Popular in many parts of the world, it is recorded as having been played as long ago as the reign of Darius I of Persia (521–486 BC).

Polocrosse Australian mounted game which is rather like a horseback version of lacrosse: the ball is scooped up in a small net at the end of a long stick and is then carried or thrown.

Pony (a) a horse not exceeding 14.2 hh at maturity. (b) the sum of £25 in gambling.

Pony Speed Test the racing of ponies ridden by light boy riders around the quarter-mile circuit at showgrounds in Australia.

Post (a) either the starting or winning post in racing. (b) to rise from the saddle at the trot.

Post and Rails a type of obstacle in show jumping and cross country courses consisting of upright posts between which are laid a number of horizontal posts. In show-jumping the rails are simply supported by the posts, whereas in cross-country events they are fixed to the posts.

Price the odds quoted by a bookmaker at a race meeting for a particular horse.

Prix des Nations an international team show-jumping competition held at an official international horse show. Four members compete in each team jumping the course twice; the three best scores of the team are counted in each round. In the event of equality after the two rounds a jump-off is held in which faults and time are totalled to give the final result. Again only the three best scores and times are counted.

Punter a racing enthusiast who bets regularly on horses.

Quarters the area of a horse's body extending from the rear of the flank to the root of the tail and downwards on either side to the top of the leg: the hindquarters.

Race Card the printed programme of a race meeting giving information, including the name and time of each race, and the names of all horses, their owners and trainers and the weights to be carried.

Racecourse a race track properly constructed for flat and/or steeple-chasing and hurdle racing, together with all the relevant facilities, such as grandstands, paddock, stables, office buildings, etc. and administered by appointed officials.

Racehorse a horse bred and trained for racing, either on the flat or over hurdles or steeplechase obstacles.

Race Meeting (a) a meeting at a given place for the purpose of holding a fixed number of horseraces. (b) the period during which this meeting takes place.

Racing Plate a thin very lightweight horse-shoe used on racehorses.

Racing Saddle a saddle designed for use on racehorses, which may range from the very light type of less than 1 kg (2 lbs) used for flat racing, to the heavier more solid type used for hurdling and steeplechasing.

Rack the most spectacular movement of the five gaited American Saddle Horse, it is a very fast even gait in which each foot strikes the ground separately in quick succession.

Range Horse a horse which is born and brought up on the range, and is never handled until it is brought in to be broken.

Rear for a horse to rise up on the hind legs.

Red Flag a marker used in equestrian sports to denote the right-hand extremity of any obstacle. It is also used to mark a set track and must always be passed on the left-hand side.

Red Ribbon a piece of red ribbon tied round the tail of a horse, especially when hunting, to indicate that it is a known kicker.

Refusal (a) in racing, the failure of a horse to attempt to jump a hurdle or steeplechase fence. (b) in show-jumping and combined training, either the act of passing an obstacle which is to be jumped, or stopping in front of it.

Rein Back to make a horse step backwards while being ridden or driven.

Reins a pair of long narrow straps attached to the bit or bridle and used by the rider or driver to guide and control his horse.

Renvers a dressage movement on two tracks in which the horse moves at an angle of not more than 30 degrees along the long side of the arena with the hind legs on the outer and the forelegs on the inner track, looking in the direction in which it is going and being bent slightly round the inside leg of the rider.

Rep a cowboy employed to search for and round up cattle which have strayed from the ranch of his employer. Such cattle would be recognizable by their brand.

Resistance the act of refusing to go forward, stopping, running back or rearing.

Ride Off in polo, to push one's pony against that of another player in order to prevent him from playing the ball.

Riding School an establishment where people are taught to ride and horses can be hired for riding, or may be taken for livery, or both.

Ringer a horse entered in a race under the name of another horse, the object being to win bets illegally on a good horse, which the public and bookmakers believe to be an inferior one.

Roan a horse having a black, bay or chestnut coat with an admixture of white hairs (especially on the body and neck), which modifies the colour.

Rope Horse any horse which is especially trained and used for roping cattle.

Run Mute said of hounds which are running very fast and thus have no time to speak.

Runner any horse taking part in a particular race.

Run Out (a) in show-jumping and combined training, to avoid an obstacle which is to be jumped by running to one side or the other of it. (b) in racing, to avoid an obstacle which is to be jumped or to pass on the wrong side of a marker flag.

Saddle a seat for a rider on horseback, made in various designs according to the purpose for which it is required.

Saddle Bronc Riding one of the standard rodeo events. The rider has to use a regulation saddle; he is allowed to use only one rein attached to a simple halter and is not allowed to touch the saddle, the horse or himself with his free hand. He must remain mounted for 10 seconds and is judged according to how hard the horse bucks and how well he rides.

Saddle Furniture the metal parts of a saddle.

Saddler a person who makes or deals in saddlery and/or harness.

Saddlery the bridle, saddle and other items of tack used on a horse which is to be ridden.

Scent the distinctive odour of the fox which is given off by the glands under the tail and from the pads.

School (a) to train a horse for whatever purpose it may be required. (b) an enclosed area, either covered or open where a horse may be trained or exercised.

Scratch (a) to withdraw a horse from an equestrian event after it has been officially entered. (b) (U.S.) to spur vigorously.

Scrub Dashing galloping after half-wild cattle in timbered country in Australia in order to round them up into a herd.

Selling Race a race immediately after which, any runner, if a loser, may be claimed for a previously stated price, or, if the winner, must be offered for sale at auction.

Service the mating of a mare by a stallion.

Shoeing the act of putting shoes on a horse. Normally a horse needs its shoes renewed every four to eight weeks depending on the type of work it is required to do, whether it is worked on soft or hard ground and how fast its feet grow.

Show (a) to compete in a horse show. (b) (U.S.) to finish third in a race.

Show Class any of various competitions held at horse shows in which the animals are judged for their conformation, condition, action and/or suitability for whatever purpose they are used, or intended to be used.

Shy for a horse to swerve away suddenly in fear (or occasionally from mere high spirits) from an obstacle or sound.

Side Saddle a saddle designed for women on which the rider sits with both feet on the same side, normally the nearside. On that side, the saddle has two padded projections placed diagonally one above the other. The rider puts her right leg over the upper one and the left leg under and against the lower one with her left foot in the single stirrup iron.

Silks the peaked cap and silk or woollen blouse, both carrying the colours of the owner, worn by a jockey in racing.

Sire the male parent of a foal.

Skate a horse of poor quality.

Skewbald a horse whose coat consists of large irregular and clearly defined patches of white and of any other colour, except black.

Sleeper a horse which unexpectedly wins a race having previously shown poor form.

Slow Gait one of the gaits of the five-gaited American Saddle Horse. It is a true prancing action in which each foot in turn is raised and then held momentarily in mid-air before being brought down. Similar to the rack and also called the single foot.

Snaffle Bit the oldest and simplest form of bit, available in a variety of types, but consisting chiefly of a single bar with a ring at each end to which one pair of reins is attached.

Snaffle Bridle the bridle used in conjunction with a snaffle bit.

Sound said of a horse which is free from any illness, disease, blemish, physical defect or imperfection which might impair in any way its usefulness or ability to work.

Speak the bark or bay of a hound on finding a scent.

Splint a bony growth which gradually forms between a horse's cannon bone and one of the splint bones as a result of excess strain or concussion.

Spread Fence in show-jumping and cross-country events, any of various obstacles which are wide as opposed to simply high, such as a hog's back, parallel bars, triple bar or water jump.

Sprinter a horse which is able to move at great speed over a short distance but is seldom able to maintain the pace over a long distance.

Spur a pointed device strapped on to the heel of a rider's boot and used to urge the horse onwards, etc.

Stable (a) a building in which one or more horses are kept. (b) a collection of horses belonging to one person, such as a racehorse owner or riding-school proprietor, or kept at one establishment.

Stale Line the line of a fox which has passed some time previously.

Stallion an ungelded male horse aged four years or over.

Stallion Hound a male hound used for breeding purposes.

Standard Event any of the five rodeo events recognized by the governing body, the Rodeo Cowboys Association. These are bareback riding, bull riding, calf-roping, saddle bronc riding and steer wrestling.

Starter's Orders when the starter of a race has satisfied himself that all runners are present and ready to race, a flag is raised to show that the horses are 'under starter's orders'.

Stayer a term applied to a horse which has great strength and power of endurance and is therefore likely to be successful over a long distance.

Steeplechase a race over a certain course of a specified distance and on which there are a number of obstacles to be jumped.

Steer Wrestling one of the standard events in a rodeo. The contestant rides alongside a running steer, and jumps from the saddle on to the head of the steer, the object being to stop the steer, twist it to the ground, and hold it there with the head and all four feet facing in the same direction. The contestant completing the event in the shortest time is the winner. This event is also known as bulldogging.

Steward an official at a race meeting appointed to see that the meeting is conducted according to the rules.

Stirrup Iron a loop, ring, or similar device made of metal, wood, leather, etc., suspended from a saddle to support the rider's foot.

Stirrup Leather the adjustable strap by which the stirrup iron is attached to the saddle.

Stock (a) a white neckcloth worn for hunting and formal occasions. (b) the handle of a whip.

Stock Class a show class for stock or ranch ponies.

Stock Saddle the high-pommelled, high-cantled Australian cowboy's saddle which has long flaps.

Straight Fence in show-jumping and cross-country courses, any obstacle which has all its component parts in the same vertical plane, such as a gate, post and rails or planks.

Strangles an infectious and highly contagious disease caused by the organism *Streptococcus equi* and occurring most commonly in young horses. The symptoms include a rise in temperature, a thick nasal discharge and swelling of the submaxillary and other lymphatic glands of the head in which abscesses eventually form.

Strike a Fox to find a fox.

Stud (a) an establishment at which horses are kept for breeding purposes. (b) any large establishment of racehorses, hunters, etc., belonging to one owner. (c) (U.S.) a studhorse or stallion. (d) a metallic head screwed into a horseshoe to give the horse a better grip on a slippery surface.

Stud Groom a senior groom, especially at a stud farm.

Surcingle a webbing belt usually 6 to 8 cm (2½ to 3 ins) wide, which passes over a racing or jumping saddle and girth and is used to keep the saddle in position, or which can be used in place of a roller to secure a day or night rug.

Sweat Scraper a curved metal blade with a wooden handle used to scrape sweat from a horse.

Sweet Itch a dermatitis usually found in horses that are allergic to a particular pasture plant, and therefore most likely to occur in the spring and summer months. It particularly affects the crest, croup and withers causing intense irritation and producing patches of thick, scaly, sometimes ulcerated skin, which the horse often rubs bare in its attempts to get relief.

Tack saddlery.

Tail the tail of the horse includes the dock together with all the hair which is usually allowed to grow about 10 cm (4 ins) below the point of the hock.

Technical Delegate the person at an international horse show or three-day event who is responsible for seeing that the competition is run according to international rules and that the course is correct. He is usually from a country other than the host nation.

Teeth when fully mouthed the horse has 40 teeth: 12 incisors (6 in each jaw), 4 canines (1 in each side of the upper and lower jaw), and 24 molars (6 above and 6 below on each side). Females lack canines.

Temperature the normal temperature of a horse is 38°C (100.55°F).

Tetanus an infectious, often fatal, disease caused by the microorganism *Tetanus bacillus* which lives in the soil and enters a horse's body through wounds, especially of the foot. One of the first visible signs is that the horse will stand with its head pointed forwards, its front legs wide apart, its hind legs straddled with the hocks turned outwards and its tail raised. If made to move the animal will walk stiffly. As the disease advances the horse may become nervous and excited and the facial muscles become so rigid that the animal is unable to open its mouth.

Three-Day Event a combined training competition completed over three consecutive days. It consists of a dressage test, a cross-country section, which includes a steeplechase course and two circuits of roads and tracks as well as a course of cross-country obstacles, and finally a show-jumping event.

Throat Lash a strap which is part of the headpiece of a bridle. It fastens under the horse's throat so as to prevent the bridle from slipping over the head. Known more correctly as Throat Latch.

Thrush inflammation of the frog of a horse's foot, characterized by a foul smelling discharge.

Time Allowed the prescribed period of time in which a competitor must complete a show-jumping course if he is not to incur time faults.

Time Limit the prescribed period of time in which a competitor must complete a show-jumping course if he is not to be eliminated.

Tipster in racing, a person who makes a business of providing information or tips about the chances of horses in races. Tipsters often work for the racing pages of newspapers.

Totalizator An electromechanical apparatus used for a form of betting in which the total amount wagered, after a deduction of a percentage for costs, etc., is divided among the holders of winning and place tickets.

Trail Horse a horse trained, bred or used for cross-country rides.

Trainer a person qualified to superintend the training of a horse for a particular sport.

Training Tracks concentric tracks inside the racecourse proper at Australian racetracks, on which the great majority of Australian race-horses are trained.

Travers a dressage movement on two tracks in which the horse moves at an angle of not more than 30 degrees along the long side of the arena with the forelegs on the outer and the hind legs on the inner track, looking in the direction in which it is going and bent slightly round the inside leg of the rider.

Treble in show-jumping, a combination obstacle consisting of three separate jumps.

Triple Bar in show-jumping, a spread fence consisting of three sets of poles built in staircase fashion with the highest at the back.

Trot a pace of two time in which the legs move in diagonal pairs but not quite simultaneously.

Turf (a) any course over which horseracing is conducted. (b) in the U.S. turf races are held over grass courses as opposed to dirt tracks. (c) the world of horseracing in general.

Turn on the Forehand a movement in which the horse pivots on the forehand while describing concentric circles with the hind legs.

Turn on the Quarters a movement in which the horse pivots on the hind legs while describing concentric circles with the forelegs.

Unentered said of a hound which has not completed a cub hunting season.

Unraced a horse which has not yet taken part in a race.

Unseated a rider who has in some way been put out of the saddle.

Unsound a horse which has any defect which makes it unable to function properly.

Unwind to start to buck.

Vixen a female fox.

Volte in dressage a full turn on the haunches: the smallest circle a horse is able to execute on either one or two tracks, the radius being equal to the length of the horse.

Walk a pace of four time in which the hoofs strike the ground in the following sequence: near hind, near fore, off hind, off fore.

Walking Horse Class any of various competitions held for Tennessee Walking Horses at horse shows in the USA.

Walkover a race in which only one horse has been declared to start. To qualify for the prize money the horse has to be saddled, paraded in front of the stand and then has to walk past the winning post.

Wall (a) an upright show-jumping obstacle made of hollow wooden blocks which are painted and stacked to look like a brick wall. (b) a cross-country obstacle built of brick, concrete blocks, sleepers or stone. Such solid obstacles are usually built as uprights, but dry stone walls may be as wide as a narrow topped bank.

Wall of the Hoof that part of the hoof which is visible when the foot is placed flat on the ground. It is divided into the toe, the quarters (sides) and the heel.

Water to provide a horse with water to drink.

Water Brush (a) a brush used to wash the feet and to dampen the mane and tail. (b) in show-jumping, a small sloping brush fence placed in front of a water jump to help a horse take off.

Water Jump a spread show-jumping obstacle consisting of a sunken trough of water with a minimum width of 4.2 m (14 ft) and a length of up to 4.8 m (16 ft). A small brush fence is usually placed on the take off side.

Weigh In in certain equestrian sports where a specified weight has to be carried, such as racing, combined training and show jumping, the rider has to be weighed immediately after completion of the race, or his round in the competition, to ensure the correct weight was carried throughout the event.

Weighing Room the place on a racecourse where the jockeys are weighed.

Weigh Out in certain equestrian sports where a specified weight has to be carried, such as racing, combined training and show-jumping, the rider has to be weighed before the race or competition to ensure the correct weight is carried.

Weight Allowance a weight allowance in racing which may be claimed by a jockey or apprentice who has not ridden a certain number of winners.

Weight cloth a cloth carried under the saddle on a horse. It is equipped with pockets in which lead weights may be inserted to achieve the correct weight.

Weight for Age a method of handicapping horses in a race by their age, the older horses carrying more weight than the younger horses.

Weights blocks, normally of lead, placed in the weight cloth and used by a rider who is not heavy enough to make the specified weight for an event.

Whipper-in in the huntsman's assistant with a pack of hounds.

White Flag a marker used in equestrian sports to mark the left-hand extremity of an obstacle. It is also used to mark a set track and must always be passed on the right.

Wind a Fox for hounds to smell the scent of a fox.

Windgall a puffy elastic swelling of a horse's knee or fetlock joints caused by an over-secretion of synovia, a fluid similar to joint oil.

Windsucking a harmful habit in which a horse draws in and swallows air, causing indigestion.

Wing one of a pair of upright stands with cups or similar fittings used to support the poles or other suspended parts of a show jumping obstacle.

Win in a Canter to pass the winning post first at an easy pace, being so far ahead of the rest of the field.

Winner's Enclosure the place on a racecourse reserved for the first three horses in a race and to which their riders have to return mounted immediately after the end of the race.

Winter Horse a horse which is kept at a home ranch for use during the winter.

Winter Out for a horse to be left out in the field during the winter rather than to be brought into the stable.

With a Stain a well bred horse but having some common blood.

Withers the highest part of a horse's back: the area at the base of the neck between the shoulder blades.

Wrangle to round up, herd and care for horses.

Young Entry the name given to young hounds before the start of the cub hunting season when they are unentered. During cubbing they are trained to hunt the quarry so that by the time the hunting season starts they are entered, usually at about 18 months old.

INDEX

A page number in **bold** type indicates the major reference to a breed discussed in the Breeds section of the book.

ACKNOWLEDGEMENTS

The Publishers thank the following for providing the photographs in this book:

Alfa 110 below; Animal Photography 15, 33, 35, 63, 64, 65, 67, 68, 69, 70, 72, 81 right, 91 right, 92, 95, 98, 99, 102, 104, 105, 108, 112, 114, 120, 124, 125, 126, 127, 147 above, 206 left, 207; Ardea London Ltd 82, 90, 91 left, 111, 145, 158 left; Barnaby's Picture Library 60, 162–3; Bio Arts 149, 150; Bridgeman Art Library 17; Bruce Coleman 4–5; Ann Cumbers 141; Mary Evans Picture Library 20, 25, 27, 28, 30–1, 32, 34, 42, 43, 45, 52; Graham Finlayson 200; Michael Holford Photographs 10–11, 12–13, 14, 16–17, 18, 19, 20–1, 22–3, 48, 49, 50; Kit Houghton 46 below, 109, 175, 180, 185, 190; Labor Pfeifer Wein 54; Bob Langrish 29 below, 32–2 below, 46–7, 56, 57, 169 below, 173 below, 174–5 above, 176, 179, 184, 187, 188, 191, 192, 192–3, 196/197, 197 below; Laurie Morton 166–7, 168, 171 above; John Moss 198, 198–9, 208–9; Octopus Library 38–9, 40–1. 76, (Kit Houghton) 61, 62, 66, 78, 80, 81 left, 84, 85 left, 86, 103 left, 106, 107 above & below, 115, 116, 117, 119, 121, 122, 134, 138, 139, 140, 143, 156–7, (Ross Laney) 103 right, (Bob Langrish) 79, 87, 88, 89, 93, 94 left & right 154–5, 164–5, 178–9, 182–3, 186, 189, 202, 202–5, (John Sims) 26–7, 40 above, 44–5, (Sally Ann Thompson) 8, 73, 74 above & below, 75 above & below, 77, 78, 96, 97 above & below, 128–9, 136–7, 146, 147 below, 158 right, 159, 160–1; Rex Features 6; Mike Roberts/Only Horses 55, 169 above, 170, 171 above & below, 174, 177, 181, 206, right; Selfridges Archive 36; Tony Stone Associates 2–3, 58–9; Elizabeth Weiland/Vision International 53, 71, 194–5, 196; Mike Williams 29 above; Youngs Brewery 37; ZEFA Picture Library (K. Hakenbury) 101, (Janoud) 110 above.